FIRE UNDER THE CARPET

D0418520

00000684081

Fire Under The Carpet

Working for Civil Liberties in the Thirties

Sylvia Scaffardi

Of course as soon as a thing has happened it isn't fantastic any longer, it's inevitable.

Voyage in the Dark – Jean Rhys

LAWRENCE AND WISHART
LONDON

Lawrence and Wishart Limited
39 Museum Street
London WC1A 1LQ

Fist published 1986

Photoset in North Wales by
Derek Doyle & Associates, Mold, Clwyd.
Printed in Great Britain by
Oxford University Press

Contents

1

Escape Into Life

Politicians today tend to sort out and tidy up recent history – still fluid and uncodified – to suit their own ends. I have heard them trot out glibly, and uncontradicted, that it was only for lack of a strong rearmament policy that the National Government failed to stand up to fascism in the thirties. They present the 'low dishonest decade' as no more than improvident, not guilty of temporising, condoning or flirting with fascist ideology. And so it may be timely now to look back fifty years and light up a patch in my own experience, to say how it was in the rank-and-file struggle for civil liberty against the dangerous tilt away from democratic principles. I played only a minor supporting role in the newly-formed Council for Civil Liberties (as it was first called), but I was there from the start, caught up in the slip-stream. It is this fundamental aspect that stands out most vividly in my memory. Much of it, I suppose, relates to work in the field – acting as an observer at demonstrations and meetings. This led on to defending cases in court, providing material for debate in Parliament, for commissions of inquiry and for publicity in the press.

But first of all, as the recorder, I must introduce myself, and then, as he came into my life, the protagonist, Ronald Kidd who started it all and who was the Council's first General Secretary.

Oh To Be In England!

It was just after the end of my first term at boarding-school in Eastbourne that suddenly on a hot summer day we were at war with Germany. The war that was to change everything! To recast the map of Europe, to give the impetus for the outbreak of the Russian Revolution, to decimate the young men of my generation – and to disillusion the survivors, to jolt insular, philistine, squirearchical Britain into a changed, sterner future, and to give women a new status and a new freedom. At the end of it, to make a peace that would plant all the time-bombs that were to explode into the Second World War.

But all I knew at the time was the cheering and the flags. We had to rescue 'brave little Belgium' from the Huns, and to bring down that arch-villain the Kaiser with the help of our old ally France.

Our family was starting a new exciting way of life on the opposite, the cold side of the Atlantic. We had crossed it once more and for the last time, not just home for a visit, but for good. We had to leave our childhood paradise in Brazil to be educated in the only place that mattered, the important centre of the world – in England!

It was goodbye to São Paulo, where I was born, and to Vovó, my Brazilian grandmother, who captured my heart in infancy with her strong vital nature, and delicious sticky sweets. Goodbye to our best and longest-lasting home in Petropolis, 2,000 feet up through the clouds above the blue bays of steaming Rio de Janeiro, to a climate radiant and fresh, with carnations, humming-birds and violets. The days too short for the blazing invitation of the garden. Mother, tolerant, unpossessive and confident, gave us our freedom to run barefoot, to climb trees, to pick fruit when we were thirsty, to make a nest in the hibiscus tree with a precious book. Washed and tidy in the afternoon, Lydia and I – Bee still at the nursery stage with Charlie and Edward – had lessons with Mademoiselle. The map of France, exact copying of a ruined castle with a pointed pencil, and out of the same funny little book that mother had learned with *her* governess, all about the gods and goddesses of ancient times – to be discovered again in art and literature. Marcolina Feliciana, Caina affectionately for short, was part of the family – we were her children. She was born in the time of slavery on Vovô's, grandfather's, coffee and sugar-cane plantation. Mother was eleven when their slaves were freed before emancipation. That only came shamefully late in 1888, an event celebrated with three days' public holiday.

1888 may well have been the year that father, Sidney James Crowther-Smith, arrived in Brazil. The son of a C of E clergyman, he had been Spartan-educated at the Bluecoat School. Determined to make his own way, he had decided on a future in this new developing country that was moving rapidly into the modern age. After eight years' hard work, he was well on his way and in São Paulo. A sociable and sport-loving member of the British colony, he received an invitation from Vovó to a tennis-party. She was ahead of her time in believing that exercise in sport was good for girls, and she even allowed her daughters to play mixed-doubles, with young men to whom they were not related! So it was on the tennis-court that father met and fell in love with my mother.

Arrived in England, mother explored the South Coast for boarding-schools. Chilled by the size and anonymity of Roedean, she decided on a small family-style school in a rambling old-fashioned building. Mrs Barber, the dignified little widowed headmistress, presided in her chintzy drawing-room with its photographs and rose-bowls. Mother recognised her at once as a woman of principle, a staunch Victorian, and devoted to her girls. We were looking forward now to the exciting life of boarding-school that we had read about in books.

At first the novelty was captivating. The cubicle bedroom in the dormitory. The snappy question-and-answer lessons on two pages of kings, battles, dates, or towns on rivers with cotton, coal or steel, and then the quick-fire competition, ticks and crosses and so much out of ten, and all wiped clean, forgotten afterwards. The glorious variety of girls! We shared rugs spread on the hot lawn, reading ripping library books.

Our euphoria lasted for that first and only term of peacetime. But when winter came! Upstairs quite unheated. As the war dragged on, with coal shortages, hot baths were cut to one a week. I thawed slowly in bed wrapped in my serge dressing-gown. We plodded in crocodile along the deserted front – grey sky, grey sea. Church twice on Sunday, I sat scratching my chilblains, waiting for release. Wartime shortages modified the once-liberal fare, eked out now with substitutes and the disgusting new margarine. We were greedy-hungry most of the time. I was learning the insular schoolgirl rules of what was done and not done, that it was sporting to be a little cheeky to the inefficient in authority and daring to break rules.

By the time I was involved in the tangle of adolescence I had lost all faith in adult wisdom. The conventional tenets about society, religion and marriage no more than a façade of adult shams. Religion expected, promised everything, realised nothing. It sanctioned in holy matrimony sensual delights that outside it were quite unmentionable, shouldn't even exist in the minds of girls. Society public-school-male dominated offered only for those young women who could make the grade, a subservient complimentary role, with marriage the only goal, and motherhood the achievement. I couldn't even picture myself as eligible, or for that matter as wanting to compete. Love and adventure – I hoped for, yes, but to make the grade in a conventional settled-down marriage – not for me.

The ceaseless struggle of the war, the relentless toll of the never-silent guns, cast a sombre shadow menacing our future, chilling us a little even in our callow youth. When at last the Armistice was declared, and the girls started to cheer and dance, Mrs Barber cut in sternly – we should be praying, remembering the dead.

Through my own small personal disenchantments, I shared something of the mood of post-war disillusion. The cynicism and resentment of the men returning after the shared agonies of the trenches into the complacencies of civilian life, their idealism muddied and bloodied. The once-respected claims of loyalty, duty, self-sacrifice – Victorian delusions no longer to be followed. What, I wondered was the point of it all? What was it that made life worth living? I was hoping to find the answer through the intellectual climate of college.

Mrs Barber, moving with the times, and to meet current secondary school standards, had engaged some qualified staff and built on a laboratory. We were entered now for the local Cambridge examinations (the Cambridge Senior roughly equivalent to matriculation). On the strength of my exam certificates and a few prizes, it was felt that I should try for a college place.

I was head girl now and rather alone in my glory. My

friends, who had left, were resolved, first of all to have a good time, and then to get married. College would at any rate postpone for me these two fearful competitive alternatives. I had been advised that my most likely entry – and somewhere where I should feel at home – would be to a women's residential college, part of London University but outside it, deep in Surrey.

Royal Holloway College, towering at the top of Egham Hill in unweathered brick was the Victorian creation of Mr Holloway of Holloway's pills – his tribute to the New Woman of his day. It provided accommodation for 200 (with a separate study and bedroom), a handsome library, a picture gallery, an impressive chapel and a sunken swimming-bath in its 200 acres of grounds. It stipulated a proper observance of the Sabbath: compulsory daily attendance at morning prayers, no cycling or river on Sundays, no male – except the visiting clergyman – to sleep under the roof, no consumption of alcohol. It offered the rigidly directed curriculum of an eight-hour working day, with compulsory lecture attendance. It was in fact a forcing-ground to qualify docile acolytes to carry the educational torch.

I was not of course aware of all this in detail when I arrived for the entrance exam, but I sensed at once inside the endless vista of corridors, the cloistered oppression, the rigid channelling of the vast Victorian foundation. And my foreboding was confirmed in the brief no-nonsense interview with the formidable man-woman Principal. And so I took my place in the big amphitheatre of the lecture hall, with a light heart. I scribbled away, indulging in long purple passages. Royal Holloway College was not for me!

But fate was against me. To the surprise of myself and my family, I was awarded a scholarship! The most modest one on the list – but it pinned me down. Now there was no escape.

I did four years at Holloway. It should only have been three, but just before the Intermediate exam – in the swotting-up fortnight – I went down with tonsilitis (the infection a legacy of boarding-school), failed in two subjects and had to go through the whole dreary syllabus again before starting on the English honours course.

The family had settled down thirteen miles outside London, Father with his golf club, Mother sadly having to make do with afternoon bridge, Lydia and I (Bee still at college) drawn into a flat round of tennis, hops to the gramophone or at the Masonic hall with the local likely lads and their sisters. So in my fourth year, as well as the threat of finals, I had two problems ahead: how to detach myself from the academic world, and also from suburbia with its relentless philistinism, its self-satisfied clichéd way of life.

The opportunity came by chance. I was active in the college dramatic society and so I took into dinner at the high table Lena Ashwell, the ex-West-End star, who was lecturing that evening. In the war she had organised theatrical and concert parties for the troops in France, and after the war sponsored the Lena Ashwell Players, designed to spread theatrical culture to the deprived areas in and around London in one-night-stands from their headquarters at the little Century Theatre in Notting Hill Gate. (This of course was before the widespread cinema circuits captured the popular audience.) I learned at dinner that the Lena Ashwell Players trained pupils and gave them an opportunity to walk on and play small parts.

My chance! A way of escape into LIFE! 'Would I', I asked her, 'be suitable?' She was a hard, handsome self-centred woman and we had disliked each other at first sight. Now she turned her eyes on me, and, as I sensed at once, dismissed me. 'Certainly,' she said smoothly. But I didn't care what she thought. This was to be my way out.

Ronald Kidd

My father without any equivocation accepted my venture, that side-stepped any advantage from my degree, and generously not only paid my premium as a pupil – a modest one – but also gave me pocket-money for bed and breakfast in London. It was never quite enough. I was always a little hungry, but after the Saturday night show I caught the train home to have a good feast on Sunday.

I stayed two seasons with the Lena Ashwell Players. After the first, as a pupil, I was kept on at a salary, and I enjoyed a summer season with them at the lovely old theatres at York and Bath. Then I launched out on my own in touring companies and provincial repertories, finding new jobs through theatrical agents and still spending the occasional summer holiday with the family in Brittany or Normandy. After one of these breaks, and after a fruitless round of the agents, I finally called in to the Stage Guild (the precursor of Equity), a notice pinned up advertised a 'high class' provincial rep with casting in progress. The actor-manager talked big and looked small, the venue was deep in Herefordshire in a town I had never heard of. All the same I felt illogically attracted to take the job of juvenile and join the rep for its first autumn-winter season.

The sleepy little market town was innocent of a theatre, the company was playing in a hall with a high platform stage, no rake, and at the back a communal dressing-room for the women and another for the men. But there was a good strong cast with a promising lovely young leading lady.

My digs, in an old overhanging house in the undeveloped part of the High Street, were almost opposite the bed-sitting room of the stage-manager. He came over to introduce himself and to have his part heard. (He had been engaged importantly as stage-director, but of course no assistant stage-manager ever materialised. And now he had been cast in the opening show – Ashley Duke's *The Man with a Load of Mischief* – on the strength of his looks and bearing, as the nobleman.)

Ronald Kidd was thirty-nine – thirteen years my senior. His almost romantic good looks were already a little worn, his crisp brown hair was receding to a professorial forehead, his sideboards greying. Dark eyes, a sensitive but obstinate mouth and a strong cleft chin. As well as the attraction of his looks, worn so casually, and his easy friendly manner revealing his interest and welcoming our compatibility, I was aware from the first of a fundamental seriousness in his nature, a commitment that claimed him, set him a little apart. (Years later his sister told me that as a very young man he had been drawn to the church and had served at the altar, but he lost his sense of vocation.) This paradox, which struck me when we first met, was still evident when he was described posthumously and variously as like the last Edwardian Bohemian or the Canon of a forward-looking diocese.

A couple of days later, coming back from rehearsal I saw him outside his digs with a slim dark woman and a little girl.

She looked up with the big brown eyes of her father. In the evening as I met him on the way to the theatre, they had already left. They had called in to see him on their way home to the West Country after a weekend in the neighbourhood. It was clear that he and his wife had drifted apart, although still friendly, and that the emotional tie no longer held them together. He spoke of his digs in London in Greek Street, and she and the child were still in their once-together home in Bristol, where for a time he had been stage and scenic director of Bristol's Little Theatre. I soon learned that he was very fond of his little girl.

Together we discovered the peaceful countryside all around, in the heavy golden calm of an autumn as sustained as in Keats's ode. The deep meadows still lush and green while the beech woods were turning in a blaze. Ronald in his old patched tweed jacket and greyers. Tea afterwards in his digs. As it turned shadowy in the narrow street, he would put a match to the fire. He showed me poems he had written, a few of them in a poetry magazine.

Ronald with the looks and the personality to attract had the susceptible Irish temperament to idealise and 'fall in love'. Now he was discovering again the 'darling girl' of his imagination. Ronald's admiration for and interest in women had made him keenly alive to their frustrated right to independence and the vote. As a young man he had campaigned in the suffrage movement – where he met Evelyn Sharp and her husband, Henry Nevinson and also F.W. Pethick-Lawrence, the doughty Old Etonian barrister, champion of progressive causes, and with his wife Emmeline, a militant fighter for women's suffrage. He was to be the last Secretary of State for India before independence, and at eighty-four to enliven the party-ending to the NCCL's twenty-first birthday celebration. Rose Lamartine Yeats, the veteran feminist, remembered Ronald's penny pamphlet, *For Freedom's Cause – An Appeal to Working Men*, as a 'bold courageous stand'. It was probably after his religious phase that he was influenced by Havelock Ellis towards sexual freedom and understanding, and an acceptance and enjoyment of sex without the barrier of Victorian guilt. He was also drawn to Edward Carpenter's idealistic outlook that disregarded social standards, conventional morals and the money incentive, in favour of a simple way of life aspiring towards universal brotherhood, and a classless outlook. Carpenter's homosexual aspect never touched him.

Ronald came of a medical family. His father, most of his uncles and his grandfather were doctors. His grandfather, who came from Ireland attended Disraeli in his last illness and had quite a fashionable practice, while remaining something of an eccentric. On occasion he would fasten his collar with string, and once, consulted by a smart lady patient, he snapped off her high french heels to help her, as he explained, to walk more comfortably.

All I know about Ronald's earlier life has been pieced together from oddments, sometimes contradictory, from letters, a few from his sisters, finally from his wife. He volunteered little himself, only the odd laconic remark, and he was the inverse of a name-dropper. I gathered that his mother had fussed and coddled him in boyhood, probably because his elder brother had died at sixteen from TB. At Heathmount School in Hampstead he was not allowed to take part in games or sport. He entered University College London as a science student, but it is not clear whether he intended to become a doctor. Ill health, it was said, prevented him from taking his degree. He did, however, receive a brief scientific training, and obtained some qualification in applied science. He was lecturing at Workers Educational Association institutes and at Toynbee Hall before he was called up in the First World War. How did he get on as a Tommy in the ranks? I asked him. 'Allright,' he smiled. At any rate he learned how to construct an outdoor latrine. They called him the Professor, because he knew all the answers. He never saw active service. When his section was due to be posted, he was told to fall out, and was sent for another medical. Finally it was decided that he was not fit for combatant duties. 'What was wrong?' I asked him. 'Nothing,' he said. 'I think they suspected TB.' His first job after leaving the army was secretary to the Wellcome Historical Medical Museum in Wigmore Street, a post normally offered to a university graduate at a starting salary of £150 a year. Ronald resigned after a year to go to the Ministry of Labour to edit a daily bulletin and later a weekly gazette. It was here that he met C.E.M. Joad, whom he roped in later as an early member of NCCL. Then he transferred to the Ministry of Pensions. His wife was hoping that he was going to make a career in the Civil Service. But the savage post-war cuts in pensions of veterans from the trenches, with claims disallowed, disputes on disabilities, sometimes to wrecked shell-shocked men, he was not prepared to administer. He resigned, to make his way in the difficult world outside. He shared a studio in Hampstead with a scenic artist-craftsman. His wife told me he had friends and contacts among journalists, artists and actors. He acted as publicity agent for some of these. He wrote a weekly column for the theatrical *Era*. He freelanced in journalism, advertising and publicity. No doubt his wife found him disappointing in the conventional role of good provider. At any rate they seemed content now to live apart. He managed tours of London productions when they left the West End, and supplemented his income with brief appearances in films: a Civil Servant behind a desk, a lawyer in court, a dinner-jacket guest and other similar roles. He had to fall out at the last minute from a well-paid overseas tour, after investing in tropical clothes, when he went down with a bout of flu. Out-of-pocket and recovered, he was glad to fix up the provincial repertory, which like me he chanced on at the Stage Guild.

Ronald and I saw the lovely autumn die in the beechwoods leaving a fiery shuffle underfoot. A tang now in the air. We were glad to get in from our rambles to the fire in his room. It was clear now that the company was running at a loss; the little theatre-hall only filled up at the end of the week. A leading man left the cast and was not replaced; the actor-manager taking up his parts – very inadequately. He was constantly running up to London on business, cutting rehearsals, fluffing his lines. Just before Christmas he went again up to London. A day went by, and then another. At the end of the week, no manager, no salaries. He had ditched the company!

Back to London. Ronald saw me off at my platform at Victoria. We parted, temporarily – Ronald to his digs in Greek Street, Soho, and I to my family. I invited Ronald to Sunday lunch. My mother was instantly at home with him. Lydia, Bee and the boys when they met him all took to him. But my father was cold, a little hostile. Ronald it is true made no special effort to defer to him or to mollify him by calling him 'Sir' – at his age this would have been a rather heavy concession, but neither did he voice any unconventional views. Yet my father divined them instinctively. He could smell the socialist, the egalitarian, and would be contemptuous of what he guessed to be Ronald's simple-life ideals, his lilies-of-the-field philosophy – anathema to a careful business man. And he probably resented Ronald's unperturbed assumption of bachelor freedom. (I had told my mother that he was married). His coldness, Ronald said, reminded him of the aversion of his first employer, a publisher of religious books, who took it as an affront that Ronald never carried a rolled umbrella. I can imagine him goaded by Ronald's romantic good looks, his big-brimmed black hat and loosely-knotted woven tie.

Ronald fixed up a summer seaside tour – Ian Hay's *A Damsel in Distress*. He was stage-managing and I was playing the nice little part of the American actress. I couldn't recognise the bright holiday esplanade at Eastbourne as the bare seafront of my boarding-school days.

Bank Holiday at Westcliff. We went to Southend to see the fun and join the crowds round the candy-floss, winkles and comic post-cards. A coachload from the Jewish East End made an exotic, dramatic entry as they turned out on to the esplanade. Mountainous Mommas, almost fairground; young mascaraed Delilahs in sleek satin, glittering with costume jewellery; startling young men in fancy suiting, a happy blue, doggish checks, with flashing ties, huge wrist-watches, rings – anticipating the fashion-freedom of the eighties! Making their own vivid assertion against the grey-mud beach, the distant flat sea. As hungry for colour and pleasure as the Brazilian blacks when they escaped from their *favelas* to join and light up the Carnival in Rio de Janeiro.

In the late autumn we joined a show leaving the West End for a final provincial tour, with Delysia, the Parisian revue star introduced by Cochran onto the London stage and now in middle-age playing it straight, and in the cast the stately ageing Violet Vanbrugh.

On this tour to the big centres I saw more of the harsh marks of poverty in the industrial north. I had already before this seen something of the hard working life in Dundee. My digs in a high-rise tenement fronted sheer on noisy cobbles, with access at the back up a network of open metal stairways that straddled the building. No bathrooms of course. I had tasted my kind friendly landlady's sparse basic food – all she had ever bought or knew how to prepare. (She was married to a tram conductor.) No green vegetables, only root crops and dried peas. In Ashington in Northumberland the street lining the shops was the only one laid down, all the rest were mud tracks, with pools in winter. In the theatre dressing-room the walls were running with damp. Clothes packed and unpacked each night. But now, in a back street in Glasgow I saw children running and playing balanced somehow on grotesque barrel legs. Deformity no cause for concern. In Newcastle, on a frosty morning, I nearly tripped over a small boy stretched out at the entrance of a shop, bare-legged, face hidden in his arms, exposing an angry red gash on his neck. He wouldn't speak. I came across him again flat on the pavement in another part of the town. In Blackpool the spill-out of a factory-outing was pressing on to the pier for the matinée. Men and women in rusty navy, mossy grey, greeny black, waddling on splay bandy legs, shapeless, undersized, foreshortened – the Glasgow children grown up – the used and the abused. A crowd caricatured by Hogarth, or savagely presented for propaganda. Inside the show their lusty appetite for comedy warmed the house; they relished unabated the jokes against their own kind – broke, drunk, twisted, snared in sex.

At the end of the tour in Cardiff, Delysia threw a fancy-dress party in the suite at her hotel. She invited everybody including old Fred the stage carpenter. Violet Vanbrugh didn't come, nor her formidable dresser who intimidated everybody. Delysia gave us a grand spread, *flambé* and the lot, the sideboard loaded with drinks. Her latest husband put in an appearance, flying over from Paris.

Back in London Ronald phoned me to cancel our meeting. He had flu and was going to sweat it out in bed. He had left Soho and had installed himself in a big bare room overlooking the river – No.3 Adelphi Cottages. Access to the three so-called cottages was in the darkness under an archway in a dead-end street, soon to vanish in Thames-side development. A massive old key unlocked a door set in the wall, and opened the way up circular stone stairs and onto the communal landing that ran the length of the three big cottage-rooms and that accommodated a sink and a lavatory. Ronald was delighted with his Beggar's Opera hideaway. My visits to London always ended there, with the big key turned in the door under the arch. There was a feeling of height and remoteness, and deep below you could hear the mysterious river-life going on its way as the London air streamed in through the three elegant sash windows, uncurtained, letting in the night. Both of us enjoyed the space and freedom of the naked room, carpetless, bare boards. Now in the empty island there was just his bed, a small camp-table, three wooden chairs stranded, a gas ring and kettle and a small box-cupboard that held behind faded chintz his basic crockery and utensils.

I had asked him when he phoned me if he had anything to eat. He didn't need anything, he had some milk. I came up the next day with a jar of chicken broth. In daytime the archway door was left unlocked by the artist-craftswoman in the cottage next-door who hand-printed her textile design on long trestle tables. Ronald was pale and unsmiling. He had some homeopathic remedies. He would phone me when he was better. I heated some milk on the gas ring. Then he was ready to sleep. Walking home along the Embankment I thought of him lying there, solemn and dignified, with something fateful about him that set him apart – something that in the end might be too big and demanding for me?

Ronald and I were now both of us pulling out of the stage. The talking cinema was stealing the provincial audience. Repertory companies were closing down, fewer tours booking out. At the same time a flood of eager well-to-do amateurs stage-screen-bitten were pressing in, ready to pay their way, work for the fun of it. My escape into life through the theatre was resolving itself. The stage with its vitality, its emotional release, its bracing discipline had pulled me out of the cold, isolated academic role of spectator critic and had made me at home in the adult world. But, for me, it represented the lighter side, a reality that sometimes was skin-deep. And now, as its opportunities dwindled, the episode was trailing towards an end. Each tentative was getting vaguer, the search for work more casual and light-hearted. It was all retreating and I was letting it go easily.

Soho Our Village

I came up to live in London. Just at first with a college friend in her ground-floor flat in Rathbone Street. Two bed-sitting rooms and a big shared kitchen-bathroom. I paid a pound a week – or was it thirty shillings? But before long I was together with Ronald in his digs.

Ronald was venturing into publishing with a firm in the Adelphi, and I was starting out as a freelance editor. My advertisement in *John O'London* – carefully worded by Ronald – attracted publishers, probably because of my very modest terms, to unload on me their neglected manuscripts for my conscientious plodded-through opinion. Some had to be de-Americanised in idiom and spelling – necessary in those days before the universal spread of transatlantic culture. A medley of amateur or semi-professional writers sent me their manuscripts for advice or work on them, and I was writing a column on fashion for a Croydon paper run by a friend.

After Adelphi Cottages had to be abandoned for demolition, Ronald had installed himself in a vacant cranny right in the hub, midway between Piccadilly Circus and Leicester Square. Dansey Yard was an ugly little open-ended cobbled mews, jammed right behind Shaftesbury Avenue and serving as a passageway between Wardour Street and Macclesfield Street. Ronald had spotted a 'To Let' notice above a film-warehouse. An open entrance led up steep metal stairs and through a flimsy snecking door into a single bare-boarded room, with a frontage designed to slide back on runnels and open flush over the yard. Below, an ancient urinal reposed in its metal cage, out of use. Sandwich-board men plodded into the yard for a breather, propping their boards, that advertised the theatres, against the blind backs that fronted in Shaftesbury Avenue.

Ronald partitioned off the back half of the room as his domestic and storage quarters, a faded no-colour tapestry curtained off the passageway. His cubicle bedroom was fitted with a Spartan tip-up cupboard bed. Too tight for more than single nightly sleeping. So with my bed squeezed in, the room was furnished. A curtained alcove outside the lavatory with an enamel basin on a shelf, and a bucket underneath by the cold tap, completed the domestic arrangements. Two big basket trunks held his personal possessions – clothes and mostly books. Heavy handed-down leather-bound topography, theology, philosophy, poetry. A handsome illustrated Boswell of 1853. Books by his missionary uncle, *Kafir Socialism*, *The Essential Kafir*, in art-nouveau covers and with photographs showing black men not starving and hollow-eyed but smooth and handsome. Books on the theatre – including experimental theatre in the USSR. A vast collection of second-hand cullings, some quaint Victoriana and Henry David Thoreau on *The Duty of Civil Disobedience*. A handsome illustrated Kelly's *Practical Builder and Workman's Companion*, weighing about five pounds, printed in 1823, and still his guide for craft carpentry. Political books, stacks of pamphlets. Ronald's half-written book on architectural treasures in London threatened by demolition, with pockets of Kodak snaps of frontages, fanlights, porticos. No novels, nothing light. A few art books with chaste nudes. Balanced on the top a smoky kettle, an old blackened iron frying-pan, a toasting-fork, broom and pan.

The fire in the main room burned flush on stone in its large old-fashioned open hearth, consuming itself, never cleared. The surrounding brickwork held the heat, the wooden room and bedroom were always pleasantly warm. There was a trestle table, a wooden bench, kitchen chairs and a creaking nursery basket-chair with heavy flocky cushions. Claud Cockburn in an amiable article in *Punch* called it 'a hovel'. Ronald, however, was pleased with it, and in pride of ownership invited to supper an artist friend from his studio days in Hampstead.

I pulled out from behind the curtain the big plates that I had stowed away unwashed, turning greenish now. I scoured them with newspaper and poured on boiling water, tilting them over the lavatory pan. The kettle was singing on the fire. On a stool by the fireplace I turned the bacon, shaking the eggs (the only dish I knew how to cook). Ronald never expected or wanted me to have any domestic skill – a waste of time. He was ready to find nourishment, fill in with anything, old brown bananas, bags of peanuts. Mostly we fed out in little cheap cafés in Soho.

It was smelling good and turning dusky in the old frying pan when we heard steps up the stairs. I dished out the grisly fare, forking out the bacon and letting the smoky fat drip back, lifting the settled eggs frilled in black. We ate with some appetite, ending up with camp coffee.

Once a fortnight, in the small hours, the crash of metal dragged us awake; I hung suspended, a stowaway insinuated behind the glamour and lights of theatreland and the all-night trade in venality in Wardour Street and Gerrard Street, waiting relaxed in a half-doze as one load of the tinned film landed in the lorry in the yard and the exchange lot hurled in thumping duller on wood. Till with the last – final – impact, I could let go and slide back luxuriously into unconsciousness.

Soho was our village, and beyond it Ronald was revealing to me the complicated and contrasting pattern of the London he loved and knew so well. He took me to the Temple, the City, the East End, the riverside at Hammersmith. He showed me Dickensian haunts, a pub for gentlemen's gentlemen from Thackeray's day, sunflowers in pocket gardens in a hidden close off the Mile End Road, unexpected elegance round corners, forgotten relics and landmarks of history. I enjoyed it all, and now it has all jumbled up in my mind to recur in dreams delightfully tangled up with earlier memories and impressions.

Ronald had opened up the Punch and Judy Bookshop in Villiers Street, with a sign hanging outside to direct you into the cubby hole next-door to the lift in Embankment Chambers. Just space enough to walk round a table, to stare at the library shelves. Fiction hired from Foyles in packing cases, so much for fifty books according to how new – but I used to go to their hiring section and hand-pick each volume. We added left-wing books – visits to the USSR (Julian Huxley's and Maurice Dobb's), *Ten Days That Shook the World*, and so on. And for people we knew, *Lady Chatterley's Lover* – unexpurgated, *The Well of Loneliness* and others. No pornography – unless you classed *Fanny Hill* as that, which I did at the time. Unreadable to me. The bright servicing heroine so patently a masculine ego-pandering creation with a fantasy devotion to her clients and her ploys.

Our customers hurrying to and from Charing Cross

underground called in for cigarettes and something to read. Friends dropped in to chat and not always remembered to buy something or order new books. We had second-hand ones too, and a constant stock of review copies. The money dribbled in, to serve as pocket-money for day-to-day expenses.

Very often after we had shut up shop, we crossed the road into the Gate Theatre opposite. Ronald had a standing invitation from Peter Godfrey to drop in any night. The entrance tilted steeply into an intimate little basement theatre and bar. The branching mainlines of Charing Cross ran overhead and an underground route below, so that every now and then vibrations shook and menaced the scene – very effectively at times – in the middle of the avant-garde experimental plays. Peter Godfrey could run his club-theatre without any censorship from the Lord Chamberlain. He put on Russian, French, Czech and German plays and some by English poets; the programmes with woodcuts by Robert Gibbings.

I remember a highly stylised *Rape of Lucrece* interpreted by French artists, with the cruel Tarquin unexpectedly prone beneath the suffering heroine, lamenting as she is raped, and still drawn to the subtly ravishing tyrant. Gwen Frangçon-Davies as Bella-Maya the cruel and tender prostitute, on a bare stage only with bed, lamp and curtain, the universal dream and prey of everyman.

Ronald and I were in at the birth of the small Soho Circus Club which started up in Gerrard Street next door to Mrs Merrick's. A young artist decorated the rough whitewashed interior of the basement-club with lively circus scenes. Boris big and puffy, and Paul, spare and bearded – jokingly dubbed as red and white Russians – ran the club, hired chairs, tables, a cash register, a piano, stocked the bar with near-beer, engaged a young unemployed North Country chef and opened up, offering very modest terms for nightly dancing, after-theatre supper and breakfast. They hoped to attract a clientele – unlike the crowd next door – of professional people, journalists, writers, artists and others. Those who turned up regularly were mostly their friends from Soho, leftist, and without much money to spend. A few strayed in from next door. A very young ingenuous red-cheeked hostess was pounced on by one of our customers, an earnest lady novelist – rather the Lena Ashwell Players type – who set out to 'save her', inviting her to the peace and safety of her country cottage. I heard from both of them their mutually contradictory stories of, on the one hand, passionate rescue and asylum, and on the other desperate boredom and escape from cold-comfort country. On Saturday night the club filled up. My brother Edward came down with a few medical students from Guy's. The piano and the man with the accordion struck up a lively quick step to attract the couples on to the polished square at the end of the room, and then melted into a languorous tango.

Towards the small hours, when Ronald had had his fill of talking and I of dancing, we broke away to emerge into the half-daylight of Sunday morning. We made for the Corner House and breakfast in the all-night restaurant. I caught a glimpse of a green comedy face in the long glass – my own! No ventilation in the basement club. A few hours of sleep in Dansey Yard, and then only half-awake we set out for the countryside. Propped against each other in the train to Leatherhead, nursing a bag of cheese rolls and oranges. In the early sunshine we started out for the bluebell woods that lead on to the grounds of Marie Stopes' house. But on the way a grassy slope invited us and we subsided on to the hard ground. And with the swing of the sky above and the pull of the earth beneath, dropped at once into insensibility. I woke slowly like a cat in the sun to feel his tweed arm and big heavy head.

Generally on Sunday Ronald came with me to my home for lunch or tea. We were both attracted to the warm centre that my undemanding, unpossessive mother created round herself. It was accepted now that Ronald and I were together.

Most week-day evenings we went to one or other of the little Italian or French restaurants in Soho, whichever was the regular meeting place, to talk away the evening on tuppenny cups of coffee and supper of eggs and chips at eightpence. Journalists would drop in and young writers and artists. George Scott Moncrieff put the Café Blue into his novel *Café Bar*. A table or so away the Soho regulars like Charlie Brooks, the ex-thief whose life a journalist was writing up, and the fierce gipsy-looking Iron-Foot Jack. And now it was politics that was the subject. Everybody was engaged, taking sides, partisan about the new world, the new thinking in the USSR. The danger of fascism. A sense of impending crisis. Up to now politics had meant nothing to me, two parties in and out, bumbling ritually on in Parliament, reported drearily in father's monopolised *Times*. And then there was a Labour Party that objected to top hats and dinner jackets. But with Ronald I was beginning to come of age politically. He never talked politics to me, but it was in the air, everything seemed to impinge on it. I had of course been aware from the first of his concern about injustice, hardship, his sense of personal involvement, the feeling that it was his responsibility to do something, not just deplore. Impossible to be with him and ignore uncomfortable facts – unemployment, hunger. Besides I had seen it for myself in Gateshead, Walsall, Ashington, the bony faces, no blood under the skin. I even had the apprentice's cheek to choose Russia as my subject for a little lunch-time talk to young typists at a bureau run by one of my literary contacts.

The Turning Point

After still another of my recurrent sore throats, my young medical brother, Edward, advised a specialist. I went into Guy's to have my tonsils rooted out. In those still primitive days of surgery, the normal sequel after the operation was vomiting basinfulls of dark blood. I emerged from hospital emaciated, and went to recuperate in Guernsey with my high-Tory aunt married to a mild husband who came of a naval family. After dinner, correct with finger-bowls, the BBC news announced, 'Mutiny at Invergordon!' Incredible! A little band started up in my head playing, pianissimo, the 'Internationale'! I broke into a grin.

Back at home, a local job turned up for me, the pay too good for a freelance to refuse: £45 a 'term' to coach a delicate backward sixteen-year-old three hours each morning and just a bicycle ride away from home. I had of course to stay in Surrey. I caught the train to London in the afternoon.

One frosty morning, on my way by cycle, I was jerked suddenly over the handlebars into a painful fog. A car behind me caught my rear wheel as it turned into a drive. Bed. X-rays. It was concussion. Recovered from my bruises, I was picking up my work again and getting ready to catch the usual train to London. But living at home, with the comfortable certainties of a secure background, had imperceptibly affected my point of view. Ronald's growing absorption in the political scene had made me understand that we had come to a turning point in our relations. Was there a hint of slackening in our intimacy? Up to now he had been the seeking lover, I at times the elusive one. I had been content to live, enjoy the present, make no plans to hold or bind the future – I thought I held the key. But now I was unsure. I had to make up my mind.

I was a little doubtful where his convictions would lead, whether I would be prepared to follow all the way in the uncertain political future. I knew his uncompromising nature, his conscience that drove him, once he was convinced, to get involved. I had seen it work out in trivial cases. Cosy together in the coach coming back at night with the company after a performance in Hereford and looking forward to moments by the fire in his digs before we said goodnight, it was discovered that a very young programme girl was missing. 'Went with a fella for a drink – in the interval,' so the other girls said. Ronald stopped the coach, got off in a dark lane to walk back, find her – too young to be left on her own. On a perfect Saturday afternoon on our way through Hyde Park to tea and then the cinema, he spotted a very sick sheep, not browsing with the others, a raw place on its side. The whole afternoon and evening spent chasing, locating the park-keeper, the shepherd, the RSPCA.

He always identified himself with the little man, lived like him from day to day. He liked to picture his forbears running barefoot on the hills of Limerick. He was tolerant to a fault, with no class consciousness. That he was never fearful about the future, always confident, optimistic, made me more wary, doubtful, insecure.

Sometimes I was cold, bored with his sense of *duty*. I had discarded the word since my schooldays, no 'must' for me outside my own choosing. I mocked his seniority, 'fussy ways'. He waited warm, undoubting for me to shed my callow, shallow mood, but he never shifted.

His chronic inability to take hard facts into account. That he had no money in reserve never limited, dictated his action, never advised a 'sensible' path. When his little girl was, he feared, dying after a pillion accident on her mother's motor-bike, and the last West-Country train from London had gone, he hired a plane.

With my comfortable background, the safety-first of suburban living, I felt a little cowardly pull towards the anchor of security, the way of life I had discarded as stultifying.

The mystery of his health. He always maintained there was nothing wrong. He had unlimited reserves of energy when there was something to be done – I tired first. He could enjoy, digest anything, postpone meals indefinitely. But the unexplained way he suddenly slipped under when we were swimming across the bathing pond in the rose garden at Ashtead; my sister and I pulled him up, half propelled him towards the bank. He was soon smiling, dismissing it – 'a little short of breath'.

At the beginning it had all been sunshine, uninhibited freedom. Venturing by happy degrees into unending pleasure with a lover who was patient and warm even when I was temperamental, who let me boss him, needed me, followed me absent with letters. Who introduced me into his congenial Bohemian London, so easy to feel at home in.

But now he was in a harder colder climate, claimed by something imperative outside my sphere. If I half-stayed outside, still expecting him to be devoted, always waiting for me, wooing me when I was difficult, he would at last tenderly, gently separate himself. I would be left behind, gradually smaller and smaller, fixed at last as a tiny little figure – all I could muster to stand up against fate.

A bird, wings fixed, slipped past my window, pulled through a streak in the sky. I went on staring into the future as the dusk turned into night, the slow dark pouring on the turning earth. After a while there would be another 'darling girl' prepared to accept and share his interests, or perhaps this time an older dear or dearest woman. This gentle Jesus, this stoical monk ready to accept any austerity, this innocent pagan happy in giving and taking pleasure, this meticulous Anglo-Saxon with his careful follow-through, his tenacity, this passionate

Irishman ready to give himself to a cause. If I wanted him, I would have to go his way. In the small hours I dropped into bed.

As I opened my eyes, my mind was empty. I waited for the tide to sweep back from the dim horizon of my sleep. Wide awake, I understood it had all been resolved. In the dangerous political scene, I had to stay safe – with Ronald. I had to be adult, to accept what I had always postponed, responsibility. I would share with him as far as I could the moral responsibility, and the consequences. It was the only way to stay alive and confident. As for hard facts – and living in my father's house they had presented themselves – I knew that nothing was more unreliable and illusory than the viability of these hard facts that were always subject to change, and surmountable – the most imponderable of all considerations.

Now, after fifty years of political consciousness, I find it difficult to recall exactly how and when it was I made the transition from ignorance to awareness, to partisanship. When it was that I started reading the papers, and to get the latest news became for me as much a necessity, morning and evening, as it was for Ronald. Nine o'clock news on the wireless was already stale and in any case mostly hand-outs. (We had no set at Dansey Yard.) Because Ronald was so tolerant and undogmatic, because he never attempted to influence me, impose his views, I was able at last to believe that I had found my own way to a contemporary left-wing outlook. And although I no longer remember the stages, I do remember vividly the first time I was drawn into, discovered and shared the confidence and conviction of the times, believed that I had found at last a worthwhile cause.

We had gone down some basement stairs to a club or a centre in Soho – or perhaps it was Bloomsbury – into an informal meeting of young people, standing, squatting on the floor, propped against tables, closing round a tough, dark young speaker. The subject the USSR. Suddenly a hostile question provoked another, and the speaker answering burst into fiery eloquence. The doubters were silenced, the cause was taking fire, the generous young going with it: the new hero, the working man! Abused, downtrodden but ineradicable (something of the noble savage, and potent as the hero in myth). Rising, toppling giants, crashing Goliath, overthrowing tyranny. Solidarity with the little man everywhere! Prejudice collapsing. A new freedom! The exciting tremors of a future with a fresh evaluation, a social purpose! The quickening of a new art, a new theatre, a new voice! In the warm ambience I felt the pull of the current, the need to abandon aloofness and a critical stand. For the first time the cold ego was melting, I was surrendering to the luxury and the warmth of involvement, the excitement of a shared emotion. A pulse, a beat, a rising tide of hope, strong and satisfying as love, it claimed and released me: Unity for the common cause! The tortured buried up to their necks, Caina's forbears, children running splayed, men and women stunted, pressed under lids – Vovó, the good, the kind, the simple – Arise! Arise! … Unite the human race!

As we left the meeting I was aware that Ronald had remained a little aloof. He had some reserve about the speaker, privately he judged him a bit of a demagogue, not altogether sound. But that didn't matter to me. In a way Ronald's reticence strengthened my feeling of independence. I was at one with the young audience. Later, John Strachey's *The Coming Struggle for Power* and then his *Menace of Fascism* gave intellectual confirmation.

I wrote long letters about the current scene and the growing sense of commitment to my Brazilian grandmother – whom I had not seen since I was a child but with whom I had an instinctive affinity. My half-Brazilian cousins on holiday to England told me of her passionate interest in world affairs.

Ronald had of course found his own fixed centre long ago. A very individual brotherhood-of-man type of socialism, based on the belief that human nature was fundamentally good, not needing repression and correction but freedom to develop. And not born in sin – he was for sexual as well as other freedoms. The ultimate good, evolution into a resolved state of peaceful anarchy. His rejection of the social restraints of accepted conventions led him into his own mild kind of Bohemianism, but his general style, his instincts, were for order, method, tidiness, his way of life civilised, courteous and considerate, and above all tolerant. He never joined a political party – in spite of the pressure of the times. He never shifted his standpoint an inch. He had the gentle obstinacy, the unyielding stubbornness, that in Tudor times would have taken him to trial and the rack. I too never overcame my instinctive reluctance to be roped in, to conform to a given line, and so I never took the decision to join any political party.

2

Unemployment at Home – Danger Abroad

Invergordon was *not* the start of the red revolution! The shilling a day cut for all below warrant-officer, well over-topped – for the lowest ranks – the ten per cent decreed by Ramsay MacDonald's 'National' government for everyone paid by the state.

'We the loyal subjects of His Majesty the King,' the subversive lower deck addressed the Admiralty, 'present earnest representations to revise the drastic cuts ... a forerunner of tragedy, poverty, immorality, amongst the families of the men on the lower deck ... quite willing to accept a cut ... within reason ... and unless this is done we must remain as one unit, refusing to serve under the new rates of pay.'

This text – not divulged of course at the time – I discovered later on in one of Ronald's books, Wal Hannington's *Unemployed Struggles 1919-1936*. Indeed the National Government had intended to suppress altogether the news of the 'demonstrations' of naval ratings at Invergordon. Friendly editors had been approached to make no mention of it in the press, but apparently the *Daily Herald* was overlooked, so that a young journalist, Ritchie Calder, was able to get a scoop for his paper. The Admiralty acted quickly. The extreme lower-deck cuts were reduced, the men were not disciplined. The economic 'mutiny' achieved its purpose.

The 1932 Hunger March

It was while I was laid up with concussion that the 1932 Hunger March came into London.

There were close on three million unemployed. They and their families were already living too near the bone even before the National Government imposed a ten per cent cut on their meagre benefit. The hated Means Test compelled their sisters, brothers in work, parents with small savings to contribute towards their keep. A British Medical Association Committee arrived at the figure of 5s. 1d. a week spent on food as sufficient to maintain existence but not enough to allow a child to develop in health. Sir John Boyd Orr found that ten per cent of the population were living on 4s. a week! Another thirty per cent on 6s., and these were still undernourished.

The objective of the Hunger March was to awaken public awareness to help win their cause against the cuts to their benefit and for the repeal of the Means Test, and to present to Parliament their million-signature petition to this effect. They came from Scotland, from Teeside, Tyneside, Merseyside, Yorkshire, the Midlands and South Wales. Some of them had already been on the road for three weeks – in all weathers, and finding accommodation along the way, sometimes on bare boards and mostly in workhouses. But they resolutely refused to accept the grim poor law regulations laid down for the casual admittance of 'tramps and vagabonds'. (To be locked up on admission, no smoking, no singing, breakfast and supper not to exceed two slices of bread and marge and a cup of tea, a task to be performed before leaving.) The march transported its own field kitchen and voluntarily adhered to its own strict discipline. And when it was harassed by police with batons to comply, it resumed its march, all through the night, to the next town.

Official London prepared for the Hunger March as though these 2,500 hardy and hard-done-by working men, and a contingent of women, offered a serious threat to law and order. Some papers even urged that they should be excluded from the capital! The March was outlawed in official eyes because it was organised by the Communist-sponsored National Unemployed Workers' Movement. It was apparently Home Office policy – Sir John Gilmour then Home Secretary – to harass and limit the effectiveness of the demonstrations and to discredit the March by associating it with disorder. On the day of the first big rally in Hyde Park, leave at Wellington

Barracks was cancelled, a large body of provincial police were drafted in and special constables were on point and traffic duties. The liberal press made comedy of the specials. Factory girls in the Borough screaming in unison: 'Kiss me sergeant!' A passer-by reprimanded by a special on point duty for colliding against his arm, elbowed him, and was promptly arrested. But the man refused to accept his arrest and walked away, the special in pursuit, the traffic snarling up!

In Hyde Park and around Marble Arch crowds had collected to support and welcome the marchers. Headed by the Scottish fife and drum band they came on in orderly grey ranks, in their cloth caps, and carrying their banners. As the last contingent passed by, there was a big surge from the crowd outside to get to the speeches. The inexperienced specials, attempting in vain to stem and control this, drew truncheons. This provoked scuffles, the mounted police came into action. In the House it was referred to as serious rioting round Marble Arch.

The *Police Review* (the organ of the Metropolitan Police) was sharply critical of the use and the performance of the specials.

> This week witnessed a wholesale departure from the original conception of what a special constable is for. He ceases to be an emergency 'ration' ... in this difficult time the appearance of the special is calculated to cause trouble rather than avoid it. At the meetings and hunger marches, the special is an irritant, rather than an antiseptic. And why this sudden conversion to the employment of special police? ... the less they are seen and used the better for everyone concerned.

And now the conservative press weighed in shrill to rouse alarm:

> The abolition of the Means Test is a pretext ... a Petition to Parliament is a blind. Hannington, professional organiser of the march, is conceited indeed if he supposes that his Communist riff-raff could make a revolution: but that they could do incalculable damage by loot and pillage in an hour or two of mob excitement is undeniable, and that bloodshed would ensue is certain ... this man Hannington ... is responsible ... for attracting the crowds which are certain to include the most dangerous elements in London ... These Communist organisers should be laid by the heels ... These

marchers are a public nuisance and a public danger.

Workers, their livelihood gone, many of them traditionally employed in the heavy industries that had built up the staple wealth of the country, suddenly transformed into public enemies, to be discredited, feared, barred from normal citizens' rights, their role to rot silently in their dead towns in passive resignation.

Hannington was indeed arrested, on the morning of the key day when the petition was to have been carried to Parliament. The police burst into the NUWM office and charged him with 'attempting to cause disaffection among the police' in his earlier speech at the Trafalgar Square demonstration. Bail was refused and Hannington was subsequently sentenced to three months' imprisonment. After arresting Hannington, the police proceeded, without a warrant, and refusing any check by Hannington, to search the premises. They seized and carried off some five hundredweight of papers. But this haul did not include a mysterious letter, delivered by hand the day before, for Hannington personally – 'he knows all about it'. This letter referred to 'the plans' for 'direct action already discussed': the waylaying of Cabinet ministers and burning government buildings. This bogus note Hannington had destroyed on the spot.

Plans went ahead in spite of his arrest. Ronald describes what he saw in his book *British Liberty in Danger* (published in 1940). Vast crowds around Parliament stretching down Whitehall and onto the Embankment. Cordons of foot and mounted police barred the way in Whitehall, and as the Hunger March advanced in their ranks, broke them up with baton charges. 'There was no violence', he wrote, 'on the part of the marchers.' As more marchers came over Westminster Bridge they were driven onto the Embankment, and then added further to the congestion in Whitehall.

It was 9.30 in the evening and during a lull that he noticed two men under the portico of the Whitehall Theatre gesticulating and 'inciting the crowd to advance towards the cordon'. They were roughly dressed in cloth caps with red handkerchiefs knotted round their necks and in heavy boots. 'There was little or no response ... 'but either they or some persons in the crowd began a certain amount of pushing and shoving.' As Ronald crossed over to get nearer, he saw that the two men 'drew regulation police truncheons from their hip pocket, laid about them, and arrested two other men ... the cordon was opened and the two men passed through straight down Whitehall, in the direction of Cannon Row Police Station.'

It had been arranged that the marchers' petition should be taken by taxi to Charing Cross Station. When the deputation of fifty finally managed to get there, the station gates were closed. They were surrounded by police and the petition confiscated. The news spread, another attempt was made to march down Whitehall, and then there was a baton charge outside the station.

Three days later, the Chairman of the NUWM, Sid Elias, was arrested. He had just recently returned as a delegate from a workers' conference in the USSR. The police in their NUWM haul discovered a letter with a Moscow address. Elias in fact arrived back in London before his letter, and received it himself; Hannington who was on the road with the Scottish marchers never saw it. Elias got two years for 'attempting to cause discontent and disaffection and ill-will between different classes of His Majesty's subjects and to create public disturbance against the police'.

Finally, in December, on the eve of the day set aside for national demonstration for the unemployed, the seventy-six year old veteran working class leader, Tom Mann, the Treasurer of the NUWM, and its Secretary, Emrhys Llewellyn, were arrested under a statute of Edward III, not for committing any offence, but as 'a preventive measure'. Both refused to be bound over and silenced and each was sentenced to three months' imprisonment.

Hitler: The British Reaction

It was the crooked symbol of fascism that was the danger. It was tilting askew accepted standards, turning lies into truth, normalising brutality, making murder an acceptable means against an unpopular opponent, vindicating violence as it achieved its goal of power.

I was beginning to understand how easily a democracy – and even a liberal government – could cave in and be taken over by a fascist dictatorship, smoothly, without a fight. It had happened in the twenties in Italy: Mussolini building up his movement, with law and order conniving, the *carabinieri*, local authorities, and even military units supplying him with arms. And when it came to the crunch – his grandiloquent March on Rome – King Victor Emmanuel himself capitulating, refusing to sign the emergency decree to call out the army. Mussolini didn't have to march, he took the train.

And now nearer home, more dangerous, the incredible, horrifying news that the unprincipled demagogue, Hitler, with his violent private army ('Down with Democracy!' 'Perish the Jew!') had been appointed Chancellor of Germany! The showman mob orator with the hypnotic power to con and hold the crowd ('people must be misled if the adherence of the masses is sought' – *Mein Kampf*) the egomaniac 'Saviour of Germany' whose fantasy fitted, the perfect tool and ally of reaction had been democratically invested with power! He had been placed there by Germany's respected hero and father-figure, Field-Marshal Baron Paul von Hindenburg, the President of the Republic betraying it to the would-be dictator. Hitler's support in votes would counter radical opposition in the Reichstag – the classic excuse, a buttress against the left.

Within a month, the sensational news: the Reichstag had been set ablaze! A national Emergency! Constitutional liberty suspended. A Communist outrage! The fall guy, Marius van der Lubbe, had been discovered on the scene, an incriminating Communist document conveniently found in his pocket. The opposition was immediately proscribed, arrested.

In spite of this, and his stormtroopers' terror at the polling stations, Hitler's vote dropped in March elections. But it was too late. With the right-wing conservative votes, he had his majority. Now, with the 'cleansed' Reichstag Hitler was in full control, the democratic machinery harnessed to his will.

We heard the ominous news from Germany. By May stormtroopers occupying trade union premises, trade union leaders arrested. The Corruption Department of the Prussian Ministry of Justice confiscating the entire property of trade unions. Property of the Social Democratic Party confiscated, and the valuable property of the co-operative societies put into 'safe hands'. And by June the announcement from the German Labour Front that leadership in the factory would be restored to the natural director, the employer.

Behind the smooth announcements were the looting, the destruction, the dragging away of victims to the cellars, the local Brown House. The bloody stories began to seep out. Facts often emerging only by word of mouth, difficult to substantiate with official denials. The source of communication sealed up with the 'Germanising' of editorial staff, the Press Association brought into conformity. The President of the Foreign Press Association of Berlin, Edgar Mowrer (of the *Chicago Daily Tribune*) expelled – in spite of protest – because his brilliant factual book, *Germany Puts the Clock Back*, described, as a reviewer put it, 'the forces dragging Europe into the abyss'. To report the facts now was an offence. 'The people who are guilty of this crime,' runs the Nazi Jewish Boycott Manifesto, 'this despicable atrocity campaign, are the Jews in Germany ... Show the Jews they cannot go unpunished if they humiliate and dishonour Germany.'

We heard the brutal facts first at left-wing meetings. The police often waiting outside, to chivvy and disperse the leaving audience, as though it was a suspect activity to condemn and to expose what was happening on the other side of the Channel. It was all set out in authenticated detail in the *Brown Book of the Hitler Terror* prepared by the World Committee for the Victims of German Fascism, with a preface by Lord Marley, a Labour spokesman in the Lords, and published by Victor Gollancz in 1933. With dates, names, signed statements, official records, photographs, it documented the appalling, sickening Nazi violence: interrogation; torture; murder; the shot or stabbed left bleeding to death, the doctor unavailable, the police impotent, complaisant. The victims: Communists, Socialists, trade union workers, Jews, progressives in all spheres, social workers, teachers, doctors, lawyers, journalists, merchants, tradesmen. It included a chapter naming and giving facts about concentration camps. (The disingenuousness of politicians who excused themselves much later, saying that they were unaware even of the existence of the camps.)

The facts about cultural vandalism, the persecution of intellectuals were publicised in the British press. The burning of books, the proscriptions, forced resignation, flight of distinguished Jews, pacifists, progressives from the universities, medicine, science, the law courts, the arts, films, the theatre, the denunciations and the post-grabbing by the second-rate.

But it was a very different reassuring picture that was presented to the wide general public. In the popular crowded cinemas, the captive audience sitting in the friendly dark waiting for the big film, heard the bland thirties ad-voice introduce Hitler in the newsreel as a new-style 'indomitable leader', an 'unflinching patriot', with over three million followers. Field Marshal von Hindenburg – once the villain and the terror of 1914 – now, respectfully, 'one of the world's greatest figures', had invited Hitler to become Chancellor, and Hitler was 'guiding Germany back to peaceful progress'. Nazi leaders appeared as jolly good fellows mingling democratically in German crowds with collecting tins, to get loyal support for party funds. Herr Goebbels was featured in an interview with the pro-fascist G. Ward-Price of the *Daily Mail*, who translated and explained Nazi philosophy. And that triumph of Nazi culture, the Burning of the Books, celebrated in May 1933, in the square outside the Berlin Opera House, with the band playing, and the Minister of Propaganda presiding, while lorry-loads from vandalised libraries were pitched into the flames, was shown on the newsreels in close-up by the flickering glare, as grinning Brownshirts fed the bonfire with what British Movietone described as 'Marxist literature'. British Movietone News was half-owned by Lord Rothermere's *Daily Mail*, and it carried Sir Malcolm Campbell's name as it flashed its caption on the screen. Sir Malcolm was himself a fascist sympathiser and flew the colours of the British Union of Fascists when he broke the land speed record in the Bluebird.

Nazi anti-Semitism was presented in a street scene thronged with strong young men in informal uniform, shirt-sleeves and breeches, outside placarded shops. The voice explained: 'Jewish shops are labelled and picketed' – not a Jew in sight – but a placard stood out prominently, carrying the Goebbels' message *in English*: 'Germans defend themselves against Jewish atrocity campaigns'. The victims turned into the aggressors!

Movietone's coverage of news from Germany never gave a hint of cruelty or bloodshed. Its excuse: that it had a duty to respect the sentiments of cinema-owners and their managers not to outrage their patrons by showing anything they might take exception to. Mosley himself appeared in a newsreel, looking inept and theatrical, plugging his own brand of fascism: 'We do not propose dictatorship, but a drastic revision of the parliamentary machine, a fight for action, for vigorous vitality and manhood, against the forces of drift and despair.'

But an independently made film by Ivor Montagu, a documentary on the German Communist leader Ernst Thälmann, was censored by Lord Tyrrell, the Chairman of the British Board of Film Censors. Thälmann was a considerable figure in German politics; he had stood as a candidate for the presidency against Hindenburg and Hitler in 1932, and headed a sizeable number of Communist deputies in the Reichstag. He was seized and imprisoned in March 1933 when Hitler outlawed the opposition. The Board of Censors explained that films about criminals were not allowed. Ivor Montagu pointed out that Thälmann had not been charged with any offence, or brought to trial. Why then was he in prison? he was asked. Why indeed! However the British public was not allowed to form an opinion. (Thälmann was to be murdered in Buchenwald Concentration Camp in August 1944, aged fifty-eight.)

Einstein had voiced a confident plea to the civilised world when his boat leaving Germany reached Le Havre in March 1933:

> The actual facts of brutal force and oppression against every free-minded person and against the Jews, the facts of what has taken place and is still taking place in Germany, have fortunately aroused the conscience of every country which remains true to the ideals of humanity and political freedom ... All friends of our civilisation which is so seriously menaced should concentrate all their efforts in order to rid the world of this psychological disease.

But by June 1934, Hitler stabilised, regularised his position in a weekend of carnage, when he eliminated the radical element in his own Brownshirts, disposing of their leader,

Gregor Strasser, and some seventy of the rank-and-file, as well as the organiser of his stormtroopers, Ernst Roehm. In 'the interests of the state' he also eliminated former government officials, who now stood in his way. His 'courage' approved by the Reichstag and the now doting Hindenburg. In Britain, the *Daily Telegraph* legitimised the murderous coup: 'The infamous character of Roehm (a homosexual) and his associates invests the stroke with a quasi-moral sanction ... General Goering can truly boast that the youth of Germany may now enter the Storm Troop ranks without fear of moral taint and corruption.' There was further reassurance for the world of business and for politicians, when it was known that the financial wizard, Hjalmar Schacht, former President of the Reichsbank, was now working for Hitler. It was to be business as usual. In these quarters therefore it was unlikely that there would be poignant regret at the destruction of the German socialist, co-operative and trade union movements and of the Communist Party. The methods might have been doubtful – but Hitler had certainly carried out a prompt tidying-up job. It was unfortunate about the Jews, but those involved were mostly left-wingers, and after all they had their own organisations to look after them.

3

The Council for Civil Liberties is Born

The *Week-End Review*, a lively but short-lived radical journal, carried an article, on 5 August 1933, 'Bandits and Bottles' by A.P. Herbert. Ronald picked it up with some interest because the bandits in question were policemen, and so-called because they were acting as *agents-provocateurs*. But reading it against the current background of the plight and treatment of the unemployed, he found the content more than he could stomach. A.P. Herbert was fulminating against the use of plain-clothes policemen to invade night-clubs, act like 'bandits' ordering drinks after hours to get convictions, to confiscate liquor. The liberty of the subject no longer held sacred! Parliament unmoved! An intolerable interference with the private lives of people who paid taxes for uncivilised and lunatic drink licensing laws, etc., etc. So much burning indignation for so puerile a cause and in the climate of the times! In a follow-up letter Ronald accused A.P. Herbert of hypocrisy and challenged him as the 'champion of freedom' to protest in defence of something worthwhile: a citizen's right to demonstrate on an empty stomach. Let him protest against the use of the police as *agents-provocateurs* against Hunger Marchers.

After a lively correspondence – featured by the editor (Gerald Barry) – APH sportingly offered to go jointly with him to the Commissioner of Metropolitan Police, Lord Trenchard, to ask for a public inquiry on the use of police *agents-provocateurs* in the 1932 Hunger March – provided of course that Ronald Kidd could substantiate his allegations.

Ronald replied that he was very ready to swear an affidavit, but he warned that at best the result would only be a white-washing departmental inquiry. On his way to the

Commissioner for Oaths by a happy chance he ran into a journalist friend who had reported that Hunger March, and who had also seen a policeman – whom he knew by name and number – acting in plainclothes as an *agent-provocateur*, in this case on the Embankment. He readily agreed to contribute his statement. And so APH and Gerald Barry had two sworn affidavits to take to Lord Trenchard.

The *Week-End Review* of 28 October spotlighted APH's article, 'Mr Kidd and the *Agent-Provocateur*', that summed up and commented in fascinating detail on Lord Trenchard's written reply. Plain-clothes police were indeed working in the crowd, and two of them did make arrests near the Whitehall Theatre, as Mr Kidd stated. But an interval of thirty-five minutes in the entries on the charge-sheets nullified, he suggested, Mr Kidd's allegation. In addition no police officer had acted 'in the manner suggested', and there were no grounds for a formal inquiry. If a policeman had acted in such a manner, he would be liable to severe punishment.

APH, as well as a playwright and novelist, was also a barrister (and a year later an MP). The discrepancy on the charge sheet, he suggested, could be accounted for in a number of ways. He welcomed Lord Trenchard's assurance outlawing police *agents-provocateurs*. He quoted a number of press reports of convictions secured by their use (among these a bookseller sentenced at Bow Street to three months' imprisonment, a £100 fine and £10 costs for procuring two obscene books, after pressure and persuasion on six visits from a young policeman passing himself off as an army officer.) He felt that Ronald Kidd had done a service in raising the issue.

Another Hunger March was coming to London early in the New Year. Ronald hoped to build on the useful publicity. If only two eye witnesses could have so much impact even after the lapse of some eleven months, how valuable to organise, say, a dozen observers on the spot, and some of them public figures.

It was while he was making plans that he decided that, as there were so many vital issues in the critical political situation, it would be much better, instead of appointing an *ad hoc* vigilance committee of observers, to have a permanent body to keep a watchful eye and take action where it was needed. This was the idea that led him in the New Year to set up the Council for Civil Liberties.

The first Vice-Presidents were Gerald Barry (soon to be Editor of the *News Chronicle*), A.P. Herbert and Kingsley Martin who was taking over the *Week-End Review* to incorporate it in his *New Statesman and Nation*.

I knew little about the early contacts, the preliminaries that led up to the inaugural meeting when the Council for Civil Liberties was set up, because at that time I was isolated with my family in the grief that overwhelmed us at the sudden death of my youngest brother. He had telephoned just before the weekend to say he was out of sorts and would not be coming to lunch on Sunday. Four days later he was dead. Edward had my mother's methodical scientific mind, her equable unselfish lovable nature, and my father's quickness and know-how, his social confidence. As a youngster he had chosen his profession, and was well on his way as a young doctor at Guy's Hospital, where he had trained, specialising in his main interest, gynaecology. My father who had identified with his youngest and favourite child – who so resembled him physically as a young man – was almost out of his mind with grief. Edward had died of dyptheria in Guy's, his throat infection treated – until it was too late – as acute quinsy.

Withdrawn, and in my bleak world, I arrived for the inaugural meeting of the Council for Civil Liberties on 22 February 1934. A dozen or so people were filing into the basement of St Martin-in-the-Fields, making for a bare table and some hard chairs. I followed with a last upward glimpse through railings to a patch of wintry sky. Two big handsome Nordic women, Dr Edith Summerskill and Amabel Williams-Ellis; a small friendly Mrs Haden Guest; Kingsley Martin; Claud Cockburn; two young barristers, Dudley Collard and Geoffrey Bing; two solicitors, David Freeman and Ambrose Appelbe; Alun Thomas of the International Labour Defence; Professor Catlin (Vera Brittain's husband) and the writer Douglas Goldring.

I was still half-numbed as the meeting opened. The speakers were voicing a common feeling, a sense of impending danger. The accepted norms of democracy: free speech, freedom of assembly and association, the democratic control of government too easily taken for granted, were all now at risk in the current climate. It was put most vividly by the half-blind Professor Frederick Le Gros Clark, who had come from Cambridge and spoke with passion of the ground 'trembling under our feet'.

Most of those present were prepared to serve on the Executive of the Council. It was suggested that this should consist of twenty-four, and meet once a month. It would be useful to include Harold Laski and Dr Ivor Jennings, and to have a good representation of lawyers, writers and journalists. Henry Nevinson, or perhaps E.M. Forster, as President – a non-party figure to attract people of all opinions. Ronald was ready to take on the work of Secretary. The immediate job now to organise a Vigilance Committee of observers to cover the Hunger March due in London in a couple of days.

In a corner of my mind I wondered how on earth Ronald was going to do all this and still find time to earn his living. He was closing down the Punch and Judy Bookshop – the short lease was running out. The publishing firm he had been engaged in for some months was folding up. He had discovered too late that his seemingly-respectable partner had concealed overwhelming debts.

The 1934 Hunger March

The 1934 Hunger March started exactly as it had done in 1932 – the same pattern. On the eve, the arrests. Tom Mann – seventy-eight now – and Harry Pollitt both due to speak at the Bermondsey Town Hall Conference before the march to Hyde Park. But this time there was so much protest that the case was adjourned and both men were released on bail. Then the Home Secretary, Sir John Gilmour, warned the public not to be at large, to keep children off the streets, when the March arrived in London. The Attorney General hinted at possible bloodshed, and the Metropolitan police advised shopkeepers to shutter up their windows.

At this moment the Council's letter appeared in the *Times* and the *Manchester Guardian*, signed by its new Vice-Presidents, including C.R. Attlee, Harold Laski, A.P. Herbert, Henry Nevinson, Lascelles Abercrombie, and H.G. Wells. It announced the formation of the Council for Civil Liberties 'in view of the general and alarming tendency to encroachment on the liberty of the citizen'. It deplored the dangerous and unjustified atmosphere of misgiving created before the Hunger March by the official public statement of the Minister and the Law Officer, and the police warning to shopkeepers. It pointed out 'the excellent discipline of the marchers' and the 'instructions of the strictest character' against 'any breach of the peace, even under extreme provocation'. The newly-formed Council for Civil Liberties would 'maintain a vigilant observation of the proceedings of the next few days. Relevant and well-authenticated reports by responsible persons will be welcomed and investigated by the Council.'

Amongst those who had agreed to act as observers at the Council's invitation were E.M. Forster, H.G. Wells, Vera Brittain, Winifred Holtby and Professor Julian Huxley. Theo Smythe, small gruff and friendly, lent us her flat behind Selfridges as a *rendez-vous*. Someone was to sit by the phone all the afternoon, to take reports and act as liaison.

Her big bare room was half-filled by an enormous divan bed. When I sat down on it, my legs vanished. The observers came up the stairs in ones and twos. Julian Huxley and his smiling Swiss wife, Vera Brittain, small dark, determined, with Winifred Holtby tall, calm and big-boned, with a strap-hanging handbag. Had she slipped sandwiches in? Something of the atmosphere of an adventurous improvised picnic. Three or four very young barristers – later to acquire the dignity of QCs, one a judge – Neil Lawson, type-cast, correct, confident; Geoffrey Bing, dark, galvanic, restless; Dudley Collard, solid, fair, a hearts-of-oak young Saxon you could picture carrying his bat in a cricket match on the village green. David Freeman, bearded, paternalistic – he had been a magistrate in the colonial service.

Ronald had arranged for some of the big guns to be collected by committee members. Claud Cockburn had been detailed to escort H.G. Wells, who had not been well, and emerged, as Cockburn told us later, wrapped in mufflers by Baroness Budberg.

In the big space of Marble Arch, a slanting grey drizzle, crowds lining the pavements, overflowing into the roadway, crossing over to join the sea of hats in the Park – caps, trilbies, hard felts, the occasional bowler. The solid rumps of the police horses, foot police everywhere, the unusual helmets of the provincial forces. Reinforcements waited in vans in the side streets. A motor cycle, flying squad cars. High on the top of Marble Arch, police manned an improvised telephone. The specials well out of the way this time.

An insignificant unit, I struggled to remain alert, observant and not to let myself be assimilated into the friendly crowd.

Banners and music. They came on in orderly informal ranks, the marching men, some with packs on their backs, in step, some singing the 'Internationale'. Ragged cheers, back-chat, the rattle of the labelled collecting tins for the journey back. More and more, turning into the entrance through the welcoming banks of the crowd on either side.

In the trodden park, the high barking voice, applause and cheers, all anonymous to me as we ranged on the outskirts, the crowds massed tight round the high platforms. A packet of cigarettes flying, and another, for a group of Welsh miners with no fags. We pressed on towards the next platform.

It was turning into a bumper Sunday afternoon in the park – the tension evaporating. The crowd was winning. Their people's day! Static, good-natured, not to be shifted, not to be denied their loyalty.

Theo Smythe's phone kept silent all the afternoon. Not a scuffle, not a baton raised. No report from anywhere of even so much as a pane of glass broken. No bloodshed! 'The most dangerous elements in London' looking just like the men who pressed onto the workmen's train in the early morning, or followed on in the rush hour, jostling each other on the way to work, any, every, day.

With the peaceful demonstration proving itself, there was a favourable swing. The public conscience was touched. 'The marchers have shamed their detractors by their dignity and surprised those who knew their grievances best, by their restraint' – the *Star*. But in the House, the tetchy prima donna, Ramsay Macdonald refused to see their deputation.

The Archbishop of York wrote in the *Times* that Christians should support the restoration of the cuts. Even the BBC – its North Regional Station – approached a returned Lancashire marcher for a short talk. But George Staunton wanted to call himself 'a victim of the Means Test'. 'Too political': the broadcast was killed the day it was due to go out.

In the March budget, Neville Chamberlain found it expedient to restore the ten per cent cuts to the unemployed. In 1935 Clement Attlee was to appear on the same platform as Wal Hannington. And in 1936, Sir Philip Game, Metropolitan Commissioner, actually paid a tribute to the conduct of the Hunger March of November 1936 as 'beyond reproach' in his Annual Report for that year.

The response to the Council was immediate. Claud Cockburn, with his flair for publicity, his panache, was the champagne that helped to launch us. (I remember too that he gave Ronald five pounds to get the phone in: 'Absolutely essential', he urged him. It was installed immediately!)

The very first members of the Council we enrolled (subscription 5s.) read rather like the pages of a cultural, intellectual and progressive *Who's Who*, and Ronald was roping in the Vice-Presidents. In the climate of the mid-thirties, a new body that intended to be active and militant for democratic rights, needed, while it was finding its feet and establishing itself, the support and sponsorship of well-known public figures. 'Democracy' as a slogan to rally support had only fairly recently acquired respectability. Ronald, in the preface to his book *British Liberty in Danger* recalls:

> I am old enough to remember the days when Conservatives, almost unanimously, did not bother to disguise their dislike of and contempt for democracy ... since the Great War, it has become expedient for those who still dislike democracy at heart to pay lip service to that principle.

Now with the current attack on hard-won liberties, Ronald was concerned to get influential backing as widespread as possible for the young Council. Vice-Presidents of the left and right: Victor Gollancz and Viscountess Rhondda, the Dean of Canterbury and Canon H.R.L. Sheppard; high and low-brow: Bertrand Russell and A.A. Milne, Professor P.M.S. Blackett and Hannen Swaffer; Labour and Liberal peers, MPs, KCs; figures from literature, the arts and the universities: J.B.

Priestley, Havelock-Ellis, Rutland Boughton, Sybil Thorndike, Sir Charles Trevelyan. By the end of the year, forty interesting, significant names to flank our notepaper, now bearing the Dansey *Place* address. (No longer Yard. Ronald had written to the Westminster City Council suggesting that in its West-End site, *Place* was more suitable, and that with the proximity to Leicester Square's conveniences, the urinal might well be discontinued. Both requests were complied with.)

E.M. Forster and the Sedition Bill

E.M. Forster had been invited to be President. Replying, he said he would call in last thing, before he caught the train back to Abinger Hammer.

The room was waiting tidy and quiet, the fire burning, the door left unlatched. The place had changed its character. No more the Bohemian haven, hidden in a neglected dead mews. Now it was a workplace, striving to conform, to be public, visited, accepted as an office. A tall sentinel filing cabinet, box-files, reference books, the telephone, a new typewriter – the old basket chair banished, crammed away.

The place didn't belong to us, we belonged to it. The day's unfinished work still on your conscience as you closed your eyes – separated only by plyboard, for a short interval, before it was all picked up again next morning. The telephone, the post. The weekly General Purposes Sub-Committee landing another load, urgently ticking up, against time.

For Ronald it was a bond of love. He was in his element. He was prepared, as Secretary, to knot his tie hard and small, to keep his sideboards trimmed, discard his big black hat, wear his town suits instead of grey flannels and a patched tweed jacket. The everyday town suit already turning shiny, fitting a little too close. The same tailor as his father and grandfather. The bill not sent in till months after delivery, and not paid, perhaps for a year, so that when another was needed, he told me ruefully, he felt conscience bound to visit him again, instead of picking up a cheap ready-made. He matched up now to our lawyers in their professional pin-stripe and black.

A QC in his eighties, looking back forty years later, to Ronald at forty-five in his response to civil liberties, said that he was like a young man in love for the first time.

Forster, as he came in, looked a little uncertain. But his face lifted as Ronald came forward. With his unconscious air of authority, Ronald was as composed and assured as if our ramshackle room was a well-appointed office suite, and the prospect outside was St James's Park. It never occurred to him that there was anything to apologise for, or any need to make excuses.

He introduced me. Forster smiled, noticed in appreciation the old-fashioned fireplace. I faded into the background, as redundant as Agnes Pembroke on her first visit to Rickie's room at Cambridge.

They stood together the two of them looking out over the yard. Forster was keenly aware of the fierce breath of the rhinoceros of fascism, the thunder of brute force to trample and overrun the sensitive humanitarian world. Not that he used any metaphor or particular emphasis, but this was the impression he conveyed in his own oblique tentative style of understatement. His lively awareness of danger and the implications for everything that mattered to him.

Ronald instanced as a flagrant attack on civil liberty the current, and already notorious, Incitement to Disaffection Bill. As drafted, the scope was unlimited, it could be used against anyone with pacifist or left-wing literature on their shelves. Forster had only just heard about it. They sat down. Now Ronald was in full spate, explaining, quoting.

I tuned out. It was all familiar ground. The campaign to kill the 'Sedition Bill' was our first all-out objective. Our lawyers had got to work at once on the Bill, and within forty-eight hours of its introduction into the House, every MP was provided with a detailed legal analysis of the dangers implicit in the measure. 'The most daring encroachment on the liberty of the subject which the executive has yet attempted at a time which is not a time of emergency,' was the verdict of the leading jurist, Sir William Holdsworth. P.C. Gordon-Walker, Tutor of Christ Church, Oxford, called it 'A Bill with a fascist outlook. It proposes steps which are fundamentally the same as those which have already been taken in Germany. There must be few people in Oxford whose houses would not be liable to search if the Bill is put into force.' The Bill in fact empowered a single JP, if he was satisfied by a statement on oath, to give any policeman the right to enter 'if necessary by force' and search any premises anywhere, and the people there, and to seize anything he decided was incriminating. And the Bill made the *possession* of literature which could be considered subversive if it fell into the hands of members of the armed forces, punishable by two years imprisonment and a fine of £200! It was in fact introducing the right of general search, abolished in the eighteenth century. All this and more was printed in our first leaflet, which had been widely distributed.

Forster was remembering his train home. He had made up his mind. 'I am prepared', he said, 'to be President' – but typically he hedged with a modest disclaimer – 'provided that Henry Nevinson [who had been ill], much better fitted than myself, really doesn't feel up to taking it on.'

Forster remembered this first meeting in Dansey Yard, when he wrote to me eight years later, after I had resigned as assistant secretary,

> I have such a vivid personal sense of all you have done, and how you and Mr Kidd have not merely served the Council but started it [too generous there as far as I was concerned]. I remember as most of our Committee cannot where the start was in a tiny room up a narrow staircase in a mews. This is the sort of place where important movements do start.

A few days later, a Quaker businessman, Harrison Barrow, on a brief visit to London, presented himself into the middle of our congested scene, the girls busy round the trestle table, fetching, stacking, folding, sorting. Ignoring the kitchen chair I proferred, he requested to be directed to Mr Kidd's private office, and was purposefully making his way towards the curtained passage-way and the domestic huddle behind it, when at that moment Ronald appeared up the stairs. As with Forster, it was instant reassurance. Ronald's calm and serenity restored confidence and order. (In his obituary Forster spoke of his gravity and courtesy.) They chatted for a while. No time for coffee. They parted cordially. His letter and cheque arrived soon after.

At first I had worked voluntarily and part-time, still tied to my coaching job – my last term. Ronald had pinned me down on the notepaper as Hon. Treasurer. Happily I was soon joined by a Joint Hon. Treasurer, a trained accountant who did all the work and kept a careful check on day-to-day finances.

Off my bike, after the morning's work, I gobbled lunch at home and caught the first train to London. I would find two or three elegant girls smelling sweet and with bangles – introduced by Cockburn – waiting for leaflets to fold, envelopes to address, sheets of halfpenny stamps. We were snowed under with circulars and literature for the delegate conference we were holding jointly with the London Trades Council on the 'Sedition Bill'. The first step to spread the protest against the Bill through national bodies, then on to branch level, and after Greater London to proliferate outwards with conferences and meetings first in the big provincial centres and then further afield.

The girls left behind with their neat stacks of envelopes a little of their glamour and perfume. The day's work finally checked, it was round about midnight that Ronald finally left with a loaded suitcase for the all-night post office in Leicester Square.

The campaign against the Bill went on all through the year. It had opened with a meeting at the Central Hall, off Parliament Square. Margery Fry had presented us with a cheque for £50 to cover the deposit on the hall. Our speakers at the meeting were E.M. Forster, H.G. Wells, J.B. Priestley and the Bishop of Birmingham. Our meeting at the Kingsway Hall could have been filled twice over. The overflow was directed into Lincoln's Inn, and a rostrum erected for the speakers after they had left the platform at the Kingsway Hall to come on again in the square. Clement Attlee was rather reluctant, he started off a little peevishly – 'I have to be back in the House ...' – but he gradually thawed to the responsiveness of the audience that had been waiting patiently on their feet in the dim square.

We intended to follow up with demonstrations in Trafalgar Square, the first to be in June. We were planning to get effective speakers and public figures on the plinth in the square. Geoffrey Bing, always bursting with ideas, had been calling in daily to the office to lend a hand. He circulated restlessly round the trestle table in the cluttered room, picking up letters and press cuttings, dropping them, his eyes focused on dazzling possibilities. He was conceiving, exploding with ideas. He tried them out on Ronald. When one fell flat, he frowned, incredulous, but with a dismissive smile, he started again. The warmth of his concern was stimulating, infectious. 'How about Bernard Shaw on the plinth?' A winning smile. 'But hasn't he recently praised Mussolini?' Bing waved this aside. I got on the phone. 'I'm too old,' the canny sage parried. 'Not at all,' I encouraged him. 'Mrs Despard in her eighties will be there.' But I couldn't persuade him. He remained cheerfully obdurate. (Bernard Shaw did in fact enrol as a member in 1939 just before the outbreak of war, and kept up his interest in the Council to the end of his life, instructing NCCL how to run its campaigns through his famous postcards.)

Trafalgar Square, before it all started, seemed so placid and immovable, so everyday with its familiar pattern of jerking pigeons in their in-and-out trot, its vacant apathetic lions. Only the perpetual splash of the fountains was reassuring and stirred a faint tropical echo. All that empty space to fill! The step-ladders and coils were already busy round the plinth. I wandered restlessly.

At last! Coming round the National Gallery, the faithful with their banners! And now clumps of people were dropping off buses, joining up into semi-circles, coalescing into solid ranks. I circulated with petition forms, directing people to the camp-tables with stacks of them and fountain pens.

When it was all over, a small group of supporters, still activated by the warmth of the demonstration, came back with us to Dansey Place to tot up the cash. Spilt out on the trestle table it looked more than when it was contained in bank envelopes. (Cockburn childishly eager to master Ronald's expert tucking-in and folding.) Too many blue envelopes with coppers, not enough buff with silver, and only a slender harvest of notes. Our supporters always with more enthusiasm than ready cash.

The *Star* gave us a good write-up. The idea that only a

section of the community opposed the Bill 'definitely killed by the Trafalgar Square demonstration'. They spoke of Quakers and Communists, 'Men of all parties and of none … People of all shades of thought gathered to fight for the right of free speech.'

Our second Trafalgar Square demonstration, held towards the end of October, just before Parliament reassembled, was a much bigger one. It was followed by a mass lobby of MPs, and then by the presentation of our mass petition against the Bill by the much-respected parliamentarian Eleanor Rathbone, Independent member for the Combined Universities.

If we couldn't suceed in killing the Bill, it had to be radically altered. Our lawyers drafted amendments that were put through by sympathetic MPs. During the Committee stage we followed up with amendments to amendments, and when the Bill went to the Lords, a rota of our lawyers took it in turn to be at hand with legal advice.

In the end the Bill went on the statute book, but considerably weakened. The young Council in its first campaign had proved its effectiveness. A search warrant now could only be granted through a High Court judge, and to an Inspector (or higher rank policeman), and with certain limitations. *Possession* of literature in itself was no longer an offence without the intention of using it maliciously and advisedly. But the Act was still a bad one. Who can judge intentions? And the onus was still on the accused to prove the absence of an ulterior intention, rather than on the prosecution to prove the commission of an offence. But the big publicity campaign, the general outcry against the measure, made it so unpopular that the government felt it expedient to put it in cold storage for the time being. It was used once in the thirties against a student who was naïve enough to attempt to persuade an RAF man, met in a café, to help the Republican side in the Spanish Civil War. His sentence of twelve months was cut on appeal. Even before the Bill became law, a timid printer had refused to set up in type a pacifist leaflet. And now both the National Peace Council and the Peace Pledge Union had affiliated to our Council.

Of all the events in our campaign against the Bill, I enjoyed most the public debate with both D.N. Pritt and Harold Laski backing each other up in brilliant form, and goading their opponent, Douglas Jerrold (whom I had always thought of as a strictly literary figure) to shed his cultured veneer and reveal himself as an out-and-out reactionary. (He was responsible in 1936 for flying Franco back into Spain from Morocco to lead the rebels in the Spanish Civil War.) His colleague, W.S. Morrison, was only shadow-boxing, no bite in him at all.

But for everybody else – looking back nostalgically in their memoirs – it was the mock trial that was the highlight of the campaign. The cartoonist David Low stood in the dock, accused of seducing the soldier, Kingsley Martin, from his duty and allegiance by his famous cartoon (auctioned afterwards). Miles Malleson was the comedy policeman. Colonel Blimp appeared as a witness for the prosecution and somebody's real-life mistress played a tart. The most uproarious fun came from the legal element. W.H. Thompson and the other civil liberty lawyers acting for the defence and the prosecution, with Aylmer Vallance (still the editor of the *News Chronicle*) the foil as the senile judge. The audience was crammed tight into Friends' House, Euston Road. It was drawn mostly from Fleet Street, the Temple and the Haldane Society, and they were all in the picture, relishing the legal in-jokes. The lawyers – for once and unforgettably — unhooking their legal corsets, letting themselves go, cocking a snook at authoritarian postures and hierarchical bigotry and pomposity in court, with justice adjusted to accommodate ancient bladders and gastric failings. They were all in the mood enjoying themselves in their verbal-intellectual-political romp.

I was rather out of it, too hungry and empty to share the fun. I had missed my lunch unable to get away from the office with its never-ending queue coming up the metal stairs clamouring for last-minute seats – sold out long ago. I could only feed them with literature and promises for the future. I could have disposed of standing room for the top price of 5s. – or was it 7s. 6d.? Doubled in price, all the seats would still have gone. But I would never have dreamed of querying the immutable masculine ideological rule of always keeping prices down to a low level with ample provision of very cheap seats for the unemployed. We could never expect to make a profit. In my rather jaundiced mood and standing at the back, it seemed to me just amateur theatricals with a lot of middle-aged men enjoying themselves and ad-libbing like mad. I found a seat outside on the literature stall, where I sat swinging my legs and waiting for the end when it could all be dismantled and I could get away to some grub.

Not any more for me was it a question of catching fire – as in the earlier meeting in the basement. Now it was a steady day-to-day grind, with regular chores. I was learning the ropes. The arrangement at first was that the Council paid Ronald rent for its accommodation, and then later on, instead, that he received a salary as secretary. I came on the paid staff towards the end of July as assistant secretary. I believe that towards the end of the year we had a part-time girl clerk. For shorthand and copy typing we had a girl from an agency working by the hour. I am vague now about what we were paid. The first balance-sheet in our Annual Report gives the expenditure for rent as £34 17s. 6d. and salaries £168 11s. 7d. (Maybe the typist came under office expenses of £30 1s. 2d.)

4

Mosley and Olympia

Mother was to read in her *Daily Mail* – along with two and a half million others, mostly in middle-class homes – that Germany and Italy under fascism were the best governed nations in Europe. What Britain needed to survive as a great power was a 'Party of the Right with the same directness of purpose and energy of method as Hitler and Mussolini'. Purely British, of course – so 'Hurrah for the Blackshirts!'

'How can you stomach it?'

· 'Don't be silly dear. I like the gardening tips, and the recipes, and I cut out the insurance coupons. Don't you take it away!'

She kept the filthy rag by her mending basket. Ready to spread it out and sit reading comfortably by the french windows, looking out at the tennis in the sunshine. And the arrests, the interrogations, the bleeding was going on.

Cook in the kitchen got a nice read of the *Sunday Pictorial*. Father provided it for her instead of the vulgar *News of the World*.

Viscount Rothermere had launched his crusade to promote British fascism a month before the Council was set up. 'Hurrah for the Blackshirts!' was the headline on 8 January 1934. His *Sunday Dispatch* and *Evening News* carried the same slant too.

My father, traditionally, read the *Times*, his link with England when he was in Brazil. Now it was his daily diet to keep him in touch with business, politics, affairs at home and abroad. But was he aware that the editor had set the Thunderer on a course of appeasement? Nothing to go in that would offend Hitler. Geoffrey Dawson, with his pro-German bias, turned it, as A.J.P. Taylor put it, 'into a propaganda sheet and did not hesitate to suppress, or to pervert, the reports of his own correspondents'. Kingsley Martin tells us in *Editor* (the second volume of his autobiography) that '*The Times* censored every anti-Nazi despatch from their correspondents in Berlin; Norman Ebbutt was the outstanding example of a brilliant journalist who lost his job because he told the truth.'

I challenged my father about the fraternisation of his local Conservative Association with the fascists. I had seen displayed on the big notice board outside their local premises an advertisement of a blackshirt meeting! My father gave a half-grin, unperturbed – boys will be boys!

And this from a man of Victorian morality, who prided himself on a keen sense of justice, and who had on his book-shelves the works of H.G. Wells and Bernard Shaw!

Fascism was in the air. It was on the winning side! The times propitious, dry tinder, tempting the ambitious adventurer in politics, the ruthless opportunist who felt in himself the power to set the flare, spread the blaze, conquer the blackened heights. Fascist parties springing up everywhere. Colonel de la Rocque's Croix de Feu, the best-organised in France, Leon Degrelle's Rexist movement detaching Belgium from Franco-British influence. In England it was Mosley.

Sir Oswald

Sir Oswald Mosley was born 'with a golden spoon in his mouth' – according to his hard-drinking estranged father, 'and never did a day's work in his life'.

He went to Winchester and then Sandhurst, where he was in the wealthy, exclusive polo-playing class. Backed by two or three friends, he took a riding-crop to another cadet who had tried to bring him down a peg, and later, escaping from the avenging sequel, jumped out of his window, broke an ankle – and was rusticated. In the 1914 war he was at first an observer in the new Royal Flying Corps. When he got his pilot's licence he crashed his plane and broke the same ankle again. He was out of it for five months, and then back with his regiment, in the trenches for another five months. His leg got infected, and in March 1916 Lieutenant Mosley, aged twenty, was out of the war – after just under a year on active service.

(Nineteen years later, at a fascist meeting, a heckler asked Mosley what was his profession, and got the answer: 'I fought in France for Great Britain so that rats like you might live.' Some of these rats were to fight, and die, in Spain in the International Brigade.)

He went into Parliament as a Conservative in Lloyd George's coalition. Then he stood as Independent.

We saw on the newsreels royalty and high society – looking incredibly heavy and dull – alighting at the Chapel Royal for his wedding to Cynthia Curzon, the heiress daughter of the Foreign Secretary, Viscount Curzon of Kedleston. She was the grandaughter, on her mother's side of the Chicago millionaire, Levi Zeigler Leiter.

Now Mosley broke with tradition and joined the Labour Party. He held office briefly as Chancellor of the Duchy of Lancaster. But impatient at the failure to get his plans for dealing with unemployment immediately accepted, he broke away and formed his own New Party. His twenty-four candidates standing at the General Election of 1931 failed disastrously, twenty-two at the bottom of the poll with lost deposits. Mosley turned his New Party into the British Union of Fascists.

'Why did you choose fascism?'

The survivor, at seventy-nine, was appearing on television – briefly in the news again – in the spring of 1975, with the publication of his biography. He seemed to enjoy the news-clips of the thirties recapping his bid to be fascist dictator: the forest of raised hands – Hail Mosley! The arrogant Semitic good looks – the Lyceum villain of melodrama! Flashing eyes, vicious mouth. His paramilitary blackshirt ranks marching, heavily escorted, insulated by protective police. The phalanx of banners, Union Jacks. The spotlight glare to focus the Leader! The batteries of loud speakers to carry the iron message of the would-be executioner of democracy!

More like a formidable old undertaker now. But still plying for hire. Still ready for the job: 'I don't feel old,' he said. The eyes in retreat now, the ugly mouth, coarsened, rapacious, had taken over, the voice with the old menace, the ugly note.

'Fascism was the only thing. I tried everything else ... I could have had power for the asking … I was always right.'

He wasn't so sure in 1949. In my *Who's Who* of that date, he ends his political career in 1930, as Labour Chancellor of the Duchy of Lancaster (he was expelled from the Labour Party for gross disloyalty in 1931.) He conveniently chose to forget his decade of high fascism. More propitious to admit to fascism in the seventies!

He took the salute in Rome with Mussolini on the anniversary of the introduction of fascism, and wrote enthusiastically about the new Italy. He backed Mussolini in his Abyssinian war, opposing sanctions with the 'patriotic' slogan 'Mind Britain's Business', while accepting a secret subsidy of £60,000 plus a year from Mussolini. The native grass huts 'opened like a rose' under the Italian bombs.

Mosley sent two of his followers to Germany to study Hitler's methods. He borrowed Nazi songs – the Horst Wessel; their slogans: 'Britain (Germany) Awake!', 'Perish Judah!'; their political violence; their anti-Semitism. And he added to the name of his movement the Nazi Party wording, 'and National Socialist'.

Hitler came to his wedding luncheon – given by Frau Goebbels – when he was secretly married in Germany in 1936 to the Hon. Diana Guinness (Cynthia Mosley died in 1933). His second wife was one of the Mitford girls. Her sister Unity, a Mosley follower, went to Germany – no doubt hoping to find someone to match up to her. The 'perfect Ayran type' she was socially accepted into the Nazi inner circle of Hitler, Himmler, Goebbels and Goering. It was rumoured she was in love with Hitler. Her sister Diana joined her in Germany.

The success of Nazi Germany stirred Mosley's blood and fired his ambition. 'Our Blood Brothers', he exulted, and 'from the bottom of my heart, "Heil Hitler!" ' (*The Blackshirt*, 27 September 1933).

There were rumours and suspicions about Mosley's financial backers. It had been estimated that Mosley paid out £20,000 in salaries in 1934. He hired a special train to take his Defence Force, stewards and blackshirt supporters to a meeting in Manchester. Funds from industrialists were mostly kept secret. Sir William Morris, later Lord Nuffield, had given Mosley £50,000 in his New Party days.

Mosley was a great litigator, and the courts were often kind to him. He was awarded £5,000 in the High Court in November 1934, for a libel in the *Star* reporting a public debate between himself and James Maxton. According to his secretary's shorthand notes, it was against the Communists, not the government, that he would be ready to use machine-guns. And he received as well a bouquet from Lord Chief Justice Hewart, who described him as 'a public man of no mean courage, no little candour, and no mean ability'.

Against John Marchbanks, General Secretary of the National Union of Railwaymen, with D.N. Pritt, KC defending, he was not so fortunate. He won his case – and the jury awarded a farthing damages.

The movement bristled with retired officers: majors, colonels, captains, wing-commanders and a vice-admiral; some of these branch leaders. It had the support of a sprinkling of Tory MPs, and of a few peers with ancient names: the Earl of Erroll, hereditary Lord High Constable of Scotland, Lord Tollemache, Lord Strathspey, and some well-connected Tory ladies in the counties. Lady Houston, the ample, wealthy self-advertising pillar of Empire who published the *Saturday Review* and admired Mussolini and Hitler, was finding Sir Oswald impressive too.

The 'Black House', Mosley's Chelsea headquarters, was a big rambling 'barracks' with a parade- and sports-ground and a gymnasium and canteen. It housed his private army, run on paramilitary lines with bugles, reveille, inspection, drill, parades. Recruits were accepted as they applied. Some of them from the former Black and Tans. A few of the young unemployed were attracted to the Black House by the prospect of free beer and fags, a uniform, cheap canteen meals and pocket money. Perhaps they had tried and failed to get in the army – in 1933 more than two-thirds of would-be recruits were turned down as physically unfit – a grim reminder of social conditions. The paid Fascist Defence Force in particular attracted bad types – six to ten expulsions a week, according to the *Manchester Guardian* of 3 March 1934. The artist James Holland captured cruelly some of the retarded types I saw at demonstrations and meetings, in a cartoon for a 1936 book calendar – illustrated also by James Fitton and James Boswell –

the lantern-jawed aggressive with no back to his head, the flat face moronic. The caption from Giovanezza (which the blackshirts borrowed from Italian fascism) ran 'Youth! Youth! Springtime of Beauty!'

All kinds of rumours circulated about the Black House. Stories leaked out about beatings-up, with castor-oil administered, for infiltrators, and about a motor corps with armoured cars – questions in the House about this. Their Leeds branch did in fact attempt to train a fascist air-unit, but was prevented as the aerodrome in question received financial assistance from the government.

For the wider public not actively engaged in politics, the image of fascism was still respectable. There was the January Club, that was founded at the beginning of 1934 'to provide a platform for leaders of Fascism and Corporate State thought'. It was accommodated at Lord Midleton's London flat and held its dinners at the Savoy and the Hotel Splendide. Its first Chairman was Sir John Squire, editor of the *London Mercury* who was acting editor of the *New Statesman* for the last two years of the 1914 war. (As a schoolgirl on my way to college, the thick *London Mercury* in its orange-yellow covers was my high-brow introduction to the modern literary scene.) Another member of the club was the writer Francis Yeats-Brown.

Blackshirts At Olympia

It was at the vast stadium of Olympia on 7 June 1934 that Mosley planned to make his most ambitious bid for publicity, introducing, as he put it 'something new in the political life of this country'. This huge rally was to be the peak event following on earlier meetings: at Brighton and Bristol in March, at the Albert Hall in London in April, at the Usher Hall in Edinburgh, again in Bristol on 1 June and in London at Finsbury Park on 3 June.

All these meetings, were accompanied by violence – except the one at the Albert Hall. After the Brighton meeting, two blackshirts, the area organiser for West Sussex, Captain Bentinck-Budd and F.W. Knowles from Chelsea headquarters, were found guilty of assault on the local organiser of the

National Unemployed Workers' Movement, whom they had invited to the meeting, and on his wife, both of whom found themselves, with their small child, 'boxed in' by fascists.

A wealthy baronet, with friends at court, Mosley had the standing to have ready access to and meet on easy terms, key people who mattered. Claud Cockburn in his news-sheet, *The Week*, with its inspired low-down on the latest in the City, and on national and international ramifications in diplomacy and politics – compulsory reading for the would-be well-informed, left and right, in the citadels of power, the diplomatic corps, even (so it was said) in royal circles – reported that Mosley was lunching with Lord Trenchard (the Metropolitan Police Commissioner) at the Savoy on the eve of his big London demonstration.

Lieutenant Colonel Sir Thomas Moore, OBE, CBE, Freeman of the City of London, Director of the World's Press News and Unionist Member for Ayr Burgs, gave Mosley a good Conservative plug in the *Daily Mail* on 27 April, asking:

> What is there in a black shirt that gives apparent dignity and intelligence to its wearer? ... There was little if any, of the policy which could not be accepted by the most loyal followers of our present Conservative leaders ... Surely there cannot be any fundamental differences of outlook between Blackshirts and their parents the Conservatives? For let me make no mistake about the parentage ... it is largely derived from the Conservative Party ... Surely the relationship can be made closer and more friendly.

Lord Rothermere topped this up in the *Sunday Dispatch* of 17 May: Sir Oswald Mosley was 'perhaps the greatest political teacher we have produced in this country'.

Invitations to Olympia were issued to people who mattered. Sir Oswald informed the police that their services would not be required inside the stadium. He had his own Defence Force of black-shirted stewards. A year earlier at the Free Trade Hall in Manchester, the *Manchester Guardian* correspondent had seen them using what looked like rubber truncheons. The police then – uninvited – had entered the meeting, segregated the stewards and restored order. Now Mosley wanted his stewards to have a free hand. A warning note was sounded in the *Sunday Dispatch*. Anyone attending the meeting who conducted himself not as the stewards wished would 'be put outside swiftly, efficiently and with the minimum of *noise*'. This substitution for the usual word, hinting that there would be no limits to the use of *force*.

The Communists, taking the lead for the anti-fascists, had made it known that they were going to be vocal in protest inside the stadium, and to demonstrate outside Olympia. They were not going to let Mosley get away with it by default. They were ready, at any cost, to expose that underneath the patriotic show and the façade of discipline, there was a policy of violence – many of them had already experienced it. A call had gone out to London workers, backed by lunch-hour and factory-gate meetings, and walls had been whitewashed with slogans for a rally at Olympia.

An hour or so before the meeting crowds were collecting outside Olympia: busmen, building workers, men from the furnishing trades, from engineering and catering, machine minders from the *Daily Mail* and the *Evening News*, the unemployed, pacifists, students, the young and committed with a burning sense of outrage against fascism, the liberal-minded, many of them with their placards and their pamphlets. Processions from the East End, escorted by police, were diverted into side streets. By the time the meeting was due to start traffic in the Hammersmith Road was almost at a standstill, and there were 760 foot and mounted police on duty in the streets outside Olympia.

Mr Skidelsky, Oswald Mosley's biographer, assiduously tracking police records, tells us that Special Branch men in the crowd were busy spotting and noting down known Communists in the crowd. In particular they listed nine names, eight men and one woman who were not only Communists but also of foreign extraction – most of them Jewish. Evidently in the thirties, people with names like Pincus Zinkin would do better to stay at home and not join demonstrations against fascism. All in good time, fascism would come to them – to their doorsteps in the East End – and even then they would be well-advised to stay indoors and mind their own business, and not come out to be provoked. Mr Skidlelsky, listing the nine names, adds: 'The fact that a significant portion of his *assailants* was Jewish was later to be given by Mosley as one of the chief reasons for his attack on the Jews. (My italics, S.S.). The upside-down cause and effect argument familiar in Nazi propaganda.

The meeting started late. A build-up of suspense with music. Five columns of blackshirts had marched from the Chelsea barracks, collected from all over the British Isles to swell the ranks. Tinned-salmon-pink drapes adorned the interior, according to the *Manchester Guardian*. Blackshirt stewards stood in the aisles, planting themselves aggressively at the end of rows. And now trumpets sounded to herald the theatrically staged entrance, and a spotlight fastened on the Leader. To cheers and applause Mosley advanced with an escort of four blond blackshirts under Union Jacks, followed by a cohort of uniformed men carrying pennons, and more of them with arms outstretched. A Conservative MP, H.K. Hales: 'Like an army marching with banners flying ... They might have been Roman warriors coming home from battle ... their leader with immobile features like the Sphinx himself.' (He was speaking in the Olympia debate in Parliament seven days later.)

Elevated on his dais Mosley gave tongue through twenty-five loudspeakers: 'Ladies and gentlemen, this great meeting, the largest ever gathered ... the climax of a national campaign ... every great city of this land. Thousands of ...'

An indistinct counterpoint had been breaking in, accompanying, competing with the amplified volume. The first brave voice had been joined by others and was picked up all over the auditorium. But it was only when Mosley stopped dead, cut out the loudspeakers, that the slogan could clearly be heard: 'Mosley and fascism mean hunger and war!' Even then, owing to the acoustics, it was not readily intelligible everywhere. But everyone was immediately aware of the reaction. The Blackshirts howled and yelled. Stewards started up all over the stadium, running, converging on the interrupters. The cheer-leaders rallied their packs to shout louder and fiercer: 'Mosley! Mosley!' But now the regimented throats met the opposition echo ... 'hunger and war!'

The spell had been broken. The fascist monopoly was shattered. The triumph was turning into pandemonium. The spotlight shifted from the platform to the audience. 'How would you like to live on fifteen shillings and threepence a week?' The voice was articulate only to those in the vicinity, but Mosley halted again, switching the interest away from the platform as blackshirts fell on the heckler, dragging him away for more punishment out of sight. Mosley, in control on his dais and with the overwhelming power of his loudspeakers, chose to adopt the tactic of highlighting every interruption, baiting, challenging – but never answering – the opposition. He ad libbed crudely: 'Red agitators', 'forged tickets', 'lowest ghettoes'. As Geoffrey Lloyd, Stanley Baldwin's Parliamentary Secretary, put it in the House: 'He was out deliberately to exacerbate interruptions and foment bitterness and fighting.' As the heckling and the disruptive incidents multiplied, Mosley threatened: 'The process of interruption becomes increasingly painful, not for us, but for the interrupters.' And sticking in the spurs: 'If there are any more reds left not sheltering behind their women they should show themselves and be dealt with.' He boasted: 'It is in the blackshirts' power today to stop any socialist meeting in the country any night we might choose.' He went on unctuously: 'Can you name any socialist meeting at which blackshirts have ever interrupted?' A rhetorical question, but it was answered six days later at Question Time in the Commons by the Home Secretary: ' … on the 24 May (a fortnight before Olympia) … a party of fascists attempted to break up a meeting held at Kilburn under the auspices of the British Anti-War Movement.'

What happened in the course of that evening at Olympia, during Mosley's halting delivery of 'one of the worst speeches I have ever heard', as Lord Winterton described it, has been well documented. The 'people who mattered', including a number of NCCL's Vice-Presidents – the Revd Dick Sheppard, Aldous Huxley, Gerald Barry, Vera Brittain, Naomi Mitchison and Storm Jameson, as well as editors, peers, politicians and others, were promptly vocal in the press. Three pamphlets full of quotes burst into print: *Blackshirt Brutality – The Story of Olympia* by Ivor Montagu, *Fascists at Olympia* by Vindicator, published by Victor Gollancz, and a fascist pamphlet, *Red Violence and Blue Lies*.

Dick Sheppard, who had assisted at Mosley's wedding, and buried Cynthia Mosley the previous year, was invited to the rally by Mosley's mother. He left early. In the corridors on his way out he saw 'men ... who had already been ejected ... treated by an overwhelming number of blackshirts in the most brutal and outrageous manner'. He went to the *Daily Telegraph* to record his horrified reaction.

Three Conservative MPs, T.J. O'Connor, KC, a one-time boxer and steeplechaser, W.J. Anstruther-Gray, a twenty-nine year old former Guards officer and H.J. Scrimgeour-Wedderburn, a Scottish MP, came together to Olympia, 'thinking that there might be a bit of fun'. They too left early because they were 'being placed in the position either of being manhandled or of being cowardly cads for not intervening'. They recorded their protest in the *Times*: 'against the ... wholly unnecessary violence inflicted by uniformed blackshirts on interrupters ... a deplorable outrage on public order'. Geoffrey Lloyd summed up in the *Yorkshire Post*: 'The blackshirts behaved like bullies and cads ... it was a deeply shocking scene for an Englishman to see in London ... I came to the conclusion that Mosley was a political maniac and that all decent English people must combine to kill his movement.'

What A.E. Coppard, the poet and writer, saw (quoted in *Fascists at Olympia*) is interesting in the context of an inquiry by the Assistant Police Commissioner into the only entry that night of the police into Olympia – and which I refer to later;

> On leaving the meeting at about 9.50 we met some blackshirts carrying one of their victims ... He was quite conscious but helpless, and seemed to have broken a limb. After passing him we met a body of blackshirts scurrying up the stairs in alarm crying out 'Here's the police!' ... We passed in the passage another poor devil who was sitting down and could not move owing to an injured leg. His face was covered with blood.

The experience of Jacob Miller was also referred to in Parliament. A student from Sheffield, given a ticket to Olympia, he ventured an innocuous remark and was promptly seized by blackshirts. He was thrown bodily over the gallery into the body of the hall – a drop of some ten feet. He lost consciousness and came to in a yard outside. 'Absolutely helpless', surrounded by blackshirts, he was beaten up with a cosh and then thrown out into the street. Dazed, bleeding, dentures knocked out, coat ripped, covered in blood, he staggered about and appealed for help to 'several policemen'. They did nothing but indicate that an ambulance was somewhere round the corner. A complete stranger took him to a doctor, who gave him first aid and drove him to St Mary Abbott's hospital, where he was detained. He was still in hospital – along with another Olympia victim – on 12 June, the date when Mosley speaking at Shrewsbury stated 'Not a single red has been detained in hospital.'

In the streets outside Olympia, the crowds, held back by the foot and mounted police away from the exits and entrances and on the opposite side of the road, caught glimpses of blackshirts manhandling victims before they pitched them into the roadway and the police closed the gates. As the incidents multiplied – the meeting went on till about eleven – indignation grew, with calls for the police to intervene, stop the violence, make arrests. A similar request was also put by members of the audience leaving the meeting. But the police, as we learned in Parliament, had been instructed to keep out of Olympia. They turned a deaf ear and kept the crowd on the move. They mounted the pavement, charged, and on occasion used their batons – although this was denied in the House. In all they made twenty-three arrests.

Richard Jeffries, writing in the *New Statesman*, saw through the opened gates a man being struck and kicked by blackshirts before he was thrown out bleeding freely, and the police closed the gates. Part of the crowd surged over, calling for an arrest. Mounted police came up to drive them back, the injured man was half-dragged, half-carried away from the horse's hoofs, and it was a young man in the crowd who was arrested – for obstruction.

Some of the 'best people' caught up in the crowd experienced for the first time contact with the police in action in a demonstration. One of the unlucky ones was Lord Berners. He was knocked against the railings by a policeman who said to him very rudely 'Get out!' and hit him over the head with some sort of weapon like a sword. His friend, a physicist, Charles Vivian Jackson, who was looking for his car, protested, 'You can't do that,' and was struck by a mounted policeman's baton and arrested. Mr Jackson said in Court:

the police assaulted him in a most aggressive manner. The crowd were not disorderly. They were certainly singing their dismal little song, but the way the police acted was the most extraordinary performance he had ever seen. He was fined 20s. for obstruction, but found not guilty of using insulting words.

The blackshirts were not to have it all their own way. Some of them, in their provocative uniform, were made the scapegoats for the brutality that had been meted out that evening. Militants in the crowd stayed on, biding their time, waiting for the final dispersal after the meeting ended. They waylaid fascist stewards and avenged the men they had seen bleeding and battered. The same tactics of reprisal had apparently been used after a recent fascist meeting in Edinburgh, when the blackshirt stewards 'were in the position of rats leaving a haystack when there is a pack of terriers waiting ...' as Mr Anstruther-Gray put it in Parliament in the Olympia debate.

After the meeting Mosley gave his dictator-in-the-wings communiqué to the *Daily Mail*:

> ... a wonderful meeting ... there were some disturbances, but the blackshirts are entirely blameless. My chief of staff wrote to the Commissioner of Police ... that the blackshirts would be responsible for law and order in the meeting ... a number of Communists and Socialists were permitted to gather outside the entrance to Olympia and there appears to have been trouble. The blackshirts ask one of two things – either that the police will keep order in the streets or we will keep order ourselves.

Mosley's arrogant either-or demands were in fact to be fully complied with by the police two years later when the scandal of Olympia had been forgotten.

The *Mail* also featured an enthusiastic report of the meeting by G. Ward Price:

> ... Red hooligans savagely and systematically tried to wreck Sir Oswald Mosley's huge and magnificently successful meeting. They got what they deserved ... The blackshirt stewards had the combination of a first-class rugby football team ... Sir Oswald spoke of people from the ghettoes ... with knives, razors, iron spikes ... never been known in England before they reached

our shores ...

The liberal *News Chronicle* praised the courage of men and women who hated fascism and through a carefully organised demonstration turned Mosley's triumph into a fiasco.

The following evening the BBC conceded a few minutes each to Mosley and Gerald Barry. Mosley spoke of brutal attacks on his stewards. He flourished the emotive razor:

> Now I put it to you, to your sense of fair play, would you have handled these reds very gently when you had seen your men kicked in the stomach, and slashed with razors, and your women with their faces streaming with blood? ... I can promise you that we at least will continue to preserve law and order.

The Home Secretary told Parliament that no hospital casualties were treated for razor injuries. Gerald Barry saw no weapons, nor did the violence originate with the members of the audience.

> I followed the ejectors out ... I saw a man lying on the floor, obviously powerless and done for, being mercilessly kicked and horribly handled. The ejection from the audience effected the stewards had no possible justification for increasing the violence out of sight and sound of the audience.

The Berlin press, according to Reuters, came out with 'Red Terror in London'. The misgivings, it said, about Sir Oswald Mosley's attitude to the Jewish question, were now at rest, and increased interest was being taken in his movement. The Nazi paper edited by Rosenberg described the demonstrators outside Olympia as 'Jewish and negroid sub-men'.

Reactions in Parliament

Questions were asked in Parliament about the Olympia meeting, and a full day's debate was devoted to it on 14 June. Labour and Liberal opposition MPs wanted government action against political violence and police inaction, and two Conservative MPs who had seen for themselves fascist law and order in action testified to the brutality. Isaac Foot for the Liberals wanted to know what government policy was, about police presence at public meetings, the assumption that stewards were there to keep order no longer held. Mosley with his private army was 'claiming almost alternative powers with the police'. Some MPs he said, were in favour of fascism, wanted to use it to crush communism. That way lay danger, with the growth of fascism, communism would be strengthened, and events abroad showed how the dykes of civilisation went down before fascism. Clement Attlee wanted an inquiry into events at Olympia. While he was entirely opposed to organised interruption there was no doubt about the 'unjustifiable brutality' used by the fascists. Political violence was part of 'the set policy of the movement'. If the police 'have it brought to their notice that illegal things are being done ... they can go in, and they ought to'. He wanted to know exactly what orders were given to the police at Olympia. Mosley had adopted the Italian method of the gang, in military style, with resounding military titles. He used *agents-provocateurs* at his meetings to incite disorder to give an excuse for violence. He borrowed Continental jargon: he was 'out to win the battle of the streets'. And he was backed by big money: 'We should like to know whether the money as well as the methods are imported.' There were beatings, disturbing incidents, he himself had been threatened because he protested against the treatment of Jews in Germany. He wanted an inquiry into the entire activities of the fascist movement, their uniforms, the whole question of their 'setting up a kind of glamour of civil war to attract youth'. What was the Home Secretary going to do about political militarization? The fascists were planning a still bigger meeting at the White City, would the Home Secretary use his powers (of binding over to keep the peace) as he had done in another case (that of Tom Mann on the eve of the 1932 Hunger March demonstration)?

But after the opposition had had its say the debate was turned another way. Earl Winterton did not believe there was any threat – as in other countries – of fascism in Britain, and 'do not let us be mealy-mouthed about the way in which interrupters are dealt with'. What did perturb him was 'the threat to free speech'. Mosley had effectively tangled the opposition case, identifying his anti-democratic fascist cause with a popular democratic appeal, and making this his main plank at Olympia: 'We are grateful to these people [the hecklers] for showing how necessary a blackshirt defence force is to defend free speech.' As Mr O'Connor put it, 'an old poacher now turned keeper'.

Mosley, with his demagogue's flair, was cashing in not only on a popular appeal but also on a grievance fairly widespread among MPs. In particular the supporters of the National Government who complained of rowdy heckling and chanting disrupting their political meetings (hardly surprising with the hardship and deprivation of high unemployment). The Tories blamed the socialists, Labour blamed the Communists, and the Liberals a bit of both. But the political free-for-all had traditional roots. In the early days of the labour movement, it was they who bore the brunt, and had their meetings broken up by young Conservatives – and sometimes by Liberals. Kingsley Griffith (Liberal) told the House how in his Oxford days he and his colleagues broke up a meeting addressed by Keir Hardie by throwing chairs, chanting 'God Save the King' and pelting the platform with potatoes and sugar lumps. But earlier violence had dwindled down (before the fascists revived it at their meetings) into shouting and rowdyism, and now it was the turn of the Tories to find themselves the target for noise and heckling. They were outraged. In spite of the huge majority of the National – virtual Tory – Government of 521 seats, in spite of all the advantages which the Conservative Party enjoyed and took for granted: the support of nearly all the national press, the traditional buttressing by the House of Lords, the 'loyalty' of the civil service, the armed forces, the established Church, they still felt affronted at cat-calls and shouting.

And so it was that the Olympia debate, where the purpose of the sponsors was to bring home the threat of a growing fascist movement (with its prototypes in the ascendant on the Continent), the explosion of political violence and the inaction of the police, was not only side-tracked by the red herring of free speech, but this 'cry' was now paradoxically linked with the fascist cause. And this was pressed home most strongly by some eight or nine right-wing Conservatives. In their eyes the danger did not come from the fascists holding their 'lawful' meeting at Olympia, but from the anti-fascist demonstrators and the interrupters who attempted to deny 'free speech'. It was they who menaced and ought to be proscribed and prevented.

The Tory Mr M.W. Beaumont, JP (Eton and Sandhurst): 'I am not a fascist, but as an avowed anti-democrat and an avowed admirer of fascism in other countries, I am naturally interested in the movement and in its application in this country.' At Olympia 'no one ... as far as I could see, got anything more than he thoroughly deserved.' Fascism, unlike 'the big organised parties ... has to rely upon public meetings for putting its case before the country, and it must have freedom of speech. To guarantee that is, I think, the desire of all quarters of the House.'

Earl Winterton saw the anti-fascist mob as 'the dregs of humanity ... the real type of revolutionaries. They may be all right at Tower Hill, but not in the streets of London.' Mr C.F. Pike (Unionist member for the Attercliffe division of Sheffield) cut in while Isaac Foot was describing the plight of the Jewish student from Sheffield still in hospital after the vicious attack by fascist stewards, 'Is he aware that that gentleman is an active member of the anti-German movement or anti-Hitler movement and is he aware that he went there specifically for the purpose of advertising his views at Olympia?'

The Home Secretary, Sir John Gilmour, answering the debate and making a case for support for the police, started off with a mollifying sop for the opposition. The police 'have a strain placed upon their judgment and sometimes mistakes are made ... but not made of evil intent.' The police had no legal right to enter a public meeting held on private premises except by leave of the promoters, and 'the fascist organisers of this meeting declined to have any police *intervention* inside the hall.' Accordingly the Metropolitan Commissioner had instructed the police, 'that they were not to go into the hall unless they had *reason to believe that something contrary to the law was taking place*'. (My emphasis, S.S.)

Evidence to this effect *was* certainly forthcoming, and from the police themselves. Plain-clothes officers *were* in fact posted inside the hall. (Sir John had tacitly admitted as much three days earlier in answer to a question by Sir Austen Chamberlain.) And public records confirm that seven Special Branch policemen were present in the auditorium, and that they all agreed that the blackshirts used very violent methods. One of them, Special Branch Sergeant Hunt saw interrupters punched unconscious. Later that evening when Sergeant Hunt was on duty outside Olympia, he saw a number of demonstrators thrown out. Speaking on the radio forty years later, he said he saw:

> Four burly fascist stewards come to the door, two holding an arm each, and the others holding a leg each, and somebody said: 'One – Two – Three' – and they swung this poor chap, to and fro, three times, and somebody said, 'Go!', and he was thrown into the air quite seven feet from the ground and he hit the pavement with a sickening thud. He laid there for a few minutes, and I should imagine he must have been injured, but he managed to struggle to his feet, and do you know that except for a sock dangling from one foot, he was completely naked.

Sir John went on to inform the House:

> In fact *information was given to the police* that certain things were happening to individuals, not in the meeting itself, but in the precincts of the meeting ... The fact remains that *the police did go in*. They found one man who had been fairly severely handled, and as they went in they observed other groups of fascists struggling with and pounding and beating up others. There was a cry of 'Police!' and the fascists in the groups ran into the Olympia. Such individuals were removed or were thrown out in various circumstances. *It was impossible for the police at that time*, without having been previously posted before the meeting began, to have really effective control or *to have apprehended anybody* who may have committed any act of extra severity against any individual. (My italics, S.S.)

This rather confused account in Parliament links up with what A.E. Coppard saw when he left the meeting at 9.50 and heard the fascists raise the alarm, 'Here's the police!' and it also follows closely the account given by the policeman who did go in.

The picture can now be filled in with interesting detail. We can contrast the account given by the Home Secretary to reassure Parliament, with the facts as presented and handled by the police hierarchy. This additional information comes from Mr Skidelsky's biography, *Oswald Mosley*. We learn that when Sir John told the House that 'the police did go in' (to Olympia) he was in fact referring to the single entry of a uniformed officer, Inspector Carroll, with ten policemen on duty outside with him. The Inspector took the decision on his own initiative and his action was subsequently queried by his superiors. Tantalisingly, Mr Skidelsky, always punctilious in giving references in footnotes, does not in this instance refer to his source. He prefaces the incident by informing his readers that 'The police were not allowed to enter the building unless they actually saw a breach of the peace taking place.' He then goes on to quote from the report made by Inspector Carroll, who with his men came on duty at about nine o'clock. Carroll took the decision to enter the premises when he saw a man 'almost unconscious' lying near the entrance. As he came in he saw six groups of six to eight blackshirts 'beating and kicking unmercifully a man at the centre of each group' generally lying on the ground. After he and his men had 'rescued' the victims, he heard 'agonising cries' from the foot of the stairs, where four blackshirts were brutally beating a weak youth lying on his back. They rescued him also. He was unable to walk away and was half-carried out by the others previously rescued. Carroll's report provoked the query from his superiors as to why he had made no arrests. Interviewed by the Assistant Commissioner, Carroll 'considerably modified his original statement'. He now said that he did not actually ·see the assaults, but that the victims appeared to have been brutally beaten. The Assistant Commissioner commented: 'I am inclined to think that Inspector Carroll's report gives a rather more serious impression of the assaults than was actually the case.' He then went on to say that none of the victims received 'any serious injuries' and all of them declined any further attention. He concluded: 'Inspector Carroll frankly admits that he wrote the report having regard to the fact that his action in entering the building at all had been called into question by fascists'.

We do not know whether the Inspector, when he was interviewed (perhaps carpeted) by the Assistant Commissioner and put on the spot as to why he made no arrests, took the line, as did the Home Secretary in the House, that in the circumstances this was 'impossible', but he must have realised that he was now out on a limb, and that it was expedient to back-pedal and tone down his report, and that the Assistant Commissioner was easing his way to an accommodation.

The Assistant Commissioner's bland comments weaken if not undermine the Home Secretary's assurances to Parliament, and they provoke pertinent questions. When, by whom and to whom was this fascist challenge to the police authority made? The only reaction at the time, as we know, was the prompt exit in alarm by the fascists involved. Why was there no mention of this fascist protest in Parliament? The Home Secretary describing the incident – as in Carroll's report – presented the police entry as a perfectly proper exercise of their powers 'on information' (of what was going on in the precinct; as he had previously stated, they had the right to enter if there was reason to suspect a breach of the peace.) There was no compromise on this or hint of criticism of the police involved, though they were, as he admitted, ineffective in the circumstances, since arrests were 'impossible'. Further, was the police criterion for the culpability of an assault dependent on the *severity* of injuries inflicted? In any case the Assistant Commissioner's criterion as to this was invalid. Injured demonstrators would be most reluctant to accept 'further attention' through the police for fear of losing their jobs. Besides, first-aid posts with doctors had been set up in the vicinity.

The truth was that there was ample and continuous 'justification' for police entry that night into Olympia. There was clear evidence of breaches of the peace witnessed by the Special Branch men (inside and outside the hall), by the police on duty at the gates (as battered and bleeding victims were pitched into the street) and by reliable people attending and leaving the meeting. No excuse for failing to check the violence. Yet the one Inspector who took the initiative to go in and do what was plainly his duty was called into question and had to justify himself, not only to fascists but also to his own hierarchy. This hierarchy was apparently disposed – and their rank-and-file required – to turn a blind eye, and to give the fascists a free hand to beat up at their leisure hecklers previously violently ejected from the meeting. And this violence was allowed to continue uninterrupted the whole evening.

Most disconcerting of all, it was a different picture that was presented in Parliament. The Home Secretary, answering the members of all parties who voiced disquiet at the implications of events at Olympia, took an uncompromisingly reassuring stand. Far from minimising or condoning fascist violence, or accepting any 'justification' for the fascists to query the authority of the police for any action taken that evening, he unequivocally condemned the fascist assumption of police powers, and he emphasised the sole responsibility of the police for maintaining law and order. He also condemned outright the action of any individual to take it into his own hands to administer rough 'justice'. He quoted a letter in the *Times* – which would appear to give the fascist version of what happened to Jacob Miller the student from Sheffield who, after venturing to heckle, was attacked, thrown over the balcony and subsequently detained in hospital. The letter runs:

> I was a blackshirt steward at the Olympia meeting. While I was stationed at the back of the lower balcony a man jumped from the upper balcony on to the people below. Spitting abuse, he slashed a girl blackshirt's face with his knife. I will leave it to the judgment of your readers as to whether the violence I inflicted on him when I eventually succeeded in throwing him down the stairs was 'wholly unnecessary'.

Sir John commented: 'If that was a true statement of the facts, that man ought to have handed the other man over to the proper authorities. There is no justification for anyone, whether a blackshirt, a greenshirt or a blueshirt to act as this man did.' However, after making these affirmations of general principles designed to restore confidence, the Home Secretary came down to the hard core of his thinking in terms of policy and action. He came out with the mildest of strictures to the fascists: 'I trust that the attitude of refusal to allow the police in any way to appear in these meetings, adopted by this fascist body ... will not be repeated. If it is, I may indeed have to take quite other lines, and I shall not hesitate to take them.' He dismissed as 'unnecessary and undesirable' a public inquiry –

as requested by the opposition – into the events at Olympia. When his government had formulated any plans they might make for action, he would welcome consultation with the leaders of all parties. But most significant of all, at the close of his speech he aligned himself with the hard-right Conservatives who had stressed throughout the debate the red herring of free speech – the popular democratic slogan misappropriated by the opportunist demagogue, Sir Oswald. Sir John stipulated: 'We should be well advised to consider most carefully how best we can serve the interests of free speech, and obtain the assurance that we shall have free speech, before we take further action.'

Five days after Olympia, Mosley speaking at Shrewsbury called those MPs who had witnessed events at Olympia 'liars and jackals' and 'a disgrace to the Conservative Party'. Questioned on television at the age of seventy-seven about the brutality at Olympia, he came back with the brazen schoolboy retort, 'We won!' It was a dubious victory that labelled the blackshirts 'bullies and cads' – Geoffrey Lloyd's epithets. The respectable British public was alienated, Mosley's credibility dwindled. Five government ministers in their speeches in different parts of the country three days after Olympia voiced their disapproval. Among them, Ernest Brown, Secretary to the Mines Department, commented that Mosley's 'was the method of the bully', Walter Elliot, Minister of Agriculture: 'We do not want dictators in this country ... whatever the colour of his shirt.' Sir Philip Cunliffe Lister, Secretary of State for the Colonies: 'Sir Oswald Mosley's clique may obtain for him a notoriety ... which his propaganda never would have commanded.'

Nevertheless the fascists, undeterred, continued their provocative uniformed parades and their policy of violence against any vocal opposition at their meetings. These indoor meetings were surrounded with an aura of intimidation and terror. It was a bold spirit that risked opening his mouth. Freedom of speech – one way – the blackshirt way. But in the thirties bold spirits were not lacking.

But after the public outcry and the shock had died down, the government took no action. Nothing was done to prevent the militarisation of politics or the wearing of political uniform.

On the Continent, where fascist parties had been springing up everywhere, political uniforms had already been banned in Holland and Sweden, and a month later Belgium was to follow suit. Lord Trenchard had indeed advised Sir John Gilmour, as early as October 1933, that political uniform should be made illegal, but his warning had been ignored. The Commissioner put the case more strongly in June 1934, stating that 'The position has become more serious ... There is no doubt that the wearing of uniform is in itself provocative and that this and other militaristic methods ... are a grave stimulus to communism.' But Sir John still refused to take any action.

The NCCL digested the lessons of Olympia. Gilmour had hinted that the government might seek further powers for the police to preserve public order. In the Council's opinion it was not an increase in power that was needed, but that the police should exercise to the full those powers that they already possessed. Olympia underlined the importance of covering such meetings with reliable observers.

It was only two months after the outrage of Olympia, and the Home Secretary's explanation that the police lacked the powers to intervene effectively, that police officers in South Wales had no hesitation in entering a perfectly orderly private meeting in a drill-hall in Glamorgan. The meeting had been called to protest against the Incitement to Disaffection Bill and to demand the removal of the Chief Constable of Glamorgan, who the previous year had ordered a low-flying plane to swoop over and disperse unemployed marching to Bridgend asking for increased winter relief. After a vote the chairman of the meeting asked the plain-clothes men who were taking notes to leave. They refused. The chairman then went to the police station to repeat his request, again refused. A sergeant accompanied him back to the meeting, and committed a technical assault on him. A charge was made against the police. It was dismissed. An appeal was taken to the Divisional Court. Lord Chief Justice Hewart, and two others, upheld the verdict.

'A Constitutional Innovation', A.L. Goodhart, a leading legal authority called it. Ronald pointed the moral in his book *British Liberty in Danger*. Judge-made law, as binding as parliamentary law, could undermine democracy. It had now established a new principle: the right of the police to enter private premises, not because an offence had been committed, but because they thought it might if something hypothetical were to be said!

Not long after Olympia, the London Trades Council and the London Labour Party called the Greater London Conference on Fascism, to affirm the party line to be adopted in view of Mosley's increased activity with his uniformed blackshirts. Ronald and I went as observers. Our red admission cards were each boldly marked in huge capitals: ADMIT ONE. As we came up the stone steps leading to Friends' House, all the swing entrances were barred by scrutineers, strictly checking credentials. No infiltrators to be allowed to challenge the platform with militant speeches.

The conference turned out to be disappointingly woolly and negative, achieving nothing. For the first hour the platform mostly confined itself to generalities about the evils of fascism, interrupted occasionally by mild boos and jeers from the delegates – in spite of the careful vetting. Herbert Morrison quoted figures showing the spectacular drop in wages in Italy and Germany under fascism. J.R. Clynes was the only one who got down to practical politics. He was not in favour of 'organised resistance to fascism'. (I scribbled it down almost disbelieving what I had heard). He went on, 'I do not advise counter demonstrations against fascists – though one can understand the spontaneous feelings of good trade unionists. If we did it would weaken our position and give the fascists sympathy.' They were getting too much attention. If they were ignored they would lose importance, fizzle out. (I thought of the young German woman who came to an NCCL weekend conference with her clever scientist husband, later a Nobel prize-winner. 'Don't make our mistake,' she had said. 'At first we dismissed Hitler as a ridiculous mountebank. And then – then, it was too late.') Clynes added: 'Appeals for a United Front are a mockery ...' (This drew the biggest opposition of all. Cries of 'Withdraw!') Then the platform speakers slipped into substituting for fascism, dictatorship, and conveniently equated, lumped together Nazi Germany and the Communist USSR. Herbert Morrison, in particular, played on this ideological theme: 'only one political theory and one political party is bad and tyrannical.' This approach effectively fudged what presumably was the ostensible purpose for calling the conference: the practical politics to be adopted in the current situation, with the threat of fascism on the Continent and at home, and its growing power and support by wealth and influence.

Ronald and I left the conference with a feeling of dismay at the lack of guidance and leadership, the negative attitude.

Mosley's ranting accusations at Olympia of socialist 'intimidation and violence' and of the 'bellowing' of trade union leaders, completely falsified the reality. The Trades Union Congress was firmly under the control of its right-wing General Secretary, Walter Citrine. The Labour Party and the TUC were content to make pronouncements and pass resolutions condemning fascism. They published a pamphlet about Hitlerism. But when it came to active campaigning, they picked up their skirts and walked on the other side of the road to avoid anti-fascists at home.

Preserving party discipline, preventing any fraternisation with Communists was more important than the menace of fascism. In 1933 they had rejected a call from the Communists and the Independent Labour Party for a United Front against fascism. Sir Stafford Cripps and his Socialist League had no more success with the Popular Front proposals. (The League was expelled from the party in 1937, and Cripps himself proscribed the following year.) The party countered by bracketing together 'dictatorships of the right and left'.

The 1934 Trades Union Congress adopted a statement about the British fascist movement demanding an end to 'the drilling and arming of civilian sections of the community' and deploring the inactivity of the police and the partiality of the Bench. This was on the eve of another big fascist demonstration planned as a monster turn-out in Hyde Park.

But when the newly formed Co-ordinating Committee for Anti-Fascist Activities – sponsored, with others, by Ellen Wilkinson, John Strachey, James Maxton, D.N. Pritt and Lord Marley, the Opposition Chief Whip in the House of Lords – called for a huge counter-demonstration to drown the fascist rally in 'a sea of organised working-class activity', the National Council of Labour countered by repudiating organised opposition. It circularised all its affiliated bodies in Greater

London advising them to stay away. The *Daily Herald* backed this up. The *Daily Worker* was militant in support of the Co-ordinating Committee. The *New Statesman* felt that the counter-demonstration should be sponsored by Labour not by the Communists. William Joyce (later Lord Haw Haw) on behalf of the British Union of Fascists went to court to try to prove the *Daily Worker* had offended against the Public Meeting Act, but failed. The National Council for Civil Liberties expressed no view for or against a counter-demonstration, but announced that it would send observers to the park.

The Metropolitan Police, after Olympia, were on their mettle (Lord Trenchard was said to have cut short his holiday) and some 7,000 of them were on duty. They escorted the uniformed blackshirts, estimated at between 2,500 to 3,000, with Mosley at the head, through the jeering crowd into a central position in the park. Here the fascists took up their stand round seven platforms. The police then sealed them off, forming a solid rectangle round them. No loudspeakers, so in effect the blackshirts were holding exclusive meetings, preaching to their own converted.

By the time we arrived, the park was swarming with people. Four anti-fascist contingents had marched in with their bands and banners, their platform meetings now were in full swing. The crowds – the biggest ever seen in the park – estimated at 100,000, were ranging freely from one anti-fascist propaganda meeting to another. Each platform urging no breach of public order. No attempt made to break into the fascist enclave.

Ronald and I had no difficulty in getting admitted through the police barrier into the fascist world inside. Blackshirts flanked the platforms, Mosley, humourless, was turning on the hate. A pallid gaunt woman, at another platform, in black, with a beret. (Was she, I wondered, his mother?) Some spectators in point-to-point style resting on their sticks; more circulating in detached groups, never coalescing; the only solid mass the attendant blackshirts, most of whom stayed put. A relief in tension to get out, leaving behind the alien regimentation, the menace of the black uniform, back into the free, untidy coming and going, the cheerful hugger-mugger of the ordinary world outside. The huge anti-fascist rally carried the day demonstrating its popular support and peaceableness, while the police force was concentrated in sealing off a fascist island in the park.

Anti-Fascists

The negative attitude of official labour, their unwillingness to pursue an active anti-fascist policy, left, by default, their militant left-wingers to be led by the Communists, already in the field.

The need, the impetus for action deepened with the sense of crisis. Turpitude and murder on the Continent roused a fervour of sympathy for the victims. The courage, the example set by Socialists and Communists, captured the imagination – Dimitrov, defying the roaring bully Goering in open court in the Reichstag Fire Trial, became an international hero. The burning issue to resist, to fight at every point every attack on freedom, and on established rights, to halt the fateful tilt down the slope that could end in totalitarian overthrow. No conflict in principle to link up, associate with Communists in the anti-fascist cause – in defence of democracy. 'Dictatorship of the left' was no more than a red herring, an empty slogan, irrelevant, an excuse to opt out, to ignore the crisis. The danger, the impending threat, was all from the right.

The anti-fascist cause embraced with the militant left, intellectuals, writers, poets, idealists, pacifists, the liberal-minded and the Liberals. The Liberals had no party inhibitions against associating with the far left in a cause they believed in. Some, temporarily, even went further – Stephen Spender in *Forward From Liberalism* published by Gollancz in 1937: 'I am a Communist because I am a Liberal ... in the modern world Communism – the classless, international society – is the final goal of liberalism.'

This was after the Moscow state trial and execution of Zinoviev, Kamenev and the other old Bolsheviks had aroused a storm of hostile anti-Soviet criticism in the Western press. The accused, found guilty of terrorist conspiracies had incriminated themselves 'with an almost abject and exuberant completeness'. This comment came from D.N. Pritt, who attended the trial and wrote a pamphlet, promptly published by Gollancz at threepence – *The Zinoviev Trial*. In Pritt's view the accused had a fair trial and were justly found guilty. Seven of them he described variously as like a German watch-maker, a book-keeper, an intelligent German prince, a British cavalry officer, a pugilist, a popular actor and an alert business man. All of them, he said, were at ease, showed no fear, strolled out of court, or spoke up when they chose. They were treated with courtesy and patience. None of them in their last words in open court retracted their confessions or said they were extracted by threats, promises or third degree. Nevertheless the confessions baffled and aroused some uneasiness on the left. I was still mystified after reading Pritt's pamphlet, even though I remembered that Bernard Pares, the former pundit on Russia, had written that public confession was part of the traditional Russian way of life.

The non-political ivory towers in Europe had been shaken, by state vandalism in Germany, by the trampling and destroying of advanced centres, the exiling and proscribing of writers and artists, the censorship and the rejection of new ideas and indeed of culture itself. Nazis thinking with their blood – and backed by rifle butts. Writers, intellectuals, their world and their public threatened by the contagion of fascism, were emerging to take sides, to unite and pool their influence. Many of them now finding a new hope and a future in the left, looking with idealism to the release in spirit of the Russian Revolution to give a new vitality and a new meaning to art and culture.

André Gide, opening the First International Congress of Writers in Paris, in June 1935:

> I claim to be strongly international while remaining intensely French ... I am a fervent individualist ... individuals and their peculiarities can best flourish in a communist society. The USSR today [is] a land where the writer can communicate directly with his readers ... In the reality around him he can find at once inspiration, a method, and the immediate echo of his work.

E.M. Forster – the first speaker:

> Love of liberty is an old English tradition but ... English liberty is a class and race liberty ... of the privileged British citizen and

not of the colonial, or the man out of a job. Great Britain is not threatened by a brutal fascism ... but by the progressive restriction of liberties ... My colleagues ... may dissent ... from my old-fashioned attitude ... talking about liberty and tradition when the economic substructure of society is at fault ... my role ... is a temporary [one]. We must continue to potter about with our old tools until the moment when everything falls about our ears. When everything crashes, nothing will serve any more. After – if there is an after – the task of civilisation will be taken up by men whose spiritual training will have been different from mine. I am more often pursued by the idea of war than by that of my own death: and nevertheless the line to adopt towards these two vexations is the same. One must act as if one were immortal and as if civilisation were eternal ... Whatever the ... divergencies between the remedies proposed for our ills, we all believe in courage ... and the courage I will find among so many men come here from so many countries can only strengthen mine ... You have guessed that I am not a Communist: perhaps I should be one if I were younger and braver, because in communism I see hope. I know that its intentions are good, although I think bad many of the acts resulting from these intentions. You have guessed that I am not a fascist – fascism does evil that evil may come of it.'

5

The Council at Work

The Council's role in this political spectrum was clear-cut. A non-party body, it had to co-ordinate and focus on the civil liberties issues as wide a range of interests and support as possible, and to work through the democratic machinery, in Parliament, the press and the courts, and, as important, it had to be active in the field in the rough and tumble to try to hold the ring, see fair play, observing at meetings, demonstrations, in the park, at the street-corner. It was a question of priorities what was most important to tackle, with our limited resources and personnel. Still only the two of us as paid officials, and a young clerk, we were supported by voluntary help, some of it from highly skilled professionals, lawyers and journalists.

W.H. Thompson and Kingsley Martin

Each week our General Purposes Sub-Committee met to plan the immediate programme. The chairman was W.H. Thompson.

Thompson was a tough Lancastrian, a big personable man with a large presence, a genial manner, the successful single boss of a lucrative solicitor's firm that specialised in the industrial field and had a thriving trade union practice. His good friends among trade union and Labour men, and his regular attendance at the annual Trades Union Congress offered very useful contacts for the Council. An uncompromising radical, a fighter against injustice and privilege, he also had friends among leading Communists. He was too rugged an individualist to toe strictly any party line. A powerful advocate, once convinced, he admitted he saw no other point of view than his own. As an opponent he would have been ruthless and implacable. His worldly common-sense judgment of what was practicable, brought decisions very much down to earth. A man's man, in a man's world, he was probably something of a philistine, with little time or place in his busy life for the aesthetic, the gentler side.

He had been interested in Mosley's New Party in its very early days. On a political weekend at Denham – Mosley's Tudor manor outside London – he was a guest with John Strachey and the writer Lawrence Meynell. After dinner, Mosley offered, with the coffee, a box of chocolates. Thompson never ate chocolates, but Meynell took one, bit into it and swallowed castor-oil instead of cream. The genial host apparently used the practical joke on guests that irked him.

'I think he was always a bit twisted,' Thompson commented.

I should guess that in this case, it was Thompson who was Mosley's intended target. Thompson who was no respecter of persons, unimpressed by rank and privilege, who had nothing of the sexual ambivalence of so many of the men who gravitated towards Mosley, and, most antagonising, who had been a conscientious objector in the 1914 war, and treasured, took away with him at weekends, the prison mug he had purloined as a memento.

Thompson was generous in the time he devoted to the Council. He turned up every week. His buoyant, decisive presence reassuring, stimulating – but demanding. He wanted results, was impatient, intolerant of delays, uninterested in the reason why – had no use for waffling, time-wasting frills.

He was Chairman also of the monthly Executive Committee. We held this in a little hotel in Craven Street, a room hired with a banqueting, or maybe it was a board-room, table. In the few minutes of chat before we sat down to the agenda, Thompson was juxtaposed with Forster. Thompson a man of the world with an air of success, a practical approach, a way of life cut down to *his* essentials, as rationalised and streamlined as his own well-integrated office. A man who, in his public face at any rate, might be mistaken for a Mr Wilcox of the left. He had the greatest respect for Forster, for his literary standing, his integrity on matters of principle, and indeed for his courage in accepting ultimate responsibility as President in such acute times, especially with his vulnerability as an undeclared homosexual. Forster deceptively hesitant, with a tentative approach that gave almost the impression of timidity. He always declined a place at the head of the table. Thompson unbending genially, making a big effort to meet him on his own plane. Almost a Howard's End encounter!

I think Forster enjoyed the contrast, moving outside his world into another of the politically committed, but an air he could breathe freely because it was pervaded with altruism and conviction. The business on the table, ideas in movement, and Ronald's contained calm that gave him confidence. He understood that fundamentally Ronald based his stand, as he did, on morals rather than politics, although of course Ronald was very much aware of the political implications.

Some of the Executive were pretty well paper members, too busy to attend. In the early days we saw little of Pritt, he remained an *éminence grise* in the Temple, available for consultation, and in the House, ready to put questions, to sponsor civil liberty issues.

Kingsley Martin, who had helped to launch us, and believed in the Council's essential role, was content, now that we were active, to stand on the sidelines. He phoned – anything really urgent on the agenda? If it was the press, the libel laws, the use of the Official Secrets Acts for censorship, he turned up. He applauded us when we were successful and made our point, when we came up in the courts and convinced the magistrate, but he excused himself – too busy – from the effort to help us get there, was chary even of publicity in the *Statesman* – till after the event. While he approved our general line, agreed that we should take an uncompromising stand on this or that, at the same time he remained anxious to preserve his own detachment – the cautious editor, never the active Vice-President. Always a little nervous, apprehensive as to where it might lead with Ronald's unworldly stubborness, his follow-through. There was, too, the embarrassment that our work in the field might tend to get the Council and its sponsors confused, equated with the 'victims' we defended, and their causes – even when these causes were also those with which he was in sympathy. Nothing must compromise his freedom to adjust a nicely balanced editorial equilibrium on the controversial fence.

We soon learned his timidity, his reluctance to commit himself first, over any issue, always waiting on events. After we had successfully canvassed, got the support of solid big names, impressive pronouncements from pundits at Oxbridge, then, reassured, he would be ready, even eager, to appear on the platform, to take the chair, to sign the letter, even to give us a little space in the *Statesman*.

On the phone, he suggested himself as chairman for our Central Hall meeting to protest against the 'Sedition' Bill, after he had seen the list of prominent speakers. Ronald very readily stood down, let him take his place in the chair – unfortunately as it happened, H.G. Wells, the star speaker, recently back from a visit to Russia, started off perversely to talk at a tangent about the denial of freedom of expression in the USSR. His high-pitched slight cockney was interrupted by a deep outraged voice from somewhere near the ceiling.

'Wot did Lenin say about you?'

Wells halted.

' 'E called you a narrow little petty BORE-JWAH!'

Dignity, the star speaker, was clipped. Proletarian impudence rebuking him magisterially. The unexpected banana skin! In the thirties it was really very funny. But most unfortunate at our meeting. The press seized on it and made much of it. (With Ronald in the chair, it might never have happened. Already as an observer he was known to the Communist rank-and-file, greeted as 'Comrade' when hopefully his presence might negative the rough stuff, the casual arrest.)

Kingsley Martin, shocked, got to his feet. His rebuke, a little too school-mastery and unctuous, provoked one or two more to join in. He sat down disconcerted. Wells, unperturbed, resumed. But he took the tip and turned his speech nearer home to the Sedition Bill and our own National Government.

Kingsley Martin, a man of the left, in principle, seemed to be always torn with doubt, tortured by misgivings, plagued with second thoughts, when it came to translating principle into current policy. His eyes haggard, his mind in a constant state of flux, seeing too many sides to every question, reason at first in one aspect, and then the contrary, swayed by the forceful argument put to him by the influential man of the moment.

Especially vulnerable if his current mentor was socially secure, economically proof against shocks. But split again, seduced towards a contrary more radical solution after the intellectual disquisition of the man he lunched with just before his last editorial conference of the week. To the left by conviction, he was always haunted by a sense of danger impelling him to reassess, retrench. Always unresolved, always in search of the touchstone to give him the ultimate correct analysis.

I began to understand the strange duality of his temperament, his ambivalence towards the left, when I read *Father Figures*, the first volume of his autobiography. His pacifist father, whom he hero-worshipped, was dependent on his stipend from the Congregational Church at Hereford, and he 'taught the duty of non-violence with a bellicose fury which drove people out of the church' and antagonised its wealthy supporters. 'My first memory', he wrote, 'was of the windows being broken on the night Pretoria fell.'

The shock and the alarm for a very young delicate child must have been traumatic. The confusion in a child's mind – how his much-loved father could bring terror and danger into the home, and rescue and safety only come with the police. His gratitude to law and order. A muddle of conflicting loyalties, emotions and fears, that left him with something disorientated in his consciousness that he could never resolve. No wonder, as he said himself, he was always afraid.

'Few weeks passed,' Kingsley Martin writes in *Editor* (the second book of his autobiography) 'in which I did not meet Ronald or talk with him on the phone.' (Ronald safely dead, he was familiar retrospectively. It was more formally 'Kidd' when he was alive and liable to make demands for civil liberty that it might be uncomfortable to refuse.) 'I never met a more disinterested man,' he went on, and it was probably this quality that made Ronald useful to him when he was getting the editorial feel of things, making his soundings, taking the pulse. Ronald at the centre of civil liberty activity, its lawyers and journalists, in touch too with academic circles, and a variety of other interests according to the scope of our current campaign, would give him an active picture, the facts, the legal angle, and a point of view unbiassed by party alignment or tied by political loyalty.

Wrongful Arrest and Suspected Persons

We were concerned now, in the autumn of '34, to prevent the Home Office from virtually killing the miniature 16 millimetre non-inflammable film. These comparatively inexpensive films were being used increasingly not just by amateurs, but for education – in schools, technical colleges, adult institutes and hospitals – for documentaries, for propaganda and for public relations. The Post Office, under the direction of Sir Stephen Tallents, were experimenting with a Film Unit. Miniature versions of many classical films were available – in spite of the attempt by the commercial film companies to check this – *The Cabinet of Dr Caligari*, *The Covered Waggon* and many of the great Russian silent films.

Now, without consulting the Board of Education, or any of the other interested parties, the Home Office announced that 'draft regulations were already drawn up ... awaiting the signature of the Home Secretary ... to put sub-standard film stock under stricter control and to bring it virtually under the same restrictions as standard film.'

Commercial inflammable films, subject to the Cinematograph Act of 1909, could only be shown under license from the local authority, and with stringent expensive safety regulations – so many exits, attendants, fireproof equipment and furniture, etc. and of course they were subject to censorship, set up by their own trade body.

Already, without any legal backing, local authorities and the police in towns throughout the country had attempted to intimidate the lessees of halls about to show on miniature film the Russian *Battleship Potemkin* (dangerous revolutionary stuff!) threatening them that in an unlicensed hall this showing would be illegal. The Council promptly made representations to the local authorities and the police in question, and no prosecutions followed the showing of the film.

A Home Office representative assured the Council that the proposal to bring sub-standard film 'under stricter control' was solely in the interest of public safety. The Council pointed out that the Home Office had no power to introduce

Regulations under the Cinematograph Act without fresh legislation. Moreover this statute, by its own terms, applied only to 'inflammable films'.

The Council brought out a pamphlet giving the provisions of the Act, the findings of scientific tests comparing inflammable and non-inflammable film as fire risks and giving publicity to some of the legitimate interests involved by reprinting correspondence from the *Manchester Guardian*.

Before the Home Office could proceed, it was essential for them to get a judicial ruling on inflammability. They selected an out-of-the-way spot in Durham. The police served summonses on eleven miners of the Bolden Colliery Miners' Lodge for showing a miniature film in the Miners' Hall, on the grounds of public safety. The Council, with financial support from the British Institute of Adult Education, undertook the defence.

In the Jarrow Police Court, a lawyer from London created something of a stir. W.H. Thompson had come up himself, and brought technical experts with him. He took by surprise the men from the Home Office who had hoped to have it all their own way. Thomson gave a demonstration in court with samples of film and matches. The celluloid of the commercial strip flared up explosively, the cellulose acetate of the miniature film crumpled, charred, refused to burn. The magistrate dismissed the case, with costs against the police. (Notice was lodged of appeal, but in due course it was allowed to lapse.)

This was not quite the end of the story. The Surrey County Council and a few more local authorities persisted in banning or attempting to ban miniature film exhibitions in their area. Sporadic police interference continued, the Council always advising that this had no legal basis. In 1938 the Council gave evidence before the Advisory Committee set up by the Home Office to look into the position of 'Slow-Burning Film under the Cinematograph Act'. The Committee reported the following year that both the content and the safety-precautions should be left to the good sense of the exhibitors and that the small minority of licensing authorities that still attempted to control them should come into line, and accept that these films were outside their jurisdiction.

With W.H. Thompson, another solicitor and three young barristers on our General Purposes Committee, legal defence for police court cases could be arranged at short notice. Thompson, the barristers, and indeed all the lawyers who acted for us, generously gave their services free.

In the spring of 1935, the National Government had thought up the Silver Jubilee as a demonstration of loyalty and patriotism – an event not celebrated since Queen Victoria's day – and indeed with little reason now (except perhaps that a general election was to be held later in the year). There was little to rejoice about, unemployment was still high, and the times were uneasy.

A branch of the National Unemployed Workers' Movement asked the Council if we would send observers to their demonstration along the route the city dignitaries would take on their way to the Guildhall celebration dinner. The unemployed were protesting against their own meagre allowance in contrast to the full-scale expensive pomp of the occasion.

Ronald and I joined a thin scatter of people waiting along the Guildhall route. The unemployed were marching in line just off the kerb, demonstrating with their placards, as the banquet guests slipped by in cars and taxis. The City police after a while diverted the main contingent into back streets. We ended up in a deserted City square. Here the men held a brief rally; a final speech, and after singing the 'Red Flag' they began to disperse. We had linked up now with Trevor Blewitt, another NCCL observer.

Just then a *Daily Worker* seller came up with a heavy satchel fresh from the press, and as fast as he could hand them out he was taking the pennies, lightening his load. This apparently offended the sergeant in charge – a stocky little bullfrog of a man. He signalled imperiously to the policeman next to the seller – I was on the other side – and now the two men, seller and policeman, were walking away together, the policeman's hand on his arm.

The smooth, easy arrest, the general acceptance – not a word or a move of protest – the normality of it – was revealing, shocking. In the thirties law and order decreed that you kept to your place, your proper sphere; if you moved out of it, into the rich man's City you were asking for trouble, especially if you were unemployed.

For a second or two I didn't connect. And then, incredulous, I butted in:

'*What* are you arresting him *for*?'

The policeman stared ahead woodenly, 'I'm acting under orders.'

The unemployed understood: the policeman had no option. Ronald was speaking to the sergeant, telling him that we wanted our names to appear on the charge sheet as three independent witnesses. And so as the small clump of policemen made their way to their station, we followed on. But, arrived there, they blocked our way. We were instructed to wait outside. A Press Association journalist came up and wanted to know what it was all about. But as time wore on and it got colder and darker, he got restive. Made off for a nip, back in five minutes.

I suggested going in to hurry them up. They agreed, no harm in trying a little sex appeal.

Down a corridor I could hear voices behind a door, just ajar. Tentatively I pushed it open. The room was full of men, helmets off, some had shed their coats. The talking stopped: 'Excuse me, could you kindly ...'

The choleric sergeant turned an outraged face, 'Chuck her out!'

An ugly raw copper grabbed me, swung me round almost lifting me, jabbed me hard in the small of my back, and sent me flying down the passage and straight out of the open door, landing on top of the two men waiting outside – instead of on my face in the road. The PA journalist had missed the fun.

But Ronald was not to be deterred. He went straight to a call-box and phoned Thompson. Thompson contacted the barrister Collard and phoned Ronald back.

Next morning, Ronald, Blewitt and I were at the police court. Collard had seen the man in the cells and was defending him, ready to call us as witnesses. He warned me not to refer to the police assault at the station.

In the witness box, the little sergeant tried to bully, trip me up.

'What would you say if I told you there was no such

number? It doesn't exist in the City police.' I had quoted an A number for the man who made the arrest. City police were B division. 'Yet you stand there and say you made a note of it!'

'I made a *mental* note,' I said coldly. 'I'm not in a position to check whether the number exists – you should know. I got your number right.'

There was a titter in Court.

The magistrate intervened. He asked the policeman who made the arrest to stand up.

'Do you recognise him?' he asked me.

'No – I don't.' (It was the ugly butcher who had assaulted me at the station! Substituted for the equable PC 'acting under orders'.)

A brief pause. Somehow it didn't look right. The sergeant's ploy was backfiring.

The police evidence, as I learnt afterwards was that a hostile 'loyal' crowd surrounded the paper-seller, wanted to seize the *Daily Worker*s and burn them! The police advised the seller to move on. He refused. Asked again, he again refused. Finally he was taken into custody for his own protection!

The magistrate dismissed the case.

I believe that this was the first and last time that one of the Council's observers was assaulted by the police.

At that time, in middle-class society, the *Daily Worker* was beyond the pale. To be seen reading it was almost as challenging as refusing to stand up when 'God Save the King' was played. Press cutting bureaux took it for granted that it was not to be covered by their service. The BBC referring to the press, blandly outlawed it – it didn't exist. W.H. Smith and the wholesalers refused to handle it. It could only be obtained – apart from its sale in the street by dedicated party members – under the counter, from small out-of-the-way newsagents.

In spite of hard times, unemployment, crime figures in the thirties give a picture of a law-abiding stable society. But the casual picking up and arresting of persons suspected of loitering with intent to commit a felony, had stepped up dramatically each year from 1930. Ronald and I had seen it happen more than once in theatreland at night. The charges often so flimsy, the evidence so thin, so stereotyped, that between a quarter and a third of the cases were regularly dismissed.

In 1936 the Council's lawyers defended a number of these cases in court. We followed up with publicity in the press, and gave MPs material for debates and questions in the House. In the parliamentary debate on the police in July 1936, the Revd R.W. Sorensen, MP referred to the case of a man arrested on suspicion, and he quoted the comments of the magistrate at the Clerkenwell Court who dismissed the case with costs against the police: 'How came this man to be prosecuted? There is no imaginable case against this man.' And in the Home Office debate in March that year Ernest Thurtle pressed home again and again 'the very remarkable figures of arrests'. Lord Trenchard's innovation of plain-clothes men were 'going out in a very large scale indeed', and to the young and inexperienced policeman 'almost every poor down-and-out man that he meets in the street will be looked upon … as a potential criminal'. And when two of his constituents from Shoreditch, unemployed men 'with nothing against their character' were picked up, and discharged without conviction, he put the question to the Home Secretary: 'Would he make it clear to the police that walking about the streets is not in itself a crime?'

At last an impact was made on the authorities, and the charges dropped dramatically. From the highest peak in 1935 with 4,877 cases (1,593 of these dismissed) to 1,164 in 1937, with 351 dismissed.

'Reform' of the Police and the Trenchard Ban

The controversial Metropolitan Police Act, steamrollered through Parliament in 1933 by the National Government's big majority – in spite of fierce opposition by the Labour opposition – was one of the factors, in that critical year, to underline the need for setting up NCCL.

The Act was the creation of Lord Trenchard, the Metropolitan Police Commissioner who had been brought in by the government as the strong man to reform the Metropolitan Police. Lord Trenchard, a dedicated disciplinarian serviceman, respected in the Second World War as the 'Father of the RAF' – his life's work to develop the army's

Royal Flying Corps into the powerful Royal Air Force – had a very different reactionary and authoritarian image in the thirties.

There were indeed legitimate causes for discontent in the Metropolitan force: the out-of-date uncomfortable accommodation in the barrack-like section houses, the 10 per cent economy cut in their pay. These grievances ventilated in the *Police Review*, the organ of their Police Federation (which was set up by the Police Act of 1919, after it was made illegal for the police to join a trade union). However Lord Trenchard's reforms, as well as introducing up-to-date methods in the detection of crime, were mainly directed to changing the character of the force and diminishing their civil rights. The main defect in his view was that the force including the officers was drawn 'solely from one stratum of society'; in fact only eleven of its 759 officers belonged to 'the educated classes'. In his view the Police Federation 'exceeded the limits of propriety in the worst tradition of militant trade union propaganda'. Grievances should go through the proper channels, through the officers, and so up to the top, to him.

The Act provided for the setting up of a Police College at Hendon specially equipped to train young men from the public schools and others of good education for supervisory positions – as announced in a government White Paper. Entry was by examination and recruits qualified directly into the grade of junior inspectors. To make room for new blood, the age for compulsory resignation for senior officers was lowered (at 'advantageous terms'), and a new intake was introduced of ten-year-service men. Membership of the Police Federation was barred to this new intake and also to inspectors and all senior grades. The Act was resented keenly not only by the Police Federation but also by the rank-and-file who saw the introduction of a new officer class as leaving the constable still plodding on the beat. Aneurin Bevan in Parliament: 'It is entirely a fascist development to make the police force more amenable to the orders of ... Downing Street ... They want to militarise the upper hierarchy of the police force because they cannot trust the police force.'

Hendon Police College opened in May 1934, and was closed in 1939. Nearly a third of Trenchard's young men from the college rose to the highest posts. One of them, Sir Joseph Simpson, as Metropolitan Commissioner, twenty as chief constables of counties, three of cities and boroughs, and scores of officers in other senior posts.

Both Lord Trenchard and his successor in 1935, Sir Philip Game, as servicemen might well have been favourably impressed by the occasional brass-hats attracted to Mosley, Captain Robert Gordon-Canning was a close adviser, Commandant Mary Allen, the co-founder of the Women's Police Force and its head from 1919 to 1938, was a fascist sympathiser. In 1940 she came out openly as a fascist, and was interned along with other leading fascists under Wartime Defence Regulations. The *Sunday Dispatch* of 13 June 1934 reported that at a meeting of Special Constables, six out of every ten were blackshirts. Hamilton Piercey, the head of the Fascist Defence Force who issued rubber truncheons to his stewards for their meeting at the Manchester Free Trade Hall on 12 March 1933, was himself for a time a Special Constable.

Police inspectors were also said to be favourably impressed by the show of discipline, the uniformed ranks, the patriotic display of Union Jacks carried by the fascists. But the bias or prejudice of individual policemen would probably count for little in a disciplined force, where the line laid down at the top passed on by their superiors, was the only expedient way for maintaining solidarity and for moving towards promotion. The policy ultimately sponsored and endorsed by the Home Secretary.

It was not long after his appointment as Commissioner that Lord Trenchard had decided that politics was a luxury that the unemployed should not afford. They could always listen to the wireless – they would come to no harm there. Ideas could stay locked in the books in libraries (far too much money wasted in opening public libraries everywhere.) The exceptional brainy ones who wanted to make good, would find them out anyhow.

Today when all the news from everywhere comes flooding in colour at the turn of a knob, it is hard to imagine the false deluding calm, the blank, the isolation of the thirties. The unutterable boredom of the BBC voice impeccably retailing neutral bulletins reflecting official handouts. Real live news only in the newspapers. And for the unemployed who couldn't afford a penny for a paper, the street was their forum, their social focus from childhood, and the street-corner meeting their way of getting the live issues in politics, the facts, the talking points that affected their lives.

But the Trenchard Ban prohibited meetings outside Labour Exchanges, even in cul-de-sacs. The slow-moving queues were not to have the right to listen. The police ban, according to the Council's legal advisers, had no validity in law. Nor was there any publication, no information about it. The Police Commissioner had taken advantage of a provision in the Metropolitan Police Act which gave him power to issue directions for the preservation of order and the protection of streets and public places on the occasion of royal and other processions. On the strength of this, he had given instructions to his police force – never made public or discussed in Parliament – forbidding meetings in the vicinity of employment exchanges.

The Council decided to challenge this attack on free speech with test meetings outside important labour exchanges. The first was at West Ham. The speaker T.E. Groves was the local mayor and MP for Stratford East. He was supported by Ronald, and the meeting went off successfully with no interference from the police.

But just two days later when men of the unemployed movement attempted to hold a meeting on exactly the same spot, the speaker was arrested. In court, he asked for a brief adjournment – even of only ten minutes – to get advice from the secretary of NCCL. (Ronald had hurried to the Court when he heard of the case.) But the magistrate refused. The Council had questions asked in the House about this arbitrary decision.

Our next test case was at Battersea. The police stepped in, and when Claud Cockburn, one of the speakers, questioned them on what authority they were prohibiting the meeting, he was promptly arrested for obstructing them in the course of their duty. (Twenty years later writing in *Punch* to celebrate NCCL's coming of age, Cockburn, in light-hearted retrospect recalled how, as they locked him into his cell at the police station, he confidently awaited Ronald's prompt arrival to bail him out. Only to remember that this was the day that Ronald was defending free speech at a traditional meeting place, threatened with closure – out in Essex, at Braintree. Nothing for it but the long dull hours ahead – and he was out of cigarettes! Interesting that the resourceful, brilliant journalist should feel that it was only the reliable Ronald who could come to his aid.) In the magistrate's court, defended by an NCCL lawyer, he was nevertheless fined 40s. The Council took the case on appeal to Quarter Sessions. Mr Dingle Foot took the case, but the appeal was lost on the strictly technical charge of obstruction, avoiding the main issue of the right to hold the meeting.

A school teacher and political speaker, Mrs Kathleen Duncan, had advertised her lunch-hour meeting on the Sedition Bill outside the Test and Task Centre in Deptford – in a cul-de-sac – and was warned in advance that she would not be allowed to speak. When she got onto her portable platform, the police pulled her down – for obstructing them. She was fined £2 with five guineas costs.

The Council decided that this was a strong case to follow up and test the principle involved. Here was an orderly advertised meeting to be held in a cul-de-sac, yet a warning was issued before it even started, with no breach of the peace, no offence committed. We sponsored an appeal to Quarter Sessions. Mr Dingle Foot again kindly appeared. But the appeal was dismissed. On legal advice we followed up with an appeal to the King's Bench Divisional court. The Council had to lodge securities of £100 – a big drain on our finances (corresponding today to perhaps £1,000).

It was not until October 1935 that the appeal was heard.

In the vast empty court – with its Dickensian atmosphere – I was waiting for the curtain to go up, to receive my introduction to the full majesty of the law. I was eager to hear the brilliant KC, D.N. Pritt, going great guns, transforming the scene, scoring echoing points for civil liberty.

'Where is Mrs Duncan?' I whispered to Ronald.

He shook his head. The witnesses?

At last the cast appeared: the triumvirate of robed, be-wigged Judges. They seated themselves in a triptych, high-backed, with Lord Chief Justice Hewart in the centre, and Sir Travers Humphreys and Sir John Singleton either side. Pritt stood on a dais to the right. In front of him, a burden of tomes piled high, with markers.

In conversational tones, that I strained to catch, he started off, detailing legal precedents, picking up volumes, slipping his finger into one marked passage after another, his manner coldly equable, strictly circumscribed, still plenty of volumes and markers ahead.

The Lord Chief Justice was staring ahead unmoved – a relentless little Buddha. When Pritt paused, he opened his mouth and in a port-wine voice stonewalled and negatived each point Pritt had carefully made and documented. The two judges either side played a considering game. They even went a little way to meet Pritt, to examine a loophole, but only to block it again, to retreat and to find themselves in aggreement with the Lord Chief Justice. After one or two more tentatives played on the same lines, Pritt putting up the propositions, Lord Hewart knocking them flat, the other two toying and feinting, but then concurring Pritt desisted, and sat down.

I was waiting for the case proper to open, after all this legal toing and froing.

And now Lord Hewart was having a private mumble with his colleagues either side, then he gave out an agreed pronouncement.

Neil Lawson who had been a spectator with us was getting up …

'What is it?'

'The case is dismissed.'

Dismissed! Not a word, no plea, no protest, no eloquence! What had this formalised ritual exercise got to do with justice for Mrs Duncan? With civil liberty? A hundred pounds for this farce! Decided before it started!

As Ronald put it in his book, this judgment

established the precedent that the police have power to ban any political meeting in streets or public places at will … The police are set up by this judgment as the arbiters of what political parties or religious sects shall and shall not be accorded the rights of freedom of speech and freedom of assembly – two civil rights which even judges of earlier times were jealous to protect.

But even when a case we sponsored on a point of principle

ended in failure it was still worth while to expose, to publicise the uncomfortable facts, to awake realistic unease. The greatest danger in these critical times – public unawareness, apathy, complacency.

In a Home Office debate in Parliament some months later, Mr Pritt challenged bluntly the right of the Commissioner of Police to ban meetings outside Labour Exchanges: 'Lord Trenchard had no more right to do that than I had. He had no right at all, and no sort of kind of justification.'

Rights of Africans and Pacifists

While we were fighting the 'Sedition Bill' in England, in the African colonies and in Trinidad English Common Law was being supplanted by repressive Criminal Code ordinances. In the Gold Coast the Governor was given the power – not to be challenged in a court of law – to declare a book or a pamphlet seditious, making it an offence to import or *possess* it.

We were pressing in the House through sympathetic MPs, including Eleanor Rathbone, for an investigation into these repressive ordinances.

And now, two delightful Africans called in to see us, delegates from the Aborigines' Rights Protection Society of the Gold Coast. They had been struggling unsuccessfully with red tape at the Colonial Office.

One of them was an old veteran, a Paramount Chief, a big powerful man with a deep rumbling voice, the other half his size, lively high-pitched. Their Society had first sent delegates to England in 1896, to Joseph Chamberlain, to petition against the annexation of their land. Successfully, they told us, and with a cordial assurance from Queen Victoria of co-operation with their Society. Now they were concerned again with land tenure, and waterworks and the welfare of the dependent communities living in the villages.

Without our help they were likely to be fobbed off and their mission in vain. A native delegation from their colony had left in the summer without any satisfaction. The Council arranged a meeting for them in the House of Commons with a Liberal group, and another at Friends' House with interested parties, in co-operation with the London Group of African Affairs.

And finally, they were able to put their case directly to the Colonial Secretary and claim his attention. This was at the General Election in November, when Ronald escorted them to Malcolm Macdonald's constituency at Bassetlaw in Nottinghamshire. (I believe that this was one of Geoffrey Bing's ideas). At meeting after meeting the Africans politely raised the points they had come to England to put to him and to get his answer. (Malcolm Macdonald lost his seat, but came back soon after at a by-election, and remained in office.)

Public polls were the new and latest thing. At the end of June 1935, the results of the 'Peace Ballot' came out: eleven and a half million for international collective security through the League of Nations (now virtually defunct) and six and three-quarter million for sanctions against an aggressor – if necessary backed by force.

In the same month, at an air display at Hendon, pacifists and anti-war demonstrators were mingling with the crowd. The Council's observers saw the police disperse them with some violence, arrest a number of peaceable people and confiscate – quite illegally – their literature.

Both the National Peace Council and the Peace Pledge Union were affiliated to our Council. From reports we had collected, there seemed to be a systematic policy handed down in the police, to make things difficult for pacifist and anti-war propagandists. Without some effective protest the illegal practice of confiscating literature might well become standardised.

Another big air display was to be staged in a week's time at Mildenhall and Duxford in Cambridgeshire, with the King – in this Jubilee year – reviewing the Royal Air Force. The Council made plans for a body of observers to go to the aerodromes.

In Cambridge, both in the town and in the University, pacifist organisations had for some time been making preparations to sell and distribute specially printed pacifist literature. A leaflet sponsored by the Society of Friends, the Fellowship of Reconciliation, the No More War Movement and others – *Air Display Special* – with a cartoon by a Spanish artist on the front page, a letter reprinted from Canon Dick Sheppard, quotations from Lloyd George, Bernard Shaw, Baden-Powell, Vyvyan Adams MP and Dr Maude Royden.

Early on the morning of 6 July the police started a wholesale confiscation of the *Air Display Special* and the leaflet. One of the propagandists who was caught was Dr Wooster of Cambridge University. A sergeant took his name and address, searched his bag and seized copies of *Air Display Special*. Dr Wooster took his number, and along with a colleague of his, Dr Hughes, obtained an interview with the Chief Constable, who informed them that he had given instructions to his officers 'to confiscate anything of a Communist flavour'.

Now the Council, through its Cambridge branch, made plans for a test case. It arranged for Dr Wooster to take out summonses against the Chief Constable and the Sergeant in question.

The case was heard in December at the County Court before Judge Farrant. In the cross-examination of Dr Wooster and his witnesses, the Judge asked, 'What would you do if the Germans invaded England?' and, of the cartoon by the Spanish artist, 'Do you seriously suggest it is artistic?' Mr Cope-Morgan, for the plaintiff, as he examined the police witnesses and to underline the irrelevance of the questions, commented, 'This is the *first* occasion today in which witnesses have *not* been instructed by his honour to answer yes or no.'

The police attempted to justify confiscating the literature on the grounds that they were contemplating bringing charges under the Incitement to Disaffection Act. Mr Cope-Morgan pointed out they had no powers of search and seizure without a search warrant from a Judge of the High Court and then only by a policeman of the rank of Inspector. The Sergeant stuck to it that he was acting under instructions and to prevent a breach of the peace – he had no thought of making a charge.

The learned judge before he gave his verdict had some be-wigged satisfaction in dismissing the *Air Display Special* as 'crude, inartistic and in one respect a childish effusion'. Dr Wooster (who was neither an organiser nor in charge) was, he said, 'supported by a bevy of satellites. Ten of these satellites wore a species of bib advertising the pamphlets, these bibs were of a reddish hue.' (Some of the literature sellers carried sandwich-boards.) He summed up:

I have little doubt in my own mind that the plaintiff hoped to attract the attention of the police to himself and to the pamphlets ... if the plaintiff's objective was notoriety as a propagandist, and if, as seems clear from his counsel's opening, he desired, if possible, to bring a test case against the police, he achieved both these objects ... and it seems, to say the least, unreasonable to expect the defendants to pay him heavy damages for doing what I infer he hoped they would do ... I consider that the Sergeant went rather beyond what in law he was entitled to do, and that, as a matter of law, he really had no reasonable ground to apprehend a breach of the peace. And I further find that a breach of the peace would not have been the natural consequence of the exhibition of these pamphlets.

He awarded nominal damages of one pound against the police.

The extraordinary upside-down contention that the case arose, not because of the illegal police action but because pacifists – who had taken time, trouble and gone to some expense to produce literature – wanted to attract the attention of the police in the hope that this literature would be seized and their propaganda negatived!

But the verdict was the thing. A victory for freedom of expression.

Northern Ireland

It was one of Geoffrey Bing's brilliant ideas that the Council should focus the spotlight on Northern Ireland. The Six Counties of Ulster were rarely in the news, meriting no more than a brief mention of the disorder attending the Orange celebrations on the anniversary of the Battle of the Boyne. The British public unaware, ignorant that on the other side of the Irish Sea, under the umbrella of the British constitution, the ruling Protestant majority had transformed a parliamentary sovereignty into virtual rule by executive decree with the unlimited delegation of sweeping powers to subordinates – all the essentials for legal dictatorship.

The Special Powers Act of 1922 suspended habeas corpus, empowered arrest on suspicion, detention and internment without trial – with no right of appeal, and with the power to hold the arrested person incommunicado without letters, visits or access to legal advice. It gave the right to impose the death penalty for crimes other than murder and treason and to refuse a coroner's inquest. It introduced the penalty of flogging for certain offences. Trial by jury was disallowed for any offender under the Act. It conferred unlimited powers of search and seizure, the examination of bank books, the confiscation of moneys. The Home Secretary was empowered to make new Regulations, create new crimes at will, and could 'delegate either unconditionally or ... as he thought fit all or any of his powers under this Act to any officer of police'.

In the words of Mr Hanna, the member of the Northern Ireland Parliament opposing the Bill in 1922: 'The Home Secretary shall have power to do whatever he likes or let someone else do what he likes for him.'

This savage assault on civil liberty was accepted as a strictly temporary emergency measure at a time when Ireland was in a state of civil war, and with the safeguard that it was to stay in force 'for one year and no longer'.

But the overwhelming Protestant majority, taking advantage of the added loop-hole 'unless Parliament otherwise determines', renewed it year by year. In 1928 there was an attempt to make it permanent. This in spite of the fact that for the last three years there had been a remarkable absence of crime in Northern Ireland. Judges and Recorders on many occasions had been presented with the white gloves, the symbol of the law-abiding nature of the district where they presided.

As a compromise, the Act was retained for another five years. Finally, in 1933 it was the very tranquillity of the Six Counties that was put forward as a reason for incorporating the emergency temporary powers permanently. By the Special Powers Act of 1933 'The Act of 1922 shall continue in force until Parliament otherwise determines.'

As a first step in the Council's campaign, barristers went to Northern Ireland to make investigations, and Ronald visited some twenty towns in Ulster. His arrival in Belfast was to coincide with the Battle of the Boyne celebrations. He was seriously warned beforehand of the risks to his personal safety; I remember his wide smile, his calm unperturbed. After his report, the Executive decided on the ambitious plan of setting up an independent Commission of Inquiry to examine the administration and the constitutional validity of the Acts, as the most effective way to discover and bring home the facts with authority.

Mr Aylmer Digby, KC, who had been a Commander in the Royal Navy in the First World War and was now a leading member of the Admiralty bar agreed to act as chairman. The commissioners were Margery Fry, who had served on a number of government committees and had been principal of Somerville College from 1926 to 1931, William McKeag, a solicitor of the High court, a director of various companies and Liberal MP for Durham and E.L. Mallalieu, a barrister and Liberal member for Colne Valley. The secretary was the barrister, Neil Lawson.

A committee in Belfast drawn from legal, academic and trade union circles with Sam Porter, KC as chairman made investigations and collected a mass of material for submission to the Commission. The Commission sat in Belfast and heard evidence. Although its movements and proceedings were discreetly monitored by men in raincoats, the Commission experienced little difficulty in obtaining witnesses. Their problem was to try to sort out planted and self-advertising evidence, but this was satisfactorily overcome. Later the Commission met at the House of Commons.

Publication of their report was delayed because Mr Digby fell seriously ill. He approved the final draft, but died before it was formally signed by the Commissioners.

The report came out early in 1936. Forty packed pages: a legal analysis of the scope of the Special Powers Acts conflicting with the limited sovereignty conferred on Northern Ireland by the Government· of Ireland Act passed at Westminster in 1920; an examination of the Regulations made under the Acts and the powers of delegation; how this affected the magistracy and the police; the crimes created by the Acts, the tribunals to hear offenders, the rights of interrogation; finally, the effect on the liberty of the subject and on political life in Ulster. The conclusions of the Commission were that:

through the operation of the Special Powers Acts contempt has been begotten for the representative institutions of government ... the Northern Irish government has used Special Powers toward securing the domination of one particular political faction and ... curtailing the lawful activities of its opponents. The driving of legitimate movements underground into illegality, the intimidating or branding as law-breakers of their adherents, however innocent of crime, has tended to encourage violence and bigotry on the part of the government's supporters as well as to beget in its opponents an intolerance of the 'law and order' thus maintained. *The government's policy is thus driving its opponents into the ways of extremists.* (My italics, S.S.)

Most significant today is the footnote to this statement in the report:

The fact that the government's opponents have not been driven to adopt a policy of systematic violence, but rather to repudiate such course, is one of the hopeful features in the present state of Northern Ireland. But at the same time there can be no doubt that large numbers of persons, particularly among the youth, who would normally owe allegiance to the constitutional Nationalist party, are being driven into the Republican movement.

It concluded:

It is clear to the Commission that the way to the re-establishment of constitutional government, the prerequisite of law and order in democratic communities, can be paved only by the repeal of the Special Powers Acts. Wherever the pillars of constitutional rule, Parliamentary sovereignty and the rule of law are overthrown there exist the essential conditions of dictatorship ...

The publication of the report had a big impact. It made the headlines in the national press. Liberal opinion in the country was shocked. There was a lively response from Northern Ireland both in appreciation and in condemnation. The controversy in the press continued for some time. (I filled a thick album with press-cuttings.) But in spite of the exposure, and the strong reaction, the Special Powers Acts remained on the statute book – with the disastrous results we see today. Half a century later, the report makes significant and interesting reading, and NCCL reprinted it in 1972.

Growing Prestige and a New Office

Now the Council's prestige was growing overseas. Roger Baldwin of the American Civil Liberties Union wrote congratulating us on the splendid work in holding the Commission of Inquiry into the Special Powers Acts and publishing the report.

But even before the report came out our reputation had crossed the Channel. We had a visitor from Paris. The Secretary of the Ligue des Droits de l'Homme warmly congratulated Ronald on the distinguished support for the Council, the well-known personalities who had lent their names. But now he was looking around sorrowfully and shaking his head.

'Forgive me ... I know how it is. We are short of money too. But I must confess I am shocked ... yes shocked. This office? How is it possible in democratic England? An organisation of this calibre?'

Ronald assured him that this was only a temporary makeshift. We were moving soon into a well-known London street. He would have no difficulty next time in finding his way to us.

But we were never to see him again. It was during the war that the news came that both he and his wife had been assassinated in occupied France.

Ronald had found new office accommodation in Charing Cross Road at a rent the Council could afford. This was high up at roof-top level and fitted into the big irregular complex that dominated Cambridge Circus, while our entrance was in Soho, the other side. Three rooms, an outer office, Ronald's room, facing the Circus, and leading out of it, a small former kitchen with sink and fireplace. This was to serve, for the time being as our living quarters. I got onto a chair, to look down far below, on to the tops of buses and taxis going round the Circus.

After supper in Soho, when we came back in the evening, we would sometimes find a formidable madam, resting her massive rump against our locked entrance door and reluctant to shift, to let us by.

In the outer general office, and Ronald's room beyond it, the floor was trodden black. I was tempted, while it was yet bare, to have a go with a bucket and scrubbing brush – the first domestic task I had ever tackled! (and something like the last, until in my seventies I learnt that it was not so difficult to be my own cleaner). I saw the floor lighten and change colour, patch by patch. Very satisfying.

Ronald bought himself a big second-hand desk, and for the outer office three inexpensive flimsy new ones in white wood. In the evening, while he was speaking at a meeting, I varnished them the approved hideous dark office brown.

I sat in the outer room with our new typist, Joy, a bonny black-eyed Susan, and later we were joined by June, a dryad-nymph with long straight hair and tender grey eyes. Both I believe in their first job. We had now acquired a gestetner that slotted out our propaganda sheets as you pumped the handle round. June was preparing the frames for our new addressograph to cope with a growing membership.

It was the thing now, apparently, to be a Vice-President of the Council. Rose Macaulay climbed all those stone stairs at lunch-time without an appointment. As it happened, both Ronald and I were out. We worked independently. He in his own room, dictating, on the phone, keeping his appointments, I in the outer office with the two girls. When I was hungry, and it fitted in best, I took my lunch. But that day we went together to Dansey Place where a little snack counter had opened up, attracted no doubt by the coming and going at our former office.

Two bouncing north-country girls, glistening in tight white summer frocks, were chatting to the girl behind the counter busy sawing the new loaf, slapping up buttery squashy sandwiches, beside the bowl of greenery. First it was Mrs Simpson and the Prince of Wales. A friend of a friend of his valet said he was mad about her. She could do as she liked, egged him on to tell funny stories, make them all laugh, make a fool of him. Then, in odd juxtaposition the Red Dean of Canterbury, looking so old and grand now, marching at the head of the procession. 'Remember,' she nudged her friend, 'he walloped you on the bum!' They recalled outings in the country when the Dean and his wife took whole families from his Manchester parish. Sweets and games. But not only the rough boys got it, he was strict with unruly girls too.

When we got back, Joy told us that the angular lady with the spiky manner had said she would like to be a Vice-President. You have to be very important, Joy warned her. She could always join as a member. Rose Macaulay obediently filled in a form, and left her cheque. In spite of Ronald's prompt letter saying we would be delighted, she would prefer now, she said, still taking the ingenuous slight to heart, to remain an undistinguished member.

When Aldous Huxley dropped in, Ronald was out. A long-jointed secretary-bird moving restlessly, his vision already impaired. Communing with his own mind, he stared unseeing out of the window, as I fed him the current clichés about civil liberty. He was not listening. No contact. But he lent his name, gave his cheque, was included on our notepaper.

Subversives!

At first I rather liked our third room – roof-top and in the hub.

It was after midnight when I heard the news: a distant cry … repeated … coming nearer … the hoarse note insistent. I stuck my head out of the window, craning down. The boy was running over the Circus with his load of papers.

The King was dead! The problematic Prince of Wales! Was he 'the people's friend', or was he sympathetic to fascism?

It was not long after this that we both, unaccountably, woke in the middle of the night feeling ill, with strange unusual symptoms. I began to mistrust the room and feel uneasy in it. First it was Ronald, who always slept soundly, awake, and in acute pain. His homoeopathic remedies had no effect. At last he decided to go to the out-patients in Charing Cross Hospital. In the morning, I woke to find him up as usual. He had been advised to stay in for a check-up, but he couldn't spare the time. He was feeling much better.

A few days later, I woke in the dark aching. In daylight I found it hurt to lift my arms, very painful to get dressed. I couldn't hold up the earpiece of the phone. Tucked against a hunched shoulder, it was worse still. I gave up. I went home to my family – to bed.

For a fortnight I struggled to find comfort, to sleep. Barbiturates only brought me out in spots. My mother spread hot poultices round my neck and shoulders. As soon as they cooled off, the pain was waiting.

When I was almost well, after massage and violet rays, mother tackled me. 'Do you know what they say about you?' Her mouth was mocking prim, as though it was something a little bit risqué. Her eyes, too often tragic in their depths, now teasing. She went on with a little malicious smile: 'Do you know what the chief policeman told Daddy? He said you are a Communist! Did he know his daughter was a Communist?'

For a moment we were both young together. Conspirators. I could see her now as a girl – unfathomable, spirited, happy to be on her own. I felt a pang of regret at her fate, caught fast in the cage, trapped.

Nonsense I told her. Rubbish. I dismissed it as gossip. What did he know about me? I was half-amused at the mistake, a little bit flattered at being included in the class that took off from the high dive, into the deep end. It was, I knew outside my range. By temperament I was not a joiner.

Five years later, when I was looking for a job, it was not so funny to have a bogus label attached to my name. Almost everything in civil liberties, it seemed to me at first, impinged on the law. I needed, in my ignorance, a short-cut to the law, an ABC on the fundamentals. I asked Dudley Collard to recommend one. Instead he told me of a course of lectures on the law he was giving at Marx House in Clerkenwell Green, starting that Wednesday at 6.30.

Clerkenwell Green still kept something of its village charm, in spite of the metropolis flowing round it. In the roomy outer hall at Marx House the girl behind the little window told me it was for members only. But she could enrol me straightaway for half-a-crown. The membership book was displayed trustingly on the outer ledge with a pencil on string.

The meeting had started. Simple points rammed home effectively. I scribbled a few notes. Tea and biscuits afterwards. Collard, something of the youthful pedagogue, a little prim, with a classic Victorian marble-mantlepiece rectitude. Cheerful learners circled round. I was too hungry to linger. College had killed my appetite for sitting and listening and taking notes. My education on the law began and ended with this one lecture.

A year later, Marx House asked me to renew my sub. Guilty at my defection from lectures – there might be another useful series ... with vague good resolutions I sent one more – my last subscription.

The Special Branch collecting the names and addresses of Marxists for their files no doubt copied down mine. I always gave my Surrey home as my permanent address. And so it came to the Surrey police, and my father, the respected local Conservative JP, was given the tip. By that time I might well too have been linked with NCCL.

As for my connections with the Communist Party, in the eight years I was on the Council's staff, I think I may have visited its headquarters in King Street twice. This would be on the eve of some big demonstration to get, for our coverage with observers, details not forthcoming over the phone. The probable number at this or that rally, likely alternative routes when obstruction or diversion altered the approved plan. And this represented my sum total of contact with the party.

But my recorded link with the Communist Party – via Special Branch, MI5 or whatever it was – may have been quite simply due to the fact that I was the Assistant Secretary of the Council. The Public Record Office apparently preserves a still more farcical Metropolitan Police record about Ronald.

I discovered this in Robert Skidelsky's biography of Sir Oswald Mosley, in which he states his purpose as making a case for him 'with sympathy and detachment'. 'Special Branch', he tells us, quoting or paraphrasing the record, 'reported that at this time [September 1934] the activities of the NCCL were directed via Kidd, from Communist Party headquarters.'

6

The Infection of Fascism

Einstein's cry to the conscience of the world, for humanity, for political freedom, had faded, died. That was in the past. Hitler was on the up and up. President now and supreme commander of the army, sworn by oath to unconditional obedience and personal loyalty to him alone. He was straddling a Germany rearmed, aggressive, demanding its lawful place in Europe and a colonial empire. His bloody methods forgotten, judged only by their results. We were going further and further down the road of compromise, condoning, normalising the hitherto unacceptable. This adjustment was standard now, the sensible attitude to adopt. We were living in a Kafka world of disquietude, where the bright façade concealed nightmare.

And so the conventional Buckingham Palace greetings were extended to Herr Hitler on his birthday. And at the beginning of December 1935, cordial relations with Nazi Germany were celebrated through the lever of sport. A Nazi football team came to play England at Tottenham. 10,000 Nazi supporters marched through London and strewed the streets with little throw-away swastikas. The approach to Victoria was thick with them – like confetti after a wedding. I was walked off the pavement near the station by two burly Nazi policemen who bore down on me arrogantly claiming their right of way and forcing me at last to step into the road. We were incensed when Sir John Simon (who succeeded Gilmour as Home Secretary) contemptuously dismissed the TUC's last-minute appeal to him to cancel the match, because, so he said, this was to introduce politics into a purely sporting context. The *Times* equated the TUC's objections with the Nazi attitude to the Jews – in each case 'intolerance'. (The matching Nazi 'intolerance' had been shown the previous season in a Nazi sporting event when a Jewish player was kicked to death by football spectators at Regensburg.) And so at White Hart Lane the swastika flag flew beside the Union Jack, the Germans gave the Hitler salute. The match (England won three-nil) was followed by a handsome dinner for the two teams at the Victoria Hotel. The toast to Herr Hitler was proposed by the Vice-Chairman of the Football Association, the 'Horst Wessel' was sung. In fact a successful occasion for Nazi propaganda.

H.A.L. Fisher, Warden of New College Oxford, had been the minister in Lloyd George's coalition government responsible for reform in state education, the Education Act of 1918, second only to the advance made by R.A. Butler in 1944. All the more shocking to find that the progressive liberal – who had joined in our protest against the Incitement to Disaffection Bill – had now aligned himself with the current accommod- ation with Nazism. In volume three of his *History of Europe* he wrote:

> The Hitler revolution is a sufficient guarantee that Russian communism will not spread westward. The solid German bourgeois hold the central fortress of Europe. But there may be secrets in fascism or Hitlerism which the democracies of the West will desire, without abandoning their fundamental character to adopt.

A crazy world where Nazi Germany could now actually stand as a bastion of freedom for democracy! Nor was Fisher alone now in flirting with the apparent advantages of venturing into a discreet Western-style type of fascism.

By the summer of 1936 Nazi Germany achieved the triumph of staging the Olympic Games in Berlin. Fifty-three nations attended. The USA taking the decision by sixty-one votes to fifty-five in the National Convention of American Athletic Unions not to withdraw from the Games in spite of Germany's violation of the Olympic rules against discrimination by excluding their Jewish contestants. The occasion a propaganda victory for German Nazism, to crown Hitler's pride and pretensions. It was celebrated with ritual Hellenic trappings, Germanic 'Grecian' maidens in tunics, marching in the vast arena, the chanting of Pindar's Ode, the torch taken with the Hitler salute, and 30,000 carrier pigeons released. At the centre

Hitler, plump, smiling, jerky with elation. Offensive notices excluding Jews nowhere in evidence in Berlin during the Games. Hitler was now presiding over a stabilised Germany. Unemployment, with wages fixed and held down, drastically cut, thanks to public works and rearmament. The economy balanced by the wizard banker, Schacht, now Hitler's faithful servant. A Germany spiritually and physically rejuvenated, freed from the liberal error of freedom of thought, rotten Jewish intellectualism, degenerate modern research and the abnormal in art. It was returning to its native Aryan folk and peasant virtues: obedience, respect, self-sacrifice – and the manly pursuits. It was cultivating the Germanic ideal of physical fitness.

Sir Frank Freemantle, the elderly Liberal MP, speaking in the House in November 1936:

> We cannot shut our eyes to the fact that in those totalitarian states, at any rate those upon the right, there is a most wonderful physique. We may object to the methods – of course we object to the methods … but the fact remains as everybody has said over and over again … the result is shown in the health of the whole population.

After the Olympic Games, Dr Goebbels launched an attack on the foreign press, threatening journalists with expulsion if they persisted in 'hysterical lies'. Karl Robson, the Berlin correspondent of the sedate, well-established *Morning Post* failed to get a renewal of his permit. In answer to a parliamentary question, the Foreign Secretary, Anthony Eden, explained baldly: 'The reason given by the Germans … is that his messages have, despite repeated protests, been unfriendly to Germany for a long time.'

Two years before the ignominious sell-out at Munich, the *Times* correspondent reported the aggressive expansionist intentions of Nazi Germany:

> The stronger Germany becomes, the more frankly – indeed impatiently – is it admitted that expansion eastward as advocated in *Mein Kampf* is regarded as natural and a vital necessity for Germany. Why should the Western powers want to prevent it? What business need it be of England's if Germany

swallowed up Czechoslovakia? ... why, after all, the Germans and the British, two virile peoples, should not share world dominion between them.

And in the House Eleanor Rathbone, Independent member for the Combined Universities, warned what would be the inevitable end to a policy of connivance with Nazi aggression:

> There is the fear of Germany's armaments, and ... Russia's economic ideas ... and the happy thought ... why not make these two fears neutralise each other by encouraging Germany to attack Russia? ... this policy would almost certainly involve the destruction of Czechoslovakia, one of the few prosperous democracies still remaining in Central Europe.

In this climate, it was not fascism that was in disrepute in solid establishment circles and in the comfortable hierarchies, it was the anti-fascists who were condemned, blamed as the trouble-makers. It was they who became the scapegoats, the legitimate target for law and order.

The blackshirts linked jingo patriotism with their foreign trappings, their 'Heil Mosley', their political violence and anti-Semitism. In their fascist demagogy they 'Put Britain First', paraded their Union Jacks, were in friendly co-operation with the police. As well as their anonymous backers in industry, they had a sympathetic group in Parliament, and, thanks to the connections of their wealthy leader, friends in high places.

Mr Duff Cooper, soon after his appointment as Secretary for War and his inclusion in Stanley Baldwin's National Cabinet, invited a few experts for an informal discussion on military politics at Buck's Club on 2 February 1936. Along with Winston Churchill, Lord Trenchard and Captain Liddell-Hart, he included the prominent British fascist, Major-General Fuller. Fuller was a close adviser in Mosley's inner circle and gave his wholehearted support to the British Union of Fascists. He marched side-by-side with Sir Oswald on demonstrations, he spoke and campaigned for the BUF, he put in writing his views on anti-Semitism:

> Because he [Mosley] struck at the Empire of Money, its satraps, conservative, labour, liberal and communist shoulder to

shoulder formed rank against him ... behind this united front there stood the Jew, the originator of the usury system, which has as its object, the economic enslavement not only of individuals but of nations.

In the climate of the thirties, Mr Duff Cooper did not feel he was in any way compromising his own position or likely to embarrass his guests – including a former service minister and the recently retired Metropolitan Police Commissioner – by admitting into the confidential enclave a militant fascist.

It was the anti-fascists who were isolated, vulnerable. In their militant role fighting for democracy they had the moral support of enlightened liberal opinion that was outraged and in revulsion against fascism, but for all practical purposes they were out in the cold. The Labour Party – unlike the Socialist Party in France and later in Belgium that made common cause with the Communists against the danger of fascism – maintained the purist line deploring dictatorships of the right and left, and rejecting a united front. They denounced fascism abroad, and at home, but they stopped short at confrontation and militant tactics. They offered no protection, no umbrella to their militant members, if they associated with Communists in their fight against fascism. They were out on their own. Law and order could be confident when it clashed with and punished the anti-fascists that they would not be treading hard on the toes of the Opposition.

The National Liberal Home Secretary Sir John Simon washed his hands clean, took his stand on *Areopagitica*, deplored fascist ideology and condemned anti-Semitism, but – he found himself powerless to check fascist violence. He lacked the police powers – as at Olympia. It was his scrupulous concern for democratic rights that tied his hands. He defended stoutly the impartiality of the police when this was called into question in the House, as it was – at first only tentatively, quoting the view of constituents, but as 1936 wore on, with increasing disquiet. But on one aspect he was uniformly resolute. He would not allow anti-fascist demonstrations to 'disturb the peace'. Against *these* he was resolute to approve and to defend the full and vigorous use of existing police powers.

He once exclaimed that 'it made his blood boil' to learn what the fascists were up to. The cartoonist David Low seized on this. He showed Sir John squatting on his heels, bony knees apart, balancing on his mean balding cranium a kettle with a wisp of steam. A civil servant in nurse's apron, hand outstretched, waiting for it to come to the boil. A nice cup of tea for the proletarian victim prostrate at their feet. Meanwhile in the background blackshirts were still scurrying down the pitch, bat raised to strike their opponents. The caption bleated 'It isn't cricket!'

Kid-Glove Treatment for Fascists

We had already in the early spring of 1936 experienced another shock in the contrast of this policy of impotence – or tenderness – towards fascists and ruthlessness to anti-fascists. A warning of what to expect from British, dinner-jacketed, boiled-shirt fascism – if we let it happen here.

This was just fifteen days after Hitler's army marched unopposed to seize and rearm the Rhineland. A victory celebrated by the jubilant blackshirts. (They were to write later in *Action* that 'the advance of the Nazis was like a symphony. The Saar the allegro, the Rhineland the andante ...')

The scene was set this Sunday in March in urbane Kensington. Ominously, unlike Olympia, it made comparatively little impact; it lacked the celebrities present to bear witness. It didn't crack the surface. The vast public unaware, uncaring. London rolling on just the same the next day. Officially, it was a non-event. The Home Secretary refused to accept that the savage baton charge ever took place. In the debate in Parliament it was resolutely fogged, side-tracked, dissipated. Calls for a public inquiry to establish the facts repeatedly stonewalled. Even today scholarly research finds it hard to uncover the truth.

It started in the Albert Hall, the staid Victorian temple of culture. Its privately-owned boxes, family preserves, handed down, and regularly filled by the same solid middle-class professional families. The Corporation of the Royal Albert Hall of Arts and Science, a public body, which had previously let the hall to Mosley, had taken the political decision to refuse it to the anti-fascists. British fascism evidently a more reputable proposition for the land of hope and glory – even after the public scandal of Olympia. And now, once again, they were providing a traditionally dignified platform for Mosley and his blackshirts.

After Olympia Mosley had boasted in his press statement to the *Daily Mail*, that his blackshirts had been responsible for law and order at the meeting, but that 'a number of Communists and socialists were permitted to gather outside ... The blackshirts ask ... either that the police will keep order in the streets outside our meetings or we will keep order ourselves.' And now all Mosley's arrogant either/or demands were met in full by the Metropolitan Police. They banned – contrary to any known precedent for a political meeting – all processions and demonstrations within half a mile of the hall. They closed to the general public two main thoroughfares, diverting traffic to the back of the Albert Hall. They conducted the blackshirts to the meeting along Constitution Hill, near Buckingham Palace, a route traditionally reserved for the Guards and royal processions.

When Ronald and I arrived, the entrance way and the surrounds of the hall were packed with police. Some of them were checking the cars as they drew up – these had been allowed through the closed thoroughfares by virtue of fascist sticker-passes, issued by the Black House. Those who arrived on foot were showing their tickets to be allowed into the enclosure.

We were in a fascist oasis, isolated, cut off. The political meeting had been turned into something of a gala occasion, an important function with the glossing of the Lord Mayor kid-glove treatment. The blackshirts confident, supreme, smiles and handshakes as they alighted from the cars; the policemen servicing efficiently.

High up, in the promenade gallery under the great dome, not a policeman in sight. There were in fact thirty in the building – in an auditorium that holds 7,000. A hundred more were stationed at the exit doors, presumably to prevent unauthorised entry.

Dingle Foot, who was at the meeting, saw a number of police

in the enclosed gallery that runs right round the hall, 'that is to say, they were within the building but not within the audi-torium'. In the course of the meeting nothing significant hap-pened in his vicinity, 'but', he said, 'I could see that from other parts of the hall people were being forcibly ejected'. Had the police been inside the auditorium, as they were clearly entitled to be, even against the wishes of the convenors, their very presence 'would have prevented the use of unnecessary force'.

In the gallery, the fascist stewards were massed in clumps; the big and tough, the short and scruffy; heavy buckled belts, black gloves (Youth! Youth! Springtime of Beauty!). A group of public school hoorah-boy-types joined them briefly, checked on this and that and then dropped away down into the lower auditorium.

The iron voice, amplified, struck out, hitting the rotundities, bouncing back, assaulting the ears, filling the head, a piston prodding relentlessly with no respite.

All the evening I heard no attempt to challenge it. No cry, no protest that reached me came from or rose as far as the gallery. Nothing to break through the barrage, to interrupt the total monopoly of the one dominating voice. (But Dingle Foot in the lower auditorium heard, from time to time, loud interruptions).

The stewards were patrolling in groups, spotting anti-fascists, reporting back, closing round them.

After about half an hour it started to happen. Rather like a nightmare old movie, the flash of action with almost no sound, the impact soft-pedalled, swallowed, rolled away in the constant volume of the loudspeakers.

I turned round. A girl had been knocked down. She was sprawling, face-downwards, blackshirts stumbling, falling over her. She was pulled, pummelled, dragged up, taken away.

Ronald in his book: 'Blackshirts whipped off their black belts and struck with the metal buckles. I saw two persons with their faces cut open in this way'.

A lanky young man passed me, head in air, as though he was hiking in the Lake District. His friend ahead looked round, he waved him on.

'That's one of them,' a blackshirt near me to another steward.

He certainly belonged to a different climate.

The steward followed up on tiptoe. I came after.

The blackshirt reached up, caught the young man on the back of the head with his gloved fist. I heard the crack.

The young man fell forward. He lay on the ground. Blackshirts ran up from all sides, surrounding, masking him. They were picking him up. They carried him forward, and out of my sight. Where was his friend?

(Ronald too had witnessed the sneak assault. The perfect case for legal action. The Council traced the victim to St George's Hospital, where he was detained for a fortnight with suspected fracture of the vault of the skull. His parents proved to be unwilling to seek any legal redress.)

While Ronald stayed, I ran off for a policeman. I took the wrong door. Nothing for it but to run on, down and down the stairs. At last, at the very bottom, just inside the exit door, a policeman. He looked through me. He refused to budge.

Upstairs again. Ronald had discovered two inspectors stationed in the enclosed back gallery. He urgently asked them to draft in more men. They reported, I quote from his book, that 'they were not present to keep order and that they had received their instructions and would keep to these instructions'. (They had no intention of getting involved like Inspector Carroll at Olympia.)

The blackshirts were attacking, without provocation, anyone they recognised as anti-fascist.

A short middle-aged man was being dragged along by blackshirts, his arms twisted behind his back. One of them jabbed a finger in his eye. His scream survived a few seconds as he passed, and then snuffed out. At the exit door, half glass, they charged him through, using him as a battering-ram, the solid glass panel smashed.

Now the flaying, remorseless voice, their link with the platform, rose on a new note. Mosley was working up for the flash point. The blackshirts stopped chatting, cocked an ear. This was the only bit of interest – the Jew bit – they wanted to hear this.

He was carrying his audience with him. In a side box, silhouetted, a chinless man in a dog-collar. I can see him today. Jumping up and down like a poodle on its hind legs, carried away, joining in the cheers, waving.

In the House at question time the next day, Vyvyan Adams,

Unionist MP for West Leeds: 'The performance in the Albert Hall last night included an anti-Jewish incitement.' Had the Home Office 'any means of dealing with this kind of dangerous incitement'?

Two days later, more questions. Why did the Metropolitan Police close free passage on a thoroughfare to the general public? Should 'a place such as the Albert Hall ... be made available for meetings likely to cause a breach of the peace and serious interference with the general body of the public'? This was from William Mabane, National Liberal MP from Huddersfield. A Unionist MP for Stockport, Norman John Hulbert asked about the cost of the special police employed. Vyvyan Adams, again, were any prosecutions to be taken 'in view of cases of violence employed by the fascist stewards in ejecting members of the audience'? Ernest Thurtle, Labour MP for Shoreditch, a First World War veteran: why, contrary to all precedent, was the fascist procession allowed along Constitution Hill, past Buckingham Palace and along Birdcage Walk?

Sir John Simon in answer: about 2,500 police were employed that evening and about 400 kept in reserve – the extra cost about £300. About thirty police were inside the hall, and in addition 100 'were posted at the doors ... and they received from the stewards the persons who were ejected and escorted them out of the building'.

'Posted' was the right word. These police remained immovable. No concern of theirs how, or why, or in what way the ejections took place. Presumably they 'received' the unconscious body of the young man we saw struck down, and that was conveyed to St George's Hospital. And all this even after the Corporation of the Hall had decided on a new policy – reported in the press a month before the meeting – to submit to the police the dates and objects of meetings, the names of chairman and speakers, and to leave it to the discretion of the police whether or not to be present at the meeting.

On the wisdom of allowing such a meeting to be held in the Albert Hall, Sir John Simon: 'I think we must face the responsibilities of living in a free country.' Mr Adams: 'Is the right honourable gentleman aware that the management of the Albert Hall refuse the use of the hall to anti-fascist bodies? ... the question of freedom of speech, therefore, does arise.'

On the question of the route along which the police conducted the fascists to the meeting, Sir John Simon denied 'that the police have been showing favouritism ... the processions of those of another view are looked after with equal care and equal courtesy.'

When we got back to Cambridge Circus after the fascist meeting, I felt tired, chastened, degraded by the experience. I had not been able to purge myself of a sense of compliance – of cowardice? As observer, as silent spectator, I had not taken any of it myself. I had not protested. I had not intervened. Every moment I had been expecting recognition as an observer. My incredible immunity had given me a sense of guilt.

'You'll feel better when we have had something to eat.'

We were going down the stone stairs when the phone started to ring.

There had been a savage baton charge in Thurloe Square – the anti-fascist meeting! Mounted police rode in without warning, drew batons. No trouble at all till then – nothing – half a mile away from the Albert Hall. The people in the crowd tried to get away, jammed, trapped in the Square, caught up against the railings, some on the ground. The police didn't touch the speaker's van. They beat up the crowd, then they rode off.

As Ronald stayed busy making phone calls, I got out the old black frying-pan.

Baton Charge in Thurloe Square

John Strachey was the main sponsor of the anti-fascist demonstration called to protest against Mosley's meeting and the Albert Hall's refusal to let to anti-fascists. Only five days before Mosley's rally, the police notified Strachey that no meeting would be allowed within half a mile of the Albert Hall. But leaflets had already been circulated calling for a protest rally outside the hall.

So when Strachey arrived in Exhibition Road on 22 March he found a crowd of some 800 to 1,000 awaiting him. He told the Inspector, who appeared to be in charge, that he proposed to hold his meeting half a mile away, near South Kensington underground station.

Strachey led the way, and the crowd followed him to Thurloe Square. The square was a residential precinct near the underground, a backwater little used by traffic, and especially quiet on a Sunday afternoon.

As the crowd moved along, there were calls of 'This way to the meeting, Comrades!' and some singing and slogans. It all died down once they were assembled round the van to listen – there was no loudspeaker. The van was parked just inside the square, near the Alfred Place entrance. By road, this was more than half a mile from the Albert Hall, but as the crow flies, measured by ruler and compass, a few yards under.

As well as the rank-and-file proletarian supporters, there was a sizeable middle-class element, a large proportion of women, and of course the Council's observers. (I myself took statements from an architect, some artists, a doctor, journalists, a barrister and I believe a clergyman.)

It was on that Sunday evening that Captain the Honourable Arthur Oswald James Hope came to dine with his mother, Lady Rankeillor, at No.44 Thurloe Square, at the corner of Alfred Place. Captain Hope, aged thirty-nine, Sandhurst and Coldstream Guards, was Unionist MP for Aston, Birmingham, and one of the five Lord Commissioners to the Treasury. He arrived at 7.50 p.m. and left his car unattended in Alfred Place outside the front door.

It was Captain Hope's testimony in the House on 25 March about the temper and behaviour of the meeting, and what happened, that flatly contradicted the evidence of the Council's observers, and the statements made by more than a hundred witnesses who were at the meeting. This gave Sir John Simon just the support he needed in his defence of the police action.

'I heard sounds of song and a certain amount of shouting outside,' Captain Hope said. 'The song as I afterwards ascertained was the 'Internationale'. I went outside ... to my car ... a motor-car came up (the speaker's van) and to my surprise a gentleman got on to the fly-board and proceeded to address the crowd.' The gentleman, he discovered, was John Strachey, his political opponent in 1931, whom he had last seen 'moaning at the loss of his deposit'. Captain Hope was hovering, anxious about his car, when ... several people very kindly said to me, 'Don't worry about your car, it will be all right.' So I went back inside. After five or ten minutes I saw twenty or thirty members of the crowd come to my car and push it backwards about twenty-five yards down Alfred Place, and put it across the road as a barrier ... I naturally ran out of the house and tried to rescue my car ...

In his speech in the Commons, Captain Hope comes back twice on this point on his quest 'to rescue my car'. The first time,

I reasoned with them, I hope persuasively, and finally was allowed to turn my car round and drive in the direction of Kensington station. When I got to my car the people round it were by no means friendly and had unscrewed the cap of the petrol tank. One man I heard say, 'Give us a match and I will set the thing alight.' Another man said, 'Give us a knife and we will slash the car.'

(In fact the car was promptly driven off unscathed.) Version number two: 'When I went to rescue my car I said to the people, "Why do you want to put a barrier across the road?" and they said, "Because the police will be after us, and will move us off." ' (But the police were in fact already there, and had been from the beginning of the meeting, at its northern end.)

Looking back at the evidence, after forty years, I am inclined to wonder whether there would have been a baton charge but for Captain Hope's precious car? Did he, after safely depositing it somewhere, get on the phone, or personally lodge a complaint with some senior police officer? Throw his weight about a bit? Give a picture of an unruly mob that knew it had no business to be there and was threatening to damage property? The verbals tempt one to speculate on this as a possibility. The Commission commented: 'We think that in his anxiety for his car Captain Hope may have exaggerated in his mind the hostility of the crowd ... he has not said that he made any complaint to the police.' D.N. Pritt made it quite clear, in parliamentary language, what he thought of Captain Hope's testimony: 'I was interested to hear what was said by the honourable and gallant Member who had the advantage of seeing a great deal of what occurred. I do not for a moment suggest that he told the House anything he did not see …'

At any event, after he had put his car in a place of safety Captain Hope made his way back to the square. This time he slipped in by climbing the area railings and got in through the area door. In the Commons, he said that the crowd was barring access to the front door. They were now 'much more impassioned … stirred up either by Mr Strachey's oratory' or because their numbers had grown. And they were in an 'ugly mood', 'yelling and shouting'.

The Council's observers: There was nothing to prevent Captain Hope going in through the front door of No. 44. Pavements were kept clear all the time. Quite unnecessary to climb in through the area. No complaints about noise or disorder were made by any householders in the neighbourhood. Indeed some of the residents came out on their balconies to listen, servants from the houses joined the crowd. The evidence was overwhelming that the meeting was orderly and quiet with occasional hand-clapping. The chairman, John Strachey, was in complete control. When he heard that rumours were circulating about disturbances in the Albert Hall, he intervened to advise the people who had joined the meeting (it had grown and was variously estimated as between 1,000 and 2,000) to stay and listen to the constructive case against fascism, and not to go to the Albert Hall. In Alfred Place, people on the very outskirts, apparently the eager-beavers keen, perhaps a little officiously, to make themselves useful and assume a role (but without any authorisation from the platform), linked arms, backs to the meeting, sometimes in one row, sometimes more. The purpose, it was said, was to contain the meeting at that end within reasonable bounds, and also, after Strachey's appeal to the crowd to stay, to discourage people from breaking away and going towards Exhibition Road. In any event the pavements were kept clear, and people passed through the 'cordon' (the formal term used in the House to describe this casual, improvised linking up) including foot police who evidently raised no objection to it. (Claud Cockburn, looking back after forty years, recalls, I believe at the beginning of the meeting, briefly joining in and linking arms with Palme Dutt and singing 'Rule Britannia'!)

At a quarter to nine, one of the Council's observers looked

at his watch. The meeting had been going on peacefully, uneventfully for close on an hour. Ted Willis of the Labour League of Youth had ended his speech. Only one more speaker. He decided that he could with a clear conscience safely go home.

At just about the same time, an Inspector came up to the northern end of the square. 'What is this place?' he asked a constable on duty (overheard by an observer).

'Thurloe Square.'

'What is this meeting?'

'Mainly Communist.'

'Where is the nearest telephone box?'

About five minutes later, when the Revd Leonard Schiff had just started to speak, a detachment of about twenty mounted police and a police van arrived in Alfred Place. The police got out of a van. The mounted man in charge approached.

A self-appointed spokesman stepped out of the so-called 'cordon' arm upraised. The mounted man bent down: 'You have had your meeting, now clear off.'

The man went back into the meeting. From the outskirts some booing and cat-calls, and shouts of 'No!'

'After a brief pause – a matter of seconds' (Mr Lazarus, a barrister, in his evidence), 'half a minute' (Mr Bird), 'barely two minutes – almost at once' (Mr Grant), the police advanced in three rows, trotted into the crowd, shouting 'Get out of the way!' Well inside, they drew batons and struck men and women indiscriminately on the head and shoulders. Some of them mounted the pavement, driving the crowd towards the northern end of the square. One police section wheeled round, cut off a large part of the crowd, who were pinned against the railings; this tactic seemingly more designed to punish rather than to disperse them. The crowd was completely taken by surprise – 'absolutely terrified', 'screams', 'horrifying' – and were only concerned to escape. Some of them tried to climb over the railings, to get into the gardens and were struck as they did so. Kathleen Wickens, pinned against the railings, was batoned over the left eye, her face cut open. She was covered in blood, felt ill for a fortnight. An elderly man crushed, another pinned, struck on the head, fell unconscious, his wife collapsed. A girl knocked down by a mounted man was lying in the road, men attempting to protect her from being trampled were harried by foot police. A man carrying a baby was heavily struck, a doctor saw a man dealt a dangerous blow on the back of the neck.

Strachey and the other speakers, who had had no warning, stayed on the van, pulling up on it a number of women. The mounted police ignored them, rode off without speaking to them.

Captain Hope from his vantage point:

> The crowd were forming a cordon across Alfred Place and were threatening the police to 'come on' ... After about five minutes mounted and foot police came up Alfred Place and dispersed the crowd ... I do not agree that the police charged the crowd, hitting people right and left ... They came at a slow pace and waved their truncheons in the air. I do not pretend to have seen everything, but personally I saw only two people struck. One was a man [a press photographer] who flashed a flashlight directly into a horse's face, and the policeman struck the flashlight out of his hand and the other was a man who aimed a blow at a foot policeman and the policeman gave him an upper cut ... I gave the police inspector a report of what I had actually seen. I do not consider that the police used undue violence and I do not believe that anyone was seriously hurt ... I believe the police were justified in moving on the crowd, and that the crowd expected to be moved on and they moved on quickly and *dispersed in a peaceful manner.* (My italics, S.S.)

Parliament Debates

The debate in the House was three days after the event. Dingle Foot and D.N. Pritt put the case for a public inquiry, with the ammunition of thirty to forty statements (the first to hand) from the Council's observers and witnesses in the crowd.

Sir John Simon had also received these statements. Earlier that day he had answered questions about the behaviour of the police. It was clear that there was a confusion in his official brief between the time and the events in Thurloe Square and those which occurred outside and, some of them, after it. But it was also evident from the first that he had made up his mind to refuse an inquiry. He remained deaf, impervious, rejecting the damaging evidence.

The case he presented in defence of the police – in answer to Dingle Foot who opened – was a travesty of the facts. His brief effectively jumbled up all the incidents that occurred that evening, elsewhere and later, and blamed the lot on the meeting at Thurloe Square, working up indignation and exonerating the police.

In the first place, he assumed that the meeting was 'in a prohibited area' and 'against the lawful orders of the police'. On the contrary, the square had been decided on for the meeting because, for any practical common-sense purpose, that is by road, it *was* half a mile away from the Albert Hall – in fact just over. Nor had the police present in the square raised any objection to the holding of it there. Apparently it was discovered by cartographical officialdom that the meeting, the speaker's van, could be shown to be ten yards inside the half-mile radius. But apart from this academic exercise, the chairman of the meeting had conformed to the spirit of the ban by containing and holding the crowd away from the disputed area and avoiding a confrontation. In the second place, Sir John Simon refused to accept that the meeting was peaceful and orderly. He made play again and again with 'my Honourable friend's motor-car', 'appropriated' to form a barrier against the approach of the police, completely misleading the House about a trivial incident resolved within minutes at the beginning of the meeting when its owner drove it away unscathed. Another trump card that he used to disprove that the crowd was peaceful was the so-called 'cordon' formed across Alfred Place. The 'cordon', a word with a militant if not a military flavour, was said to be a threatening and provocative tactic to keep the police at bay.

There was no 'cordon' at either the northern or southern limit of the meeting in Thurloe Square. And in Alfred Place if the 'cordon' had presented any obstruction, the police would no doubt have drawn batons right away. But from all accounts, including Captain Hope's evidence, the police were able to advance straight into the crowd without any difficulty or obstruction. It was only when they were well inside that they drew and used their batons against the surprised people trying to escape.

But Sir John Simon gave a picture of 'a very dangerous situation and a vast accumulation of people'. He referred to a bottle thrown at a policeman (this was a later and separate incident in Exhibition Road and a man was fined for it) and to the attempted rescue of another arrested man when a policeman was said to have been 'kicked in a most horrible manner.' No one was arrested and no policeman was injured in Thurloe Square itself.

Having thoroughly confused and prejudiced the issue with these red herrings, Sir John Simon then gave the helpful advice to any member of the public who had a grievance. The Commissioner of Police, he said, 'is always prepared … to examine any complaint which is made and supported by evidence against any policeman'.

He ended by recapping the steps taken by the police before they broke up the meeting confirming that no warning or request to close the meeting was given to the chairman or the speaker on the van. 'I have already pointed out', he said, 'that the crowd was barricading the entrance to Thurloe Square' (Captain Hope's long-vanished car multiplied now to present a formidable barrier). The mounted man in charge addressed himself to 'a man' who stepped out of the cordon and 'appeared to be in authority' (the people at the very outskirts of a political meeting are hardly likely to be 'in authority'). The policeman then waited 'ten minutes' (even Captain Hope spoke of five minutes) before he and his mounted contingent rode into the crowd.

The Home Secretary saw no grounds at all for holding an inquiry.

The Council assembled a formidable body of evidence with statements from 113 witnesses. (I spent all my time interviewing. In the end I almost felt I had been there myself.) The case presented in our dossier was so strong and complete, revealing the violent police action as totally unnecessary, and such a flagrant abuse of police powers, that the Council felt an official public inquiry must be conceded. It continued to press the Home Secretary, keeping him supplied with all the material. Perhaps by now he himself was aware how damaging an inquiry might prove to be. He persisted in his refusal.

The NCCL Commission of Inquiry

Now the Council had to decide – lawyers and journalists were divided – whether to rely on the force of public opinion and hold a big public meeting to reveal the facts, with key witnesses and victims – but already some weeks after the event. Or to set up our own unofficial Commission of Inquiry, with the long-term prospect of bringing more weighty influence to bear on the government with the publication of its report. It was this latter that was decided on.

But a Commission of Inquiry is not assembled or set in motion as quickly or as easily as a public meeting. It was not until 10 and 14 July that it held its two public sessions under the chairmanship of Professor Norman Bentwich with Mr Harrison Barrow, Professor F.M. Cornford, J.B. Priestley and Eleanor Rathbone, MP as commissioners and Dudley Collard the secretary.

As an unofficial body its powers were limited. It could not call for documents or summon witnesses. The police refused to co-operate, to give evidence, or even send an observer. Captain Hope also refused to appear.

The report came out at the end of July. It concluded that

the crowd was perfectly peaceable and orderly ... that no attempt was made by the police to get the speakers to stop the meeting, although the police would have had no difficulty in approaching the speakers. That apart from an order to a small portion of the crowd in a side street, which the police did not allow time to be obeyed, no warning was given by the police to the crowd to disperse. That there was no necessity whatsoever for a baton charge, that the baton charge was carried out with a totally unnecessary degree of brutality and violence, that serious injuries were caused ... That the crowd offered no resistance to the police. That a serious riot might easily have been caused ... for which the police would have been solely to blame. That the account of the incidents in Thurloe Square given by the Home Secretary in the House of Commons can only have been based on substantially inaccurate information, and on confusion of incidents which happened elsewhere. That the facts call for an official public inquiry into the conduct of the police.

Professor Harold Laski, a member of the Executive of the Labour Party, wrote a strong Preface to the Report:

There is no use denying that there is an ugly body of suspicion abroad about police behaviour in dealing with the problems created by the Fascist movement. To deny an inquiry in circumstances like the present is to raise the grave presumption that it is denied lest, under examination, the charges should prove justified.

But the report did not receive anything like the press coverage of our Northern Ireland Commission of Inquiry on the Special Powers Acts. It related back to events some months earlier, and 1936 was an eventful year – the Spanish Civil War had just erupted, and a controversial monarch Edward VIII was on the throne. In spite of repeated questions in the House the Home Office remained adamant. The shocking injustice was officially passed over and blotted out. But the anti-fascist resentment built up and was to explode later that year.

7

Anti-Semitism

The contagion of anti-Semitism was spreading.

As early as August 1934, Sir John Simon, who was then Foreign Secretary, found it expedient to deny in the press that he was a Jew. Rumours and statements current at home and abroad had suggested that his ancestry had powerfully influenced the policy of the National Government. Sir John Simon was careful, after denying the imputation, to add that he himself had no sympathy with anti-Semitism, which he utterly condemned.

At this time Nazi Germany was spending the equivalent of £13 million in propaganda (stepped up to £21 million in 1937). German nationals and settlers, and their consulates and embassies all over the world, were roped in as centres, to play their part and to operate as Nazi communities with anti-Semitic barriers. An agency at Hamburg circulated articles translated into a number of languages for free publication overseas, and sent propaganda direct to likely lists of civil servants, service officers and others. In Catholic countries the bogy of Bolshevism was exploited and Nazi Germany's role as the saviour of Europe from this menace. The World Service Bureau at Erfurt concentrated exclusively on anti-Semitism. Information sheets in eight languages 'the intellectual armoury of every Gentile' exposed 'the machinations of the Jewish underworld'. The Service brought into currency again all the old lies and forgeries – ritual murder, the Protocols of the Elders of Zion, 'quotations' from the Talmud and so on. In May 1934 Julius Streicher, the head of an anti-Semitic publishing house, featured ritual murder in a special issue of his paper *Der Stürmer*. The Archbishop of Canterbury in the *Times*: 'It seems incredible that such a publication recalling the worst excesses of medieval fanaticism should have been permitted in any civilised country.' Germany attempted to prevent this issue circulating abroad.

I have a *Der Stürmer* publication for the indoctrination of German children. A cloth-bound picture book 'for young and old', the Gothic script in verse, with attractive bright colour plates. 'God made the world' and Jesus Christ says the Jew is a murderer, no other race could be found to torture him to death, and so the Jews were the Chosen People. The Talmud, their book of law, they learnt from their father the Devil. Squat, shifty, repulsive, the Jew is contrasted with the upright honest German. In his filthy butcher's shop, cigar in mouth, the Jew cuts tainted offal for the trusting German simpleton in patched breeks. The Jewish lawyer defrauds the young couple up from the country. The Jewish doctor poisons Gentiles in hospital to find the right remedy for his Jewish patient. Top-hatted he attempts to seduce the German maiden. The willing German peasant girl slaves for her Jewish mistress. The smart German teenager – surprisingly – hopes to marry the rich Jew. Her father, who has always kept his race pure, explodes in anger: 'One never yokes a good cow together with a dachsund.' But now to the rescue! Julius Streicher appears in his brown uniform! A bevy of little ones offer him a bunch of flowers. The Jewish children, ugly and rude, are driven from the schools with their teachers. *Der Stürmer* placards warn and show the children where it is and is not safe to shop to avoid the Jews. Sunny beaches exclude the Jews. At last the Jews are seen making a grand exodus, dispatched to a mysterious land 'in the far south where once stood the cradle of the Jews … How they roll their eyes as they waddle along.'

Nazi Germany made capital out of the libel action won by Lord Camrose and the *Daily Telegraph* against the British Union of Fascists' weekly paper *Action*. The then editor, John Beckett, wrote an article to show that the British press in general and the *Daily Telegraph* in particular was controlled by Jewish financial interests. Lord Camrose it alleged was a Jew and the Berry family connected by marriage with business interests controlled by Jewish financiers. The damages awarded totalled £20,000. (Action Press Ltd, however, was a dummy company with a nominal capital and worthless.) The Nazi official guide to Berlin, presented to all who registered at hotels, pointed out how far anti-Semitism had progressed in England. The extent of the damages proved that it was now a deadly insult to call a man a Jew. It went on to exclaim at the gullibility of foreigners who believed that the Jews were persecuted in Germany!

The deliberate stimulation of anti-Semitism, not only abroad but in this country – 'the will to hate' – with the objective of 'depriving Jews of that equal status which the British sense of justice still – thank God – upholds, the vilifying of the Anglo-Jewish community, all this decided the Board of Deputies of British Jews to sponsor an informative defensive publication, *The Jews of Britain* by their press officer Sidney Saloman. It set out the contribution of British Jews to the arts, literature, music, the stage, to sport, and the part they played in the First World War. It traced and exposed the lies, forgeries and superstitions used in the dissemination of anti-semitic propaganda. It was published first in hardback in 1938, and then in Hutchinson's sixpenny pocket edition.

It was in 1936 that Mosley's anti-Semitic campaign came to the boil – in the Jewish East End of London. It had been steadily building up since the end of 1934, when Mosley was adopting an anti-Semitic posture. The Jew was an insidious alien, part of an international world-wide conspiracy dominating the sources of power, including the old gang in the Conservative Party. At the same time Jewry controlled Bolshevism in Russia, and international socialism with its British Labour Party – in 1934 Mosley had said 'behind the Communist and socialist mob is the alien Jewish financier supplying the palm-oil to make them yell.' Jewry threatened and persecuted the gallant and patriotic British Union of Fascists, the only champion determined 'To Put Britain First'.

British Fascist policy as it crystallised stood for stopping Jewish immigration, and deporting Jews guilty of anti-British conduct, that is of putting their own interests before the British interest. Jews innocent of this could remain as second-class citizens, without the full civil rights of the British. A European conference would have to find a suitable territory where the stateless Jew, 'the parasite of humanity', could be accepted for deportation.

It was in a speech in April 1935 that Mosley made his position clear on anti-Semitism. He won his spurs and gained approval in Germany from the arch anti-Semite who had previously been coldly critical. The notorious Julius Streicher sent him a telegram of congratulation.

He responded with alacrity to Julius Streicher (was he looking for a subsidy from Germany?): 'I greatly esteem your message in the midst of our hard struggle. The forces of Jewish corruption must be overcome in all great countries before the future of Europe can be made secure in justice and peace. Our struggle is hard but our victory is certain.'

But Mosley's heroic role championing fascist justice and peace in 'the modern age', challenging the big battalions of Jewish corruption – when it came to practical politics – was cut down to size. This wealthy aristocratic David found it expedient to confine his attacks on Goliath to cold print and speech-making at a convenient distance from the City and Mayfair. For campaign tactics and vigorous action he prudently chose a more vulnerable target. From the first the enemy was to be hit at his weakest point.

'The big Jew puts you out of employment by the million, the little Jew sweats you in Whitechapel.' The little Jew attacks with the big Jew's gold – all part of the same system of usury. A specious justification in a speech at Sheffield Town Hall in the summer of 1935.

Mosley's East End Campaign

Mosley announced that he would open a ring of 'barracks' in East London.

The vulnerable, overcrowded, poverty-ridden East End, hard hit by unemployment and by trade leaving the area. Struggling to survive, living on its own doorstep in ramshackle derelict old property, much of it a hundred years old. Stepney had the highest concentration of Jewish residents, but still in a minority – about thirty per cent. Bethnal Green next and after that Shoreditch and Poplar, with Jewish families spreading sparsely into Hackney, Bow and the streets around. 'Practically the whole of Stepney is a slum,' a housing official cheerfully commented in the thirties. The promise in the names of

Stepney's Paradise Row, Fleur de Lys Street, Flower and Dean Street was contradicted by their squalor. Paragon Mansions with naked gasjets flaring on the stairways, the children jumping up to light paper at them, and when the gas blew out the fumes escaping into the building. Rotten floors and falling plaster, the damp wall in a shared lavatory exuding into the living quarter the other side. Slum landlords did no repairs or decorations, but with the congestion in the area there was no shortage of tenants. Some of them lived in insanitary basements, sharing a tap and a WC in the rat-infested yard. There were two-room bug-ridden tenements where the whole family cooked, ate, lived and slept, the bugs – endemic in the old buildings – a torment and a stink in the airless summer nights. Babies born at home, with a hard pillow for the mother to bite on, the wall around blood-spotted with the traces of bed-bugs. No place to store food. The street markets open on Sundays a necessity and an attraction in Club Row, in White Horse Road, in Stepney High Street, and Petticoat Lane. Phil Piratin, recalls Stepney's

> virility, its movement, its bright shops, its cafes and restaurants open up to two, three and even four in the morning, its informality, its thousands of evening strollers on the broad pavements of Whitechapel Road …. Stepney folk had their own Cockney gaiety, and with a few bob in their pockets found their own means of escaping the grimness and the drabness around them. But without a few bob …

Whitechapel had at one time been filled with common lodging houses, the first Rowton House was opened there, attracting the down-and-outs and 'vagrants'. With its proximity to the docks, Stepney was cosmopolitan and polyglot. Sally, born in a tough street where many of the male members had at one time been 'inside', recollects her childhood friends in the thirties to include 'Catholic, Muslim, Chinese, Lithuanian, you name them, they were there'. (She was writing to her good friend Edith Ramsey, whom I visited in her Stepney home when she was in her eighties. Miss Ramsey came into the East End in 1920 as a Cambridge graduate to devote herself to educational work, fell in love with the people and stayed there for life.)

Mosley's racialist campaign in the East End was not the first. There was a big influx of Jewish immigrants seeking asylum from persecution in Tsarist Russia, Poland and other central European states in the late nineteenth century. They had arrived without any English, children with labels round their necks, some of them expecting, hoping to find themselves in New York and discovering instead the London docks. In 1901 the Tory member for Stepney, Major Sir William Evans-Gordon, led the so-called British Brothers League in a campaign to stop Jewish immigration: 'The rubbish shot from the dustbins of Austria and Russia, destroying Sunday, sleeping eight to a room, debasing national life, corrupting morals'.

The second generation of Jews born and grown up in the East End had outlived the native antagonism aroused by their incursion and by the campaign launched against them. With the tolerance and the neighbourliness shown by the very poor and with the daily familiarity of proximity, they had been accepted as part of the local life. All of them rubbing shoulders with their fellow cockneys, in the street markets, the small shops, the workshops, costermongers, traders, skilled and unskilled workers, competing in the hungry daily pressure to survive. Dan Frankel MP, born in his constituency of Stepney, recalled in the House in 1936, the anti-Semitism of thirty years earlier, the battle every evening coming home from school. His election to represent Stepney was in itself evidence of the decline of that anti-Semitism. But now Mosley's East End campaign was again stirring up racial feeling and isolating and alarming the East End Jew.

The clothing industry, traditional in the East End, had attracted the Jewish immigrants, who brought their own expertise and skill to bear in it, running the trade against the handicap of the bad local conditions and the keen competition outside. It developed with a proliferation of small workshops and small masters; workers and boss eked out a living as best they could with hectic work in the peak season of the fashion trade, and underemployment in the slack. The workshops crammed into the congested area were ill-ventilated, shutting out the light and air, built onto houses and in back yards with communicating bridges on different floors. The master tailor or dressmaker who made good preferred not to move out but to stay in the neighbourhood beside his work; his car and his style of living in contrast to the poverty around made him conspicuous, 'ostentatious'. It was easy for the fascist street-corner demagogue to make the Jew the scapegoat, to identify him as the bad employer, the sweater, responsible for the prevailing misery, the bad conditions endemic in the East End – for 'the ghetto the Jews have turned it into'. Sally again, as she recollected her youth:

> the real cockney people, Gentile and Jew, had one thing in common that bound us together, poverty, of course there were Jewish people that were better off than us, both Jew and Gentile were in their employ ... in the rag trade. But still you did a day's work and you got a day's pay ... When me and my friend was hungry, we went to the Jewish Soup Kitchen in Butler Street, they gave us soup, bread and butter, they did not ask us what our faith was, all they knew was we were hungry ... But when I look back one thing I do know. Poverty does not discriminate. That is what I meant when I said Mosley was not successful in our area. Jew or Gentile we were in the same stream of life, fighting together the same tides of life. We were too busy (I say we including our parents) keeping alive to have time to hate anyone.'

After the general election of 1935 Labour won control of nearly all the East End constituencies and their MPs included three big guns: George Lansbury, Clement Attlee and Herbert Morrison. The veteran Liberal, Sir Percy Harris held South West Bethnal Green which he had represented since 1922. The Communist Party had a radical following in the East End and held regular street meetings.

William Joyce, Mosley's leading lieutenant, (later, in the war, the Nazi spokesman 'Lord Haw Haw') rented a room in the East End in 1933. The first fascist branch was set up in Bow in 1934, another in Shoreditch in 1935, and then in Hackney. But it was into Stepney and Bethnal Green, with a branch in Green Street, that the fascists infiltrated and campaigned most pugnaciously. The branches had a full-time organiser and offered facilities for recreation, funds were available to make weekly payments to the recruited unemployed once they were active members. A fascist organisation was set up at Burdett

Road Labour Exchange in Limehouse to contact the unemployed.

The NCCL, pledged by its constitution to oppose radical, religious and political discrimination, consulted with its lawyers on the feasibility of checking anti-Semitism at its source through legislation making it an offence to foster hatred on racial or religious grounds. Discussions went on, in particular with D.N. Pritt. There was the difficulty of phrasing and interpretation and the risk of a civil liberty body sponsoring legislation which if amended and loosely interpreted might be misused in a repressive context divorced from its original purpose. Meanwhile, as the lawyers discussed, the Council in its day-to-day campaign was active in the field. Observers attended meetings and demonstrations and collected information. Dossiers were prepared to serve as ammunition for MPs and to raise infringements of civil rights in questions in the House. Whenever possible first-hand material was used for publicity in the press. The facts were printed in *Civil Liberty* and provided material for speakers' notes. Most important of all, prompt legal advice was available from a key panel of lawyers who generously gave their services free, and who provided defence in the courts in suitable cases.

Ronald was in touch with the dedicated Anglican priest Father Groser, who felt that the fascist danger in the East End was the most serious in his experience in all his years there. Before the blackshirt incursion, he had seen only two cases of mild Jew-baiting. But it only needed the will to exploit quiescent anti-Semitism at a time of economic depression to inflame it. For three weeks young blackshirts paraded just outside his vicarage in Watney Street, which was lined with Jewish-owned stalls and shops, selling their papers and urging people not to buy from the Jews. Then they held a street-corner meeting. It looked as though trouble was imminent. But he and his helpers were able to persuade the police to get the blackshirts out of the way and let him handle the crowd. He used his influence in the parish to succeed in dispersing the crowd peaceably. After that he anticipated scheduled fascist meetings, he and his helpers getting up to speak. Finally the blackshirts moved away and left the area in peace.

However the blackshirts only shifted their activities away to Duckett Street, where they held regular meetings. It was to prove a familiar posting for NCCL observers.

The Ben Jonson School in Harford Street was close to Duckett Street. Edith Ramsay, the Principal of the Stepney Women's Institute, ran afternoon and evening sessions there, sponsored by the Institute, for the local girls and women 'from 14 to 90'. She received anonymous letters at the school, pressing her to 'be British, ban the Jews'. One night the caretaker warned that there was a crowd waiting outside. She let the women and girls out unseen through a side door, and then she and her colleagues came out at the front. The crowd dispersed. 'The only Jewish family living in Duckett Street', she told me, 'were afraid to go home at night, until they could creep in unnoticed.'

Menacing PJ (Perish Judah), and swastika stickers appeared overnight plastered on windows, doors, lamposts. Notices outside shop windows: 'Come in and be Robbed', 'Stinking Jews', 'Boycott Jewish Shops'. A small café was threatened if it continued to serve anti-fascists. J.J. Mallon, Warden of Toynbee Hall in a letter to the *Times* in October 1936:

> The Jews are subjected to a continuous battery of abuse in which their influence in the community is denounced ... They are described as 'Yids' as 'alien offal', as persons occupying or seizing positions which belong properly to persons of British antecedents. The East London population is invited to 'crush the Jews'.

Police Partiality

The hate propaganda spilling out day after day stirring up prejudice and passion erupted inevitably into violence. By March 1936 the situation was serious enough to justify Herbert Morrison, MP for Hackney South, raising in Parliament on the Home Office vote the 'safety and security' of Jewish East End citizens from 'attacks ... by persons who appear to be members of Fascist organisations'. Keeping back names and addresses, he gave details of harassment, threats and physical assaults on a 'law-abiding' community, one man so badly beaten up that he was a fortnight in hospital, traders and shopkeepers molested, threatened with murder and arson, their business damaged, customers warned off by shouting gangs of fascists. A local councillor waylaid at night by a group of blackshirts waiting for him outside his home – 'I assure you,' he protested, 'I have never given these people any cause to insult me, and have never visited any of their meetings'. He was afraid now to go out at night on his own. When he reported a number of incidents at Old Street Police Station, seeking protection, he was advised when he next saw the fascist ringleader to get his name and address and take out a summons! Morrison instanced the case of a leading local fascist, arrested for a speech likely to cause a breach of the peace, who had a record of housebreaking, larceny and obtaining property under false pretences. He was bound over by the magistrate. Morrison commented that 'If a man with that record had come before a good many London police court magistrates and had happened to be a Communist, he would not have been bound over, but would probably have been given "time".' John Beckett, Mosley's director of publicity, in answer to the question at a street meeting in Hackney: 'Could a Jew under fascism become naturalised and use a British name?' replied,

> Certainly not. It is preposterous. We must get rid of this muddle-headed idea that the Englishman is a Jew and the Jew an Englishman … Foreigners … it is not our habit to beat them up – if they live here, it is under three conditions: first that they are decent citizens; secondly that they do not interfere in British politics; and thirdly that they do not do work which is keeping a Briton out of employment.

Winding up his case, Morrison conceded,

> I hold no brief for Jews as such. They all have their little ways, but so have we, and so have every other race in the world. If the nation takes the view that the Jewish population should be excluded, Parliament should face that issue, but it is certain that no Parliament is likely to wish to do any such thing. That being so we simply cannot tolerate a situation in which these people are taking the law into their own hands and making Jews feel, that when they go onto the King's highway, that they are not free from molestation.

These final remarks give a little insight into the uneasy aspect of the thirties when the contagion of Nazi 'righteous', 'patriotic' anti-Semitic propaganda crossing the Chanel had effectively presented, focused the Jew in a *racial* context, and put him on trial.

Ernest Thurtle, MP for Shoreditch, speaking in the same debate cited a speech delivered in Victoria Park:

> When there are any jobs going who is it that gets the jobs? The Isaacs, the Cohens, the Solomons and the Jacobs. They are robbing the British worker of their daily bread ... The Jews among us are the cancer and every foul disease. The situation calls for surgical operation. We will extirpate them thoroughly from our life.

F.C. Watkins, MP for Hackney Central, pointed out that it was not only the Jew who was attacked and persecuted. An ex-serviceman crippled in the war had had his late-night café's windows broken because he served Communists and had been threatened that if he continued to do so his shop would be smashed to pieces.

In his reply, Sir John Simon gave an unequivocal assurance: 'I say that in this country we are not prepared to tolerate any form of Jew-baiting.' But he then went on to qualify this, to speak of 'very great difficulties in dealing with the matter effectively' without impinging on civil liberties and free speech. He entirely agreed that 'if there is a proper case and the police have proper evidence they ought not to leave it to the individual to prosecute.' He promised a strengthening of the police presence in the East End. He absolutely denied that the police 'discriminate in favour of the fascists' or that 'they are trying to use their power in a partisan spirit'. He played down the extent of the fascist danger: 'The information which I have does not give the slightest ground in support of the view that this movement from which these things come is on the increase – not at all; very much the opposite.' Both the Home Office and the police, he stressed, 'have nothing to do with people's political philosophies'. Nevertheless he felt obliged in discussing the role of the police to bring in the main anti-fascist opposition, the Communists. In their 'philosophy' they too 'may be disposed to seek their ends by forcible methods'. As always in reviewing law and order, Sir John Simon was as concerned with the reaction of the opposition as with the fascist provocation. This was quite uncalled for in the East End context. Neither Mr Morrison – no friend of Communism! – nor any other MP had referred to the Communists as presenting any threat whatever to order or good relations in the area, nor indeed did knowledgeable welfare and church workers take that view. However the debate ended with the MPs who took part in it reassured by the Home Secretary's rejection of Jew-baiting and his promise to strengthen the police force in the East End.

But Mosley promptly challenged Sir John Simon in a letter to the press invoking his constitutional rights of free speech if the police were to be used to check 'criticism' of the Jews.

The British Board of Deputies, resolutely confident that the forces of law and order, British tolerance and liberal traditions could be relied on to counter anti-Semitism, reacted to the Parliamentary debate with unshaken equanimity and expressed its appreciation of the Home Secretary's condemnation of Jew-baiting and sincere gratitude to the MPs who had raised the issue.

The press also was reassured by the Home Secretary. The *Daily Herald* commented enthusiastically:

> Uniformed men with special knowledge of the district will emerge today on duty in plain clothes. They will patrol night and day ... Orders have been issued for the immediate arrest of any person who appears in any way likely to provoke an incident.

The *Economist* pointed out that the emerging anti-Semitism was damaging to Great Britain's reputation. It dismissed contemptuously Mosley's 'great concern for the rights of free speech'.

The NCCL was not so sanguine. Police measures invoked – ostensibly to check fascist provocation and violence – were very often turned in full strength against its most militant opponents. Until then the police presence in the East End had not calmed the tension or reassured the Jewish residents. A Metropolitan Police record dated September 1936 states:

at about 60 per cent of fascist meetings … organised opposition in the form of continuous heckling, singing, shouting of slogans, jeering at the speakers and generally attempting to prevent speakers from obtaining *a proper hearing* has been actively conducted by the opponents of Fascism. (My italics, S.S.)

Whether the Metropolitan Police assumed that it was part of their duty to obtain 'a proper hearing' for fascist anti-Semitic propaganda in the East End, or quite simply that it was easier to prevent an incident by dealing with those provoked rather than attempting to check the provoker, they did in fact adopt the policy of clamping down firmly on the anti-fascist opposition. They escorted the fascists as they marched in (a favourite blackshirt chant: 'The Yids, the Yids, We gotta get rid of the Yids!') and they policed their meetings, acting virtually as stewards. Sir Percy Harris, the Liberal MP for South-West Bethnal Green, described in the House on 10 July, the tactics which the police used:

I have been speaking in the open air for more years than I remember … and have never asked for police protection … I hope I shall still have a good deal of interruption … In the case of the fascists however, the speakers make the most provocative statements. They … indulge in abuse of the Jews trying to stir up bad blood and … if any member of the audience, whether Jew or Gentile interrupts, the police – I do not say this in criticism of them, it may be they act because they are afraid of trouble – immediately elbow the interrupter out of the crowd, and sometimes, I have been assured by the mayor of the borough, the interrupter is even taken to the police station. There is a feeling going right through the East End that somehow or other the police are acting in collusion with the fascists.

On one particular occasion, towards the end of 1935, the police even went so far as to close down a Communist anti-fascist meeting, turn it away from its regular pitch in Walthamstow in order to instal in its place a fascist contingent escorted from its own meeting place about a mile away by a strong body of police headed by mounted men. This incident, following on a number of others in the locality roused

indignation in the borough council and the local organisations. D.N. Pritt brought the matter up in the House, and Sir
John Simon went so far as to admit that the police action was
'an error of judgment'.

The unpopular role which the police regularly adopted was
in direct contrast to the tactics which Father Groser, with
police co-operation, found successful in keeping order in his
own parish. Yet the police who were present at anti-fascist
meetings did not apparently feel it necessary to extend the
same protection to these speakers. Ronald Kidd writing in *Civil
Liberty* (April 1937): 'Fascists are permitted by the police to
create actual disorder and to break up the meeting, and in very
few cases have the police taken action against Blackshirt
disturbers.' In Cambridge Road in East London, he saw
blackshirts come into an orderly anti-fascist meeting, let off
fireworks, edge towards the platform, threaten to break up the
meeting. The speaker twice appealed to the inspector in
charge, but with no result. Eventually about seventy police
arrived, charged the crowd and arrested the anti-fascist
speaker! In the same street on another evening at an
anti-fascist meeting addressed by a councillor, blackshirts
came in singing their songs to disrupt the meeting; they grew
bolder as repeated requests to the police from the speaker were
ignored, and all but knocked him off his platform. The police
then warned him that if he could not control his meeting it
would have to be closed down. Yet, as the speaker pointed out,
not a hundred yards away any attempt at heckling at the fascist
meeting was pounced on by the police and might even be
followed by an arrest.

In Bethnal Green in August 1935, a fascist speaker read out
an anonymous letter naming Councillor A.E. Turpin as going
round the streets preaching Communistic propaganda and
using bribery and corruption so that Jews instead of
Englishmen got the jobs. As soon as Mr Turpin heard about
this he came into the meeting to get the speaker to repeat the
libel to his face. He was arrested for insulting words and
behaviour and for assaulting the police. Counsel for the police
stated that, 'P.C. Shiels got in front of Turpin and pushed him
back, and immediately felt two blows on the small of his back.
He turned round and saw the prisoner with his fists clenched.'

Three witnesses testified that Mr Turpin had not struck the policeman. The magistrate dismissed the minor charge, but, on the assault charge, he 'was obliged to accept the police evidence'. He fined Mr Turpin £5 with £3 3s. costs.

The Bethnal Green Borough Council meeting in June discussed witholding the police expenses levy for the year 'if the police continued to show partiality to the fascists'. Councillor King a JP: 'When trouble broke out – caused not by the anti-fascists but by the fascists – then the police took sides and arrested many anti-fascists.' Councillor Turpin wanted adequate protection for all sections of the community reporting that 'every day locally [there] were further cases of Jews and anti-fascists being brutally assaulted'.

By mid-summer, MPs faced with the alarm and protests from their constituents decided to raise the matter again in Parliament. Since the last debate in March, and only a fortnight after it, there had been the shock of the unprovoked baton charge in Thurloe Square, coupled with the exceptional facilities laid on by the Metropolitan Police for Mosley's Albert Hall meeting, and the refusal of the police to intervene in the Hall.

There was another case of police partiality towards the fascists at a meeting in Oxford in May. There the chief constable refused to identify and charge the blackshirt stewards who had attacked hecklers, and instead arrested two anti-fascist undergraduates. The meeting was not chaired, and R.H.S. Crossman, then warden of New College, got onto the platform to ask Mosley to remove the fifty or so blackshirt stewards, and found himself on the floor. Frank Pakenham, now Lord Longford and an Oxford don at the time, was violently attacked when he went to the assistance of an undergraduate being attacked by the fascists. His attempts to charge his assailants were dismissed by the police.

There was the earlier Trenchard ban on public meetings, the illegal seizure of pacifist literature at the Duxford Air Display and the widespread arrest of suspected persons. All these abuses prompted the opposition to call a debate on the police vote and to link this with civil liberty. In a day-long session on 10 July, Labour and Liberal MPs brought home the situation in the East End and prodded the government to act and make use of *existing* police powers to check fascist provocation and incitement.

Dingle Foot speaking on this: whatever the niceties of the law, in practice the police had complete discretion in what street meetings were allowed. 'It is a very dangerous thing if people believe, even without foundation, that there is some kind of favouritism as between one side and another on the part of the police.'

There was also the power to bind over to keep the peace, a deterrent, as Lansbury pointed out, that the police were not slow to use against the left. Lansbury wanted to know whether note-takers were busy at fascist meetings as they were at the Communists', by now they should have amassed a formidable dossier to bring to the notice of the public prosecutor. He cut in sharply to a bland rejoinder from Sir John Simon, 'if you have not, or if you have and the public prosecutor has not been called in, you have treated the fascists differently from the Communists.' Fascists were inciting others to attack the Jews, to treat them as 'people outside the pale'. D.N. Pritt, who opened the debate, said that the police made 'elaborate and costly arrangements to protect the holding of fascist meetings', and that within limits this was right. But 'as soon as it becomes evident and established by precedent that the fascists are using these meetings to cause breaches of the peace and to utter insulting language, the protection must cease.' He went on:

> A far more serious charge is that there are frequent cases in London and the country ... that the police stand cheerfully by while Fascists 'beat-up' – and I use the word advisedly – bystanders or listeners or hecklers – and there is nothing unlawful in heckling ... I have this from Stepney, that in the presence of the police indeed, a speaker threatened the hecklers that he would have them removed by the police if they objected to what he was saying.

A.P. Herbert, the member for Oxford University, was concerned that dons who had been 'brutally treated' at Mosley's Oxford meeting in May, had been unable to obtain redress. Fascist meetings where the show of 'brutal cruel force' was 'common form', with stewards disciplined and drilled in 'this technique of intimidation and violence', were 'very near to being unlawful assemblies'; he quoted legal precedents to bear this out.

Sir John Simon's reply was very much in the same bland disarming vein as in March. He welcomed the debate, agreed with much that had been said, felt 'deep concern', and repeatedly exonerated the police of any bias. In this he had the support of 'important people interested in the matter, including those who speak with very great authority in respect of Jewish organisations', who 'made no allegation against the police of prejudice or bias'. The police had a very difficult task, if 'they make a mistake, I do my best to say so'. He had kept his promise of detailing plain-clothes men into the East End and he believed the gravity of insulting remarks had been toned down. He showed his remoteness from the scene, when he could not understand why fascist assailants at indoor meetings were not identified and charged. (Three Tory MPs at Olympia had learnt the alternatives: to remain – silent and anonymous, to speak out – and join the victims, or to leave the meeting). East Enders he advised to 'stay away' (from their own streets, homes, shops, stalls?) and to have the courage to come forward as witnesses. (Mr Watkins had quoted the case of a young East Ender and his girl challenged at night – 'Are you a Jew?' – and assaulted; the girl, hardly able to stand, frightened of reprisals, persuading her young man not to go to the police station with the PC who had caught one of the gang.) The legality of political uniform and military marching was out of order in the context of this debate, and he dismissed the matter lightly with a reference to a European country where uniforms were banned and the fascist marchers adopted clipped Hitler moustaches. One positive measure: there would be note-taking at fascist meetings 'in cases where it seems proper', and 'if such a case [of prosecution] arises it should be presented before the Court with all possible authority ... by a skilled and learned person ... with the intimation to the court that the Executive regards this as a grave matter'. He closed with a tribute to civil liberty and a quotation from *Areopagitica*.

There was little this time round to encourage East Enders and small comfort for their MPs to take back to their constituents.

Three days after the debate, the London Trades Council

sponsored a big East End demonstration 'Against Fascism and War' with A.M. Wall, its secretary, Herbert Morrison, two other local Labour MPs and the Earl of Listowel to take the platform at Victoria Park. Contingents from all parts of the East End formed with their banners in a mile-long procession lead by a brass band and with the Mayor of Poplar and three Labour MPs at the head. As the procession came through Bethnal Green and passed the fascist branch in Green Street, blackshirts on the roof showered down bags of soot and flour and threw eggs. The following month, on 30 August, a rougher reception was aimed at another big anti-fascist demonstration: an ex-servicemen's movement – veterans wearing their medals – Communists, Jewish bodies, trade unionists, marching to Victoria Park. As they halted at Old Ford Road for a contingent, soot and flour were thrown followed by stones, the speakers Sylvia Pankhurst and James Hall, MP were struck, and two other men had head injuries. There was fighting outside and at the entrance to the park. While the meeting was going on, blackshirts were doing just as they liked in Green Street – cars were stopped and the occupants were spat at and insulted, people were half-pulled off buses because they were Jewish. The premises of the Young Communist League was broken into and smashed by blackshirts in uniform, and two shops that were open on the Sunday afternoon were raided and the stock knocked about. Two Jewish boys aged between eight and nine years going through Green Street to Victoria Park were badly beaten up and had to be driven home by the police.

How many times, at the end of an anti-fascist meeting, did I see the police move aggressively into the dispersing crowd, chivvying, breaking up a last chat, treading on heels, even putting a horse onto the pavement! One evening Ronald and I went to an anti-fascist meeting in the Kingsway Hall with Edith Summerskill. A small German woman sitting at the back of the platform came forward to give her testimony in a bleached monotone and in German. Her missing anti-Nazi husband was delivered on her doorstep, his broken body in a sack. We emerged onto the deserted pavement of Kingsway – its broad thoroughfare almost empty of traffic. A sizeable group of waiting policemen moved smartly into the exiting crowd. Edith Summerskill confronted by a heavy constable unceremoniously shoving her on, stood her ground outraged: 'Do you know who I *am?*' He didn't care. Evidently she was anti-fascist and to law and order anti-fascism was a suspect activity, only to be tolerated – at present – and on sufferance. Its participants, likely trouble-makers, its audiences not free as audiences from the theatre, concert or cinema to take the night air and linger for a moment on the pavement.

In September, the police did in fact take action against a fascist speaker. The fascist prosecuted was not the local cockney Mick Clarke who made most of the running in the East End and who was the District Leader of the BUF in Bethnal Green. Clarke had abused the Jews as 'filthy', 'scum', 'the lice of the earth that must be exterminated'. He had spoken threateningly of organising 'an unofficial pogrom'.

The speaker arrested was the so-called 'philosopher' of the BUF, Alexander Raven Thomson who expounded fascist ideology in pamphlets and booklets, certainly a rabid anti-Semite, but not, as Clarke, at home on the street-corner soap-box. He was warned by the police before he started to speak that if he used insulting words he would be arrested. Thomson confined himself to foreign affairs: Palestine, Lawrence of Arabia – the Arabs fought a damn sight better than the Jews – and to the South African War – the Jews stayed at home and made money out of it. The crowd grew. There was shouting, boos and cheers. The police force strengthened. Eventually Thomson was arrested. At Old Street, Sub-Divisional Inspector Bohan, asked by prosecuting counsel whether he considered the arrest was justified, replied, 'I did not hear the words he [Thomson] used but judging by the crowd, I concluded that he had aroused the feelings of a certain section of the crowd. We had to draw a police cordon to divide the Communists and fascists of the crowd.' The magistrate dismissed the case:

If fascists come down and make wholesale attacks on a law-abiding community they will be punished ... if on the other hand, a coterie of Jews or somebody else claiming to associate with Jews challenge the remarks, Thomson is free to deal with the challenge.

The Crisis Point

All through that summer and into the early autumn local indignation was mounting. No success had been achieved through Parliament by Labour and Liberal MPs. The President of the Board of Deputies took the view that 'The Jewish community not being a political body as such, should not be dragged into the fight against fascism as such.' From the first the Communists had challenged the fascists in their East End adventure. They had been active in the field before the fascist incursion, and now they waged a continuous day-to-day campaign against them. The militant elements in the community, Jew and Gentile, Labour and Liberal, who, whether they liked it or not, had been 'dragged into the fight against fascism' in their own streets, their shops and cafés, were attracted by this as the only effective opposition, to co-operate with them and follow their lead. At the end of July, a radical group set up the Jewish People's Council. This non-party body took the lead in the local Jewish community to fight fascism, not only to oppose anti-semitism but also to defend all civil rights fundamentally threatened by fascism. It was to co-operate with the NCCL in its fight against racialism.

The crisis came when the fascists announced as the culmination of their East End campaign an anniversary rally on Sunday 4 October to celebrate their success in a grand demonstration march through the East End ending with four open air meetings addressed by Sir Oswald Mosley. Huge posters appeared on all the East End hoardings. The operation was planned as a military exercise with directives issued by the 'Officer in Command' of BU's (British Union – 'of Fascists' now prudently dropped) Southern Administration: assembly in uniform and military formation at Royal Mint Street, near Tower Hill, the western tip of the East End. A column to parade for inspection by the leader. After the march, the columns to divide and proceed to four large open air meetings in Shoreditch, Limehouse, Bow and Bethnal Green. Operation Headquarters for the day: the fascist premises 22(a) Green Street, Bethnal Green with Sir George Duckworth-King in charge.

As soon as the news broke the East End was in a ferment:

anger, protest and, in the families of the young and the elderly – fear. Local authorities were alarmed at a demonstration on that scale in the explosive situation of the East End. The Home Office was bombarded. Five East End mayors led by Stepney urged that the march should be banned – or failing that diverted. 100,000 signatures for banning the march were collected by the Jewish People's Council and presented by the MP for Whitechapel with the support of the London Trades Council and Father Groser. Lansbury wrote warning Sir John Simon against a march through Aldgate and Whitechapel High Street.

The result was a stalemate. Mrs J. Roberts, JP of Stepney was shuttle-cocked between the Home Office and the police with no satisfaction from either. Finally with no sign of action from the authorities, and with a last-minute stepping up of intimidation in window smashing and assaults, Mrs Roberts appealed to the people of East London 'to remain level-headed and keep away from the demonstration'. Lansbury in the interest of peace and order gave the same advice. The *News Chronicle*, the *Daily Herald* and the Board of Deputies all cautioned the East End 'stay away'.

But it was too late for temperate, negative advice. Appeals to law and order had failed. The East End had had enough, it was not going to take any more. The Independent Labour Party and the Communist Party took the lead to channel and organise all-out a concerted drive to stop Mosley's march. They adopted the Spanish rallying call 'They Shall Not Pass!', invoking the spirit of Republican Spain's improvised citizen army that together with the International Brigade was resisting the organised forces of fascism in Spain. In a year of democratic retreat and compromise with fascism, the Spanish example was an inspiration and a motive force.

The big fascist posters were torn down and replaced with a fresh appeal: 'Bar the Road to Fascism!', 'They Shall Not Pass!', 'Remember Olympia!', 'Aldgate Sunday 2 pm!' The message was spread in whitewash, and reinforced with leaflets, at propaganda meetings, appealing to trade unions, trades councils, Labour Parties. The call was for a mass rally at Gardiner's Corner Aldgate, to block the key junction commanding the main routes into the East End, and to face

Mosley with an impassable human barrier if he attempted to march in through the main stream and not to creep in at the back door. Cable Street – another possible route into the East End – was to be secured as an advance line of defence by putting up street barricades. A disused lorry in a yard nearby was earmarked to be overturned, together with piles of timber, junk, old furniture, bedsteads and matresses. Dockers living in the Cable Street area were called on to co-operate. Riders on motorbikes and bicycles were to report back to headquarters the latest moves 'from the front'. First-aid posts with doctors and nurses in charge were set up in shops and houses in the neighbourhood.

Very late on Sunday morning, Ronald and I, after gobbling a breakfast-lunch, made our way to act as observers. Why we were not up early this very day I no longer remember. Perhaps just because it *was* Sunday. Six days of the week we pulled out of a heavy sleep to plunge into the choppy sea of work, never quite getting abreast, smacked by the next most urgent job before we had found our feet, scrambled up from the last. Still at it on Saturday, after the office, very often observing in the afternoon, and for Ronald most likely a speaking engagement in the evening. Sunday was our anchor, a respite, and a lovely lazy lie-in. The stress and the challenge Ronald accepted with Olympian calm and disregard. My impatient vehemence, my revulsion at the daily diet of injustice, clamoured for cries of rage, anger at the turpitude of the times. Ronald's unruffled and leisurely serenity was sometimes maddening, but his tranquil temperament resolved and soothed the abrasions of hate and anger.

We made for the fascist rallying point as the most likely focus for action. In the autumn sunshine, in Royal Mint Street, the build-up and the tension slowly evaporated; it flattened out into a false calm. The focus point was generally near the fascists, but this time we were wrong. We found ourselves impacted into a police enclave, a static scene dominated and controlled by officialdom. With the generals and away from the action. The only confrontation that day between fascists and anti-fascists was very early on. East Enders had collected near the fascist assembly point, and when the first contingent arrived by coach, windows were smashed and the blackshirts got a taste of their own medecine before the police arrived in strength to clear the site. The anti-fascists fell back to swell the congestion in Aldgate and the police cordoned off Royal Mint Street making it a safe base. For the next two hours the blackshirts gradually assembled, formed ranks and paraded in military formation, awaiting their leader.

Now the only movement was the uneasy shift of the Metropolitan Police. Foot and mounted men blocked access to or from Aldgate, through Leman Street or Cable Street. They wedged, almost concealed the fascists. The uniformed lines of blackshirts stood silent, awaiting instructions. Interest was diverted away from them to the police. They hogged the show. We were on the look-out for the senior man in a trench-coat who could give orders.

In this scene, Mosley himself, absent or present, was no longer the operative factor. He too was a pawn. In his campaign to gain popular support promoting street-corner anti-Semitism, in his bid to win 'the battle of the streets', he demanded and to a certain extent relied on the goodwill of law and order. The police who had reacted with ruthless severity against the propaganda of the organised unemployed – binding over their leaders, arresting speakers, using *agents-provocateurs*, making baton-charges, even illegally entering their headquarters and seizing property from the National Unemployed Workers' Movement – in contrast, showed themselves unfailingly punctilious in observing and respecting Sir Oswald Mosley's aggressively asserted democratic rights of free speech and assembly for his blackshirts. They were assiduous in the course of duty to escort and protect them and to enforce and maintain a 'proper hearing' for their propaganda, and they found themselves impotent to check the 'insulting words' of fascist speakers. It was the extent of this lenience and accommodation (in contrast to the lip-service assurances in Parliament) and the implications behind it that carried the real threat to the future of civil liberty, and not Mosley himself.

Just about 3.25 a car drew up, escorted by motor-cycles and police. Over the helmets and between the shoulders I snatched a quick glimpse of an aggressive profile under a peaked cap. Mosley was making it smartly between police, sporting his new uniform – grey breeches, military jacket, jackboots. A rumour circulated that the windscreen of his car had been shattered.

The minutes crawled by.

And now the police were on the move! They were ... thinning out. The enclave was opening up, showing gaps. Behind them the blackshirts ...were ... disappearing! Marching away! In retreat! The grand military exercise, the triumphal celebration – up the spout!

The papers the next day filled in the details: it was 3.30 when the Commissioner, Sir Philip Game, who had been on the scene most of the afternoon, sent for Oswald Mosley – who had just arrived. In all the surrounding streets, dense crowds were being held back by foot and mounted police, and to the South and East there was a hostile determination that the fascists 'should not pass'. It was at a street corner, opposite the Royal Mint, that the Commissioner instructed Mosley 'that the march must be abandoned forthwith'. The procession of 2,500 blackshirts, 'isolated and guarded by police', were turned westward, marched to Charing Cross and was dispersed.

Now for Ronald and me the way was clear. We went up Leman Street to Gardiner's Corner. The wide junction ahead was swarming with people. On the move now, scattering, going their own ways. Not a policeman in sight! It was all over. The East End was getting back to normal. Nothing more to observe. Victory was in the air with a feeling of sober jubilation. The roadway was slowly opening up. And now a bus was crawling by. But people were still on the alert. When a rumour started that blackshirts had been spotted, half the top deck dropped off to follow the scent.

'They Shall Not Pass!'

How it all happened on that Sunday that the old East End will never forget, has been told from the inside by Phil Piratin, organiser and participant, in his book *Our Flag Stays Red*.

Early that morning the East End was on the move. At 7 a.m. speakers were standing by platforms at the four points where Mosley was to halt and deliver oratory – the traditional East End way of reserving the site. Loudspeakers roused the streets, and then the band of the Young Communist League, led by Harry Gross, later killed in Spain. The Jewish Ex-Servicemen's Movement were on the march wearing their medals and decorations and carrying the British Legion banner. Half a mile from Gardiner's Corner they came up against a police cordon and into a struggle for the right to march in their own borough. Their Legion banner was seized and smashed. Piratin comments: 'The police had begun "to maintain law and order".'

Long before the fascists were due, East Enders were blocking the streets in Aldgate. The numbers swelled into the greatest East End crowd that anyone present could remember. At the Leman Street junction with Commercial Road a tram-driver got down and joined the crowd. Two more trams following him were also abandoned, effectively blocking the roadway. At first the police just shoved the crowd around, then the force moved in in strength – estimated at 6,000 – with the whole of the mounted division, all posted between Tower Hill and Whitechapel, wireless vans reporting as they cruised, an observation aeroplane flying low overhead. After repeated baton charges the police had cleared Leman Street and the Minories. Now they were concentrating on breaking a way through for the fascists to march by Aldgate. Time and again they charged the crowd, the windows of neighbouring shops giving in as people were pushed through them. But the crowd held. The police could make no impression on the immense human barricade.

Then it was the turn of Cable Street. Someone shouted 'Get the lorry!' A stationary lorry about 200 yards away was pushed over (in mistake for the one in the yard nearby), and it was piled round with the made-ready box-room junk. As the mounted police advanced marbles were scattered, and the foot police climbing and circling the barricades were pelted with milk bottles and stones from the roofs and windows of the small two-storey dockers' homes overlooking Cable Street. Housewives pitched in with anything to hand. According to Piratin, the police had not got their heart in it to go in and arrest local housewives, and 'a number of police surrendered. This had never happened before, so the lads didn't know what to do, but they took away their batons, and one took a helmet for his son as a souvenir.'

The ILP pamphlet celebrating the Cable Street victory

reported that just after three o'clock, Fenner Brockway, later Lord Brockway, made his way from Gardiner's Corner to a phone box in Whitechapel to call the Home Office to alert the Home Secretary: 'There are a quarter of a million people here. They are peaceful and unarmed, but they are determined that Mosley's provocative march shall not pass. If you permit it yours will be the responsibility for the serious consequences.'

The active part played by the dockers in the 'Battle of Cable Street' was significant. Piratin:

> Never was there such unity of all sections of the working class as was seen on the barricades at Cable Street. People whose lives were poles apart, though living within a few hundred yards of each other, bearded Orthodox Jews and rough-and-ready Irish Catholic dockers – these were the workers that the fascists were trying to stir up against each other …

Dockers, the key workers in the East End, with the militant traditions of the great strike against the miserable conditions of 1899 when to win their tanner they paralysed the Port of London, were incorporated in the powerful Transport and General Workers' Union. Now for the first time since the fascist campaign in the East End, a prominent union leader intervened. Ernest Bevin, chairman of the TUC and General Secretary of the TGWU, sent a telegram to the Prime Minister, Mr Baldwin, from Geneva (where he was attending an international conference). This was on 14 October after the fascists in revenge for their humiliation on 4 October unleashed their most serious bout of hooligan attacks and window-smashing:

> View with grave concern renewed disturbances in East London. Transport Union represents thousands of members employed in East End, and is concerned that if government permits fascist provocation to continue, grave industrial unrest and serious dislocation of industry possible. Urge you take immediate action to protect peaceful citizens against uniformed fascist attack.

At its annual conference opening on 5 October the Labour Party passed an emergency resolution urging the government to take 'stronger action to suppress fascist activities'. NCCL asked the government to consider whether aggressive military-style fascist demonstrations breached the law relating to unlawful assemblies. The London Trades Council called on the Home Secretary to suppress the fascist movement. Even Ramsay MacDonald in Edinburgh raised his voice advocating measures to prevent 'deliberate planning to create disorder under the cloak of freedom of speech ... to insult the Jews and arouse unnatural passions'.

Late on Sunday 4 October Scotland Yard issued its official statement, playing down the situation and attributing the vast turn-out to the weather! 'A fascist assembly was held in the East End today, and largely owing to one of the finest days of the year, many people were *attracted to it* including a large number of women and children.' (My italics, S.S.).

The Public Order Act

The East End crowds were to prove more effective than their representatives in Parliament in pushing the government into action. As soon as Parliament reassembled after the summer recess the Public Order Bill was introduced. Its main clauses made illegal the wearing of political uniform and the militarisation of politics, but it also gave additional powers to the police of control and prosecution.

NCCL strongly opposed these clauses in the Bill. Existing powers had not been used to avert the recent crisis – and some of the new powers could be used in situations very far removed from public order. For instance the extension of the 'insulting words and behaviour' charge – the policeman's friend – commonly used against hecklers. Up to that time it was operative only in certain areas of the metropolis but now it was to cover the whole country and with penalties stepped up from £2 5s. to £50 and or three months' imprisonment. In debate an attempt was made by the ILP MP Campbell Stephen to tack on to the charge of insulting words the amendment 'calculated to excite racial or religious prejudice'. Earl Winterton opposing: 'It would be an intolerable abuse of public liberty if people were not permitted to make speeches which showed either racial or religious prejudice ... It has existed in this country for hundreds of years and will always exist.' Mr J.H. Hall, MP for

Stepney Whitechapel, in support:

> In the East End of London during the last few months ... racial animosity has given an impetus to hooligans ... the Jewish people have been constantly insulted and the speakers who have been responsible for it have had the protection of the police while doing so.

The amendment was negatived. NCCL also strongly objected to the blanket banning of *all* processions if one threatened the peace.

While the Bill was being debated in Parliament, the Special Branch made a report – in November 1936 – on the situation in the East End following 4 October, assessing the relative standing and prospects of the fascists and the Communists:

> The general cry of the anti-fascist press was that the 'entire population of East London had risen against Mosley and had declared that he and his followers should not pass', and that they did not pass 'owing to the solid front presented by the workers of East London'. This statement is, however, far from reflecting accurately the state of affairs regarding fascism in the East End. There is *abundant evidence* that the fascist movement has been steadily gaining ground in many parts of East London and has strong support in such districts as Stepney, Shoreditch, Bethnal Green, Hackney and Bow. (*No attempt has been made by the BUF to hold meetings or spread its propaganda in the immediate vicinity of Aldgate where the disorder occurred* on the 4 October.)
>
> There can be no doubt that the unruly element in the crowd ... was very largely Communist-inspired ...
>
> While attempts by the Communist Party to raise enthusiasm over the 'fascist defeat' were *comparative failures*, the British Union of Fascists, during the week following the banning of their march conducted the most successful series of meetings since the beginning of the movement ... *On 11 October*, Sir O. Mosley addressed a meeting of 12,000 at Victoria Park Square, and was enthusiastically received, later marching at the head of the procession to Salmon Lane, Limehouse, without opposition or disorder ...
>
> In contrast, much opposition has been displayed at meetings held by the Communist movement's speakers ... *it has been necessary for the police to close some meetings* to prevent breaches of the peace ...

> Briefly, a definite pro-fascist feeling has manifested itself throughout the districts mentioned since the events of 4 October ... *It is reliably reported* that the London membership has increased by 2,000. (My italics, S.S.)

The evaluation of the facts in this report to give a very favourable asessment of the fascists' standing – at a time when there were clear signs of the decline of the movement – lends some colour to the then widely-held suspicion that the Special Branch in particular was sympathetically inclined towards the fascists.

For instance, the assumption at the end of the first paragraph that there was any significance in the fact that the 'disorder' on 4 October in Aldgate occurred in an area that had not immediately been covered by fascist propaganda. The huge anti-fascist crowd *collected* (but was not drawn just from Aldgate), and assembled at Gardiner's Corner, Aldgate, because this was the key junction for the passage of the fascist march on its planned route. In fact, fascist and anti-fascist meetings were held regularly some two miles away. This far-fetched face-saving plea to attempt to explain away the fascist 'defeat', might well be expected to appear in fascist *Action*, but hardly in a police report.

As to the 'comparative failure' of the Communists to raise enthusiasm after the fascist 'defeat', the *Times* of 12 October reports the anti-fascist East End Victory March on 11 October: 'About 5,000 marchers ... gained a big following during the long march to Victoria Park'. There were large crowds round three platforms in the park. 'A party of fifty or more fascists made some attempt to interrupt the meeting ... but when they were still about 100 yards away the police charged them, and they turned and ran.'

The Special Branch's contention that the fascists were gaining ground and membership in the East End was soon put to the test. Mosley's next campaign was to concentrate all his resources to promote six fascist candidates in the LCC elections for three East End constituencies: South-West Bethnal Green, Stepney Limehouse and Shoreditch, each with two seats. Mosley himself wrote the British Union election manifestos: 'Our Challenge to Jewry', 'Mind Britain's

Business', 'Let East London Lead', tactfully omitting any reference to fascism. The campaign was fought with a ruthless exploitation of anti-Semitism and a saturation of propaganda meetings. The results in March 1937 showed Labour returned in all three constituencies. Later, forty rank-and-file fascist candidates stood in the local borough elections. None was successful. In Spitalfields – a fascist stronghold according to the Special Branch – a Communist was elected for the first time, Phil Piratin. Nor was his popularity short lived. In the 1945 general election he defeated the Labour parliamentary candidate to represent Stepney Mile End as the Communist MP till 1950.

A fortnight after the LCC elections Mosley cut his salaried staff from 143 to thirty. Two of the axed, John Beckett and William Joyce, former leading lieutenants and editors of fascist publications, broke away to set up a rival fascist body and gave a press conference criticising their ex-leader. More resignations followed, including two of Mosley's carefully selected LCC candidates, J.A. Bailey and Charles Wegg-Prosser. Wegg-Prosser, a young Catholic lawyer, voiced his criticism of Mosley and the tactics used in the LCC campaign in a pamphlet published later by the Jewish People's Council:

> I watched with dismay the mentality which said, 'Get rid of the Jews, and you will automatically get rid of unemployment, slums, sweating.' Further, I have always loathed the spirit which says, 'He is a Yid, therefore bad'. I know and you know, that vile unprovoked assaults have been made on single Jews by a group of fascists, even looting has occurred.

Special Branch refers to the 'disorder' on 4 October, and to the unruly members in the crowd as largely Communist-inspired, but makes no mention at all of the anti-Semitic hooliganism for which the fascists were responsible. On 11 October, while the police were attending the Victory March in Victoria Park Square, Jewish shops in the Mile End Road were attacked and looted, a Jewish tradesman and a child were thrown through a smashed shop window, a car overturned and set on fire. This news was covered in the local and national press, which also reported the steep increase in Lloyds riot damage insurance, so that in certain areas of the East End, owing to the frequent hooligan window-smashing, it was practically unobtainable.

Ronald and I attended Mosley's 'enthusiastically received' meeting at Victoria Park Square – followed by a march to Salmon Lane and another meeting. This was on 14 October. The square, surrounded by its terraced houses was solid with people. The spiked pennants and drooping flags of the blackshirts were hemmed in by helmets and buttoned tunics, horses wedged tight in the crowd of men and boys, a scattering of women's hats. Mosley's relentless voice echoed back and front from the metal mouths on the speaker's van parked flush against the pavement. It knocked against the houses, doors and windows. I can feel again the stretched tedium. At that time I didn't have to lock my mind against the turgid rhetoric, the amplification, thickened, blurred it all. When the pitch rose into the hunting cry, the blackshirts responded, arms raised, 'Mosley! Mosley!' The crowd stood silent. Were they resting on their recent victory? It had cost them eighty-four arrests and two or three hundred injured. Or were some of them swallowing it, drinking it in? Impossible to tell, with the heavy silencing police presence. But one small incident still vivid in my memory showed the change in spirit since the watershed of 4 October.

Mosley stood silhouetted – in his Mussolini stance – hands on hips, legs apart – close up against the backing terrace of houses. Suddenly just above him a window opened, a woman appeared, head and shoulders, buxom, fair. An instant live Punch and Judy Show! Punch juxtaposed threatening, the comely Judy facing up. She said something straight at him, taunting him. (At a guess: 'Why don't you and your effing blackshirts bugger off and leave us in peace!') Any speaker with a popular appeal would have exploited the comedy of the situation – confident of his command of the air and the woman's relative inaudibility – to jolly her, pull her leg, raise a chauvinistic belly-laugh from his supporters. Mosley, humourless, arrogant, turned a dictator's face contorted with rage. The leader insulted! He answered her back, speaking directly into her face. The amplifiers didn't pick it up.

The window space was blank again.

Two minutes later, there she was! At her front door, shaking her duster. She was right in it now! Outside the safety of her house. Three blackshirts stepped up smartly. I felt a pang of fear. Then another intervened, checked them. Too public – she wasn't a Jew. She stared round contemptuously – slammed her front door.

In the meeting that followed at Salmon Lane, Ronald's notes show how disciplined was the 'enthusiasm'. As Mosley was expanding on friendship with Italy and Germany, a man ventured to ask, 'Doesn't Italy want to dominate the Mediterranean?' He was promptly warned by PC N221 to be quiet. He tried again soon after: 'Well Germany wants our colonies ...' and was seized by PCs N221 and M507 and ejected from the meeting. (*Civil Liberty*, April 1937.)

Mosley's first appearance after the passing of the Public Order Act at a fascist meeting at Hornsey Town Hall brought no change to the violence of his stewards or to the reaction of the police to turn a blind eye. (The clause in the Public Order Bill making it illegal to equip or train persons for the use of physical force to promote a political object, was specifically amended in debate to exclude stewards.) An inspector on duty outside refused to go in and identify the assailants of two of the injured ejected from the meeting. One of these a local resident of seventy years a member of the Liberal Party, attacked for trying to get out to call in the police. He followed up with a solicitor's letter to the Commissioner of Police. The NCCL investigated and reported to the Home Secretary and MPs called for a public inquiry. This was refused. A private inquiry was held which exonerated the police. But the climate had changed. Representations were evidently made, and this was the last fascist *indoor* meeting at which violence of this kind was reported.

On a Sunday morning, at the height of the fascist LCC election campaign, I made my way as an observer into the East End. At the wide Mile End Road, deserted then, a group of young men came swinging by (no longer of course in the outlawed uniform) just as two dark Jewish girls were passing by on the opposite side of the road. The youths jeered and one of them snatched up two empty milk bottles and hurled them one after the other across the road. The startled girls backed as the glass shattered on the pavement – and then hurried on.

The NCCL's forebodings about the use of the additional police powers under the Public Order Act were confirmed when the 'insulting words and behaviour' charge under the Act were first used – in an industrial dispute. This was the bitter lock-out and strike at Harworth Colliery in Nottinghamshire, where the underlying cause of the disturbances against strike-breakers was the refusal of the owners to recognise the Nottinghamshire Miners' Association (NMA) – affiliated to the Miners' Federation of Great Britain – and their determination to recruit their workers into the tame company union.

The strike started in September 1936 over working conditions, when two miners were sacked for refusing to accept a modification to their snap-time for food in the mine. It then widened into the key issue of the Harworth miners' right to join the union of their choice.

Eleven years earlier, a former trade-union official and Labour MP, George Spencer, had set up the breakaway Nottinghamshire and District Miners' Industrial Union, in rivalry to the NMA. This Spencer union was fostered by the employers and developed as a company union. The colliery companies maintained that the Spencer union was the only representative body and refused to recognise the NMA.

This key question of the representative union was tested in November 1936 by secret ballot, counted and checked by disinterested public men. The result showed, 1,175 votes for the NMA and 145 for the Spencer union. But the company still persisted in its refusal to recognise the NMA.

The NCCL had received reports of high-handed action by the police in the dispute, and so Ronald went to Harworth to get first-hand information. The purpose of his visit was announced in the two local daily and two evening papers. He planned to interview leading individuals and organisations, including the police and the county council, and, of course, the miners and their wives involved in local incidents.

The NCCL published his report in March 1937. The Harworth mining company, Messrs Barber, Walker & Co., he reported, had built and owned the greater part of the village of Bircotes that adjoined the Harworth pit. They also owned the land where the church, the parish hall and the Salvation Army hut stood. As well as the power of eviction, the company controlled much of the activity in the village, so making it difficult for the striking miners to carry on their propaganda and their communal life. Only once, at the beginning of the strike, were they or their wives allowed the use of the parish hall, and from the start they were locked out from the Miners' Institute. The company chairman, Major Barber, was also chairman of the county council.

Between 100 and 150 policemen were drafted into the village of Bircotes – at an estimated cost of £120 a week. The police adopted a threatening attitude, warning off the street – and even searching – men and women 'not in any way disorderly', going about their ordinary business: buying fish and chips, making visits or on their way to catch a bus, when this way took them through Scrooby Road, leading to the mine. Inevitably, the police interfered with legal, orderly picketing. Men were taken to the police station, and detained, with no charges being made. In one case a man was arrested with no cause in the presence of an MP. However the MP followed up with a complaint at the police station, indicating that he would be a witness in court. Thereupon the man was released and no charge brought against him. Summonses against men charged a month earlier were served with no more notice than twelve or thirty-six hours for attendance at court some ten miles away. Some of the men could ill afford a bus or train fare, and they were left no time to consult a lawyer or to arrange for attendance of witnesses. In at least six cases the men were charged with the new and far-reaching 'insulting words and behaviour' offence under the Public Order Act.

The composition of the Bench was almost exclusively of persons whose social and economic background was that of the coal owners. In cases of conflicting testimony, the Bench relied almost entirely on police evidence. At Quarter Sessions, the judges were of the same character, so the men had no confidence in lodging an appeal.

NCCL's report was presented to the Home Secretary by J.D. Bellenger, MP and a number of questions were asked in the House arising out of it.

About a month later, picketing at the pit gates – which apparently had been meeting with some success – was interrupted. Individual strike-breakers could no longer be approached when the tactic was adopted of a collective entry of the eighty strike-breakers with an escort of police – no more than thirteen. This however effectively prevented any verbal contact. As the strike dragged on, the frustration of the miners eventually vented itself.

On 23 April, stones were thrown, the windows of two buses were broken and a superintendent struck – but not incapacitated, he continued on duty, and later testified that the missile had in fact been aimed at the bus. A strike-breaker received bruises and cuts. Later that evening more stones were thrown in the village, windows broken in the houses of some of the strike-breakers, and in the Miners' Institute, and some damage done to garden walls, but no injury to persons. Sixteen men and one woman were arrested.

The following night at 10.30 a powerful force of police raided the local club and dance hall in order, it was said, to arrest five men implicated in the previous night's events. These were all men whose homes were known to the police and who could have been charged at any time during the day. The raid, it was alleged, was carried out with such violence that a number of people were injured and property damaged, although the men arrested offered no resistance.

The matter was urgently referred to the NCCL. And Ronald went again to Harworth, with Geoffrey Bing from the Council's legal panel. They spent a week investigating and their findings were submitted in a dossier to MPs at the House of Commons with a view to holding an inquiry. Sir Stafford Cripps agreed to appear in defence of the seventeen people previously arrested.

Thirty-two men and one woman finally came before the Magistrates' Court. Seventeen of them were referred for trial at Quarter Sessions, and the remainder were either dismissed, bound over or sentenced for short periods.

It was the conduct of the trial at Quarter Sessions before Mr Justice Singleton and the extremely heavy sentences he imposed, together with the refusal of an appeal led by D.N. Pritt, which prompted NCCL to organise a petition to the Home Secretary for a remission of the sentences.

Michael Kane, the president of the Harworth branch of the NMA, received two years' hard labour, two rank-and-file strikers, fifteen months, another, twelve months, and the remainder terms varying between four and nine months. Mrs Hymer, the respected Sunday School teacher, was sentenced to nine months' hard labour. In this mass trial, complicated by a number of different charges against each of the accused, the jury – after the judge's summing-up – spent exactly fourteen minutes to decide their guilty verdict. The police evidence, (contradicted by the defence) was that a serious riot took place on 23 April, when 1,500 to 2,000 men armed with sticks and bottles charged the strike-breakers who were cordoned by the police. In fact only thirteen policemen safely escorted all the strike-breakers into the pit gates, *without even drawing batons*. No sticks or bottles were produced in evidence, none of the men charged were accused of using them. The defence maintained that 'the attack' consisted mainly of boos and shouts. After the guilty verdict, and before sentences were imposed, the Superintendent gave evidence on the records of the prisoners. He repeated again and again that the accused had played an active part against the strike-breakers. In the case of Michael Kane he quoted the opinion of his employer (with whom Kane was in disagreement) that Kane was 'a bad workman'. As though either this, or the normal conduct and propaganda of a strike, was evidence of criminal behaviour. The chief evidence against Michael Kane, that he was responsible for organising the demonstration, came from a strike-breaker who, at his window, said he saw 'Michael Kane moving about'. He went on: 'I opened my window slightly to see if I could hear anything. *I think* I heard him say, "On the green tonight boys, at nine o'clock and bring your sticks and bottles".' In his summing-up Mr Justice Singleton, quoting this evidence, ommitted the qualifying, 'I think'. In the case of Richardson the Judge summed up:

> It may be that someone said he was in the crowd at some time but I do not remember anyone saying that Richardson was doing anything actively in the crowd ... bringing my memory to bear on the case as far as I can, I do not think there is much evidence against Richardson except that he was in the crowd.

This man he sentenced to four months' hard labour.

The Home Secretary, in response to NCCL's petition, which was backed up by public support, finally granted a small diminution of the sentences.

Later in the year, on 14 July, the Public Order Act was invoked against local Jewish residents in an orderly crowd at a small fascist meeting. The fascists had been escorted by the police into the Jewish area of Stepney Green – no heckling allowed – while some 100 yards away there was an anti-fascist meeting of the Ex-Servicemen's Movement. One man at the Fascist meeting was charged under the Public Order Act for putting two fingers to his mouth and letting out a whistle, another for blowing his nose in a disrespectful manner – both charges dismissed in court. The attitude and temper of the police who drew batons and used them against the crowds at both meetings led to the immediate investigation by NCCL lawyers followed up with a meeting in the House, at which East End MPs put the facts to Sir Samuel Hoare, then Home Secretary, calling for an official investigation.

As late as 31 July 1939, a Jewish Reserve Army Captain summonsed a fascist speaker under the Public Order Act for insulting words and behaviour. The fascist who was wearing a swastika had, he said, attacked the Jews and their religion and had accused them of using their 'controlled press' to incite to war. He had shown photographs of Jews being beaten in Germany and South Africa. His whole speech in its violent abuse was a direct incitement to people to attack the Jews.

The magistrate, Mr Herbert Metcalfe, at Old Street: 'It has nothing to do with your opinion. It is a matter for me. Why didn't you walk away?'

Complainant: 'Because I was so outraged.'

The magistrate: 'What's it got to do with you? You're not a police officer. It is no part of your job to interfere with people, whatever they say.'

Finally the magistrate gave his decision: 'What nonsense this is and what a waste of my time! This wretched summons will be dismissed at once.

In September 1936 Ronald had represented the NCCL in Paris at the International Conference Against Anti-Semitism speaking on civil rights for Jews in Britain. The following year the NCCL organised in London a conference on anti-Semitism. Ronald was now joint Secretary of the British Committee of the World Congress against Anti-Semitism, together with J. Pearce of the Jewish People's Council.

8

Drifting Into War

Financially, the NCCL for the most part lived precariously from day to day. But each new campaign we embarked on attracted fresh support, and gradually we were building up a more solid base. And now we received a very generous offer of accommodation at a modest rent in Upper Regent Street, quite near the BBC. This was in an impressive office block with its uniformed commissionaire in the foyer with tubs of greenery, porters at the lifts and central heating. We occupied four rooms on the sixth floor.

Ronald found a convenient third-floor 'bijou' flat in a tiny block tucked away in the small streets behind the BBC within easy walking distance of our new office. We were too busy to use it for more than a parking place at night. A perambulating breakfast in the morning, eating off the wooden top over the bath in the narrow one-way kitchen-bathroom.

The day's incentive started, as we made our way to the office, with a fresh breeze from Regents Park flowing past the Epstein figures on the BBC and streaming down Regent Street, as we turned into our handsome block. The work was easier now with ordered space and services; office hours for both of us more conventional, now that late working had to involve the night porter with special arrangements for exit. But the volume of work was increasing enormously. Cases defended in court almost every week, and a fixed day each week for a rota of lawyers to give legal advice. Activities in our branches raised civil liberty issues further afield, and there was the regular work of preparing dossiers for MPs for debates in Parliament and for questions in the House. Now there were social activities too. A civil liberties dance at the Suffolk Galleries – with the popular 'cockney' actor Gordon Harker doing a turn for us.

The next one was at the Burlington Galleries and Ronald Frankau and Cyril Fletcher generously provided a cabaret. Civil liberty lunches at the Comedy Restaurant – Jawaharlal Nehru one of the speakers. Weekend conferences and discussion lectures at the Kingsway Hall. Some of this work was delegated to sub-committees with voluntary helpers lending a hand.

The regular tenor was broken for Ronald when a car speeding down Hampstead Hill on a Sunday evening in November 1937 caught him half-way over a pedestrian crossing knocking him down and breaking his leg. Forster wrote asking me 'was the accident really accidental?'

Ronald came out of hospital with a heavy plaster cast from ankle to thigh, and went straight back into his usual routine. Last thing at night he dragged up three flights into our flat. W.H. Thompson was acting for him to get some compensation for the accident. Visits to specialists revealed an irregular heart condition. He was advised to slow up.

In the summer, Ronald took his holiday in Czechoslovakia, on his own this time to save expense. This was the fateful year when that 'far off country' was the focus of Nazi aggression. Hitler, after his seizure of Austria, was now demanding the key Czech fortified border area with Germany, which had a sizeable German-speaking population. Henlein, his agent in Sudetenland was provoking incidents, exploiting 'grievances', working up public demands for union with the 'Fatherland'. Ronald had long been a warm supporter of Czech democracy. A year or so earlier he had made the acquaintance of Benes who had called on the NCCL when he was on a visit to London. Ronald spent the first part of his holiday recuperating in the beautiful Tatra mountain region. And then he devoted himself to the real purpose of his visit. In Prague he had introductions to leading figures in politics and the Jewish community. Then he went into the Sudetenland, getting first-hand information about Nazi provocation and the concessions made to them by the Czechs. He crossed into Romania and Hungary, the latter already succumbing to Nazi propaganda, with bookshops full of Nazi literature and squares renamed Mussolini and Berlin. He came back to London with full notebooks, maps, literature and snaps he had taken. But by September this material was academic. The

Czech crisis exploded and the fate of the country was locked and lost in the shameful surrender forced on Czechoslovakia for the farcical 'peace in our time'. In Prague, at the last minute, Ronald had called in at the post office, and two young Jewish Czechs helped him with a language problem. Learning that he was leaving for London they asked his help to get themselves out of the country. Ronald noted the essential facts and on his return found a sponsor in Ruth Fry. After asylum for a while in England both of them found a haven in the United States. The NCCL was actively pressing for the right of asylum for refugees from Czechoslovakia. The government finally granted a block of 350 visas for the most endangered refugees.

In the uneasy peace of 1939 I snatched our usual August holiday for the two of us in Brittany. The beach hotel at Tréboul had vacancies only for the end of August running into September. We both loved France and I was rather absurdly hoping to recapture before it was too late the spirit of early carefree summers abroad.

Just as it used to be: espadrilles slapping along the wooden floor, the sun streaming through slatted blinds and coffee and croissants in bed. But Ronald was not well. The first few days he had to spend in bed. And then we wandered down the long white road leading into the little sardine and tunny-fish port of Douarnénez. On the sparkling quayside ruddy red-headed fishermen mending the fine blue sardine nets outside their white cottages – just like Cornishmen, but colourful in blue-striped vests and red canvas tops and slacks fading to orange and pink. A heavy black tunny-boat sailed in silently, the cruel great hooks hanging over the side, decks stacked with the solid decapitated fish, up-ended fin-tails up, like a cargo of smooth grey bombs. A scare next day that a periscope had been sighted in a neighbouring bay. We visited the savage Pointe du Raz and on the way back strayed into the annual religious-secular celebration of that isolated region. The procession with its banners and effigies accompanying the religious leader (to play a brave part in the Resistance) was entombing itself in the ancient edifice, dwarfed by time – was it the relic of a one-time cathedral? Flocks of children attending first communion, shining girls and good little boys with slick hair, ranks of tradesmen and notables in black with bony foreheads and hard eyes, halting in the porch for the trade in thick white candles. The dusky interior glowing and shimmering with hundreds already alight, flowering in sheaves at the foot of a saint and clustered in aureoles above; a warm core burning, resisting the ancient shell, and even threatening it. Outside, the fun of the fair: booths, sweets, trinkets, a primitive roundabout, mystery and horror tents – small boys nudging, half in awe of the man-sea-monster rolling in its green tank.

In the mornings lying on the sand we read the papers. The body relaxed, the mind unquiet – it seemed silly now to be on the wrong side of the Channel. The newsboy threading his way along the beach called and sold the Communist *L'Humanité* along with the other papers. But not today. And no more, after the bomb-shell of the Nazi-Soviet pact! The shock that put paid to the right-wingers' and the fascists' dream of Hitler – true to *Mein Kampf* – marching east to annihilate Bolshevism, and the Western powers accommodating and co-existing in a 'safe' Europe. Now the tables had been turned. It was the USSR that was expediently standing aside to give a free hand to Nazi Germany to embroil the capitalist powers! For us and for France it was now or never. We had to stand up to the mad dog of Europe – but now without the thirty-five Czech divisions and without their Skoda armaments, working instead for Germany.

We took the train back to St Malo to be on the spot for the Channel boat. That evening we walked along the ancient sea ramparts. The sunset was eclipsed, dying under a heavy sky, engulfing, black, ready to deluge and drown. The sea livid with refracted light, sailing up at very high tide, light as air. A fantasy in the strange light that sea and sky were reversing their roles in a world turning upside down … it held, electric with foreboding, until the anonymous dark blotted it all out.

In the morning sunshine we went to spend our last francs in the old town. I bought a tiny silly white and yellow skull-beret to perch on one side. As we sat down to lunch, I found I had dropped it on the beach, the tide would swallow it. The hot close room was full of sun and the smell of good food and the rattle of eager knives and forks. A door burst open, the son of the house brushed past the crowded tables to cry to his mother behind the hatch: '*C'est fini! C'est fini! La Pologne est envahie!*'

We were almost the first on the boat. Hanging over the side, we watched them coming, the queue stretched out of sight. Cars abandoned, and now trunks. Passengers only, and carrying their hand luggage. At nightfall, crammed to capacity, the boat gave its long warning, the gangway lifted. Packed tight on deck and in the dark now, we heard the loudspeaker calling: 'No Smoking on the Deck'. As we chugged out to sea I had the buoyant feeling that we were making for a new world. I was daring to hope that we had seen the last of our 'low dishonest decade'!

Civil Liberty In Wartime

In the early morning as we manoeuvred into our berth at Southampton, the workers on the quayside booed us – the idle rich coming back sun-tanned! They were already war-minded.

It was deflating in London to find the dubious peace still holding. Chamberlain teetering, hoping against hope.

On Sunday morning, the air-raid alarm woke us – unaware that a crest-fallen Prime Minister had just spoken on the wireless to tell the nation in lugubrious accents that as the deadline had expired we were now at war with Germany.

Down in the side street I could see people running, and now a bicycle wobbled by, the rider calling peremptorily, 'Take cover! Enemy aircraft!'

Ronald refused to budge.

The all-clear went as I was getting dressed.

The phoney alarm was the prelude to the phoney war. Crisis defensive measures were taken against no reality of war – little or no action anywhere – draconian Defence Regulations, Parliament sitting only three or four days a week, gas masks to be carried everywhere all day – and identity cards. The blackout, no street lighting, no headlights on cars. Children evacuated. Cinemas closed.

For the NCCL there was an immediate compelling part to play. In a single afternoon, the Emergency Powers (Defence) Bill was rushed through, giving the government dictatorial powers that swept aside all civil liberties, including habeas corpus. In comparison, the Defence of the Realm Act regulations of the 1914 war were child's play. The opposition, by common consent, waived its function, there was no criticism or dissent. The NCCL lawyer who had come to the House armed with essential amendments to put to MPs found that *no* amendments were to be raised!

But this was only a temporary set-back to the NCCL's long slogging campaign to annul or amend objectionable Defence Regulations. Dingle Foot moved a Prayer in the House and a promise was extracted from the government that the Defence Regulations should be reconsidered in their entirety. Dingle Foot sent his good wishes for the success of the delegate conference that the NCCL called in November on 'Civil Liberty in Wartime', and thanked the Council for its 'informed and vigorous' support. 'If the new draft (of defence regulations) shows provisions which are dangerous to the free expression of opinion and the essential rights of the subject, I am sure NCCL will be foremost in opposing them.' This indeed was to be one of the major preoccupations of the Council in the early war years. Restrictions were of course inevitable but the NCCL believed that it was fundamental in wartime to preserve a Parliament free to criticise and expose, a press free to maintain informed opinion and, for the effective use of manpower, a voice for the trade unions and the right of representation and access. The NCCL was to be busy providing constant legal advice and help in wartime law. Already petty dictators were taking advantage of the situation and abusing the emergency powers. Auxiliary Fire Service workers engaged on a seven day week at 10s. a day wrote to their Superintendent querying pay of £3 (instead of £3 10s.) and asking whether they were not entitled to a free meal a day, as in other brigades. Instructed to report to divisional headquarters, they were marched before the chief constable sitting with an army officer, asked to verify their signatures to the letter and informed that they were liable to a fine of £100 or six months' imprisonment for subversive activities. Instead, they were to be instantly dismissed. (There were still over a million unemployed.) All this during the phoney war.

By the end of the year the NCCL had outgrown its

accommodation in Regent Street. It had doubled its income, and with a staff of nine now was tackling an increasing volume of work. Ronald had found inexpensive roomy premises in a tall Georgian house in a terrace in Great James Street near the Inns of Court. The entire bare, unheated building was vacant, except the ground floor. By Christmas we were installed, with blackout curtains, lino and gas radiators. I adapted the bathroom as my own small room. The top-floor lavatory with its ancient plumbing froze hard the first cold winter.

Chamberlain's unwilling war was trailing on unconvincingly. Half of the evacuated children had dribbled back. Cinemas reopened. Gas masks lost or dumped in the junk cupboard. In March the NCCL held a Leap Year dance, and in April a weekend conference in the sunshine in Brighton on 'The Press, Civil Servants and Trade Unions in Wartime'. Francis Williams, ex-editor of the *Daily Herald* was speaking on the press. A voluntary censorship was in operation: news editors sent articles which *might* infringe defence regulations to the Censorship Bureau of the Ministry of Information, and were liable to very stiff sentences if something not submitted was judged against the national interest.

Ominous trends in once-democratic France – our close ally – were of deep concern to the NCCL. We were dismayed at the collapse in France of all the fundamental liberties that we were fighting to preserve: parliamentary rule abandoned, the Chamber of Deputies suspended – rule by decree; drastic and direct press censorship; no recognition of conscientious objectors; pacifist and anti-war propaganda subject to imprisonment and fines; 'enemy' aliens, including well-known anti-fascist refugees, interned – as indeed many of them were in Britain, the NCCL actively campaigning for their release – but in France in appalling conditions in the internment camps. Trade union vacancies filled by appointment subject to the confirmation of the Minister of Labour, wages fixed, many workers on soldiers' pay and subject to military discipline. Draconian action had been taken in October 1939 against the group of Communist Deputies. They were detained in the Santé prison, along with common criminals, on a charge based on opinions they expressed in the Chamber – before its suspension – which normally would have been protected by parliamentary privilege. After three months they were tried in camera by a military court, thirty-five of them sentenced to the maximum five years' imprisonment and the remainder 'released' and promptly interned. A legal observer who attended the preliminary open sessions of the trial for the NCCL was of the opinion that the charge (of propagating orders from the Third International – based on a letter sent by the Communist Deputies to the Speaker asking that the Chamber should discuss the Soviet-German peace proposals) would not have stood up in open court. The prosecution conceded that all their evidence related to events that had taken place within the Chamber. In Britain the pronouncements put out by the Communist Party adjusting and correcting its policy to meet the implications of the Nazi-Soviet pact were no danger to anyone or anything other than its own credibility. In April a savage French decree authorised the death penalty for 'Communist propaganda, pro-Hitler propaganda, and eventually any propaganda evidencing the same characteristics which may manifest itself' – significantly avoiding specifically incriminating 'fascist' propaganda. The NCCL organised a written protest signed by twenty-one Vice-Presidents including H.G. Wells, Sybil Thorndike, J.B. Priestley and George Bernard Shaw (a member then but not a Vice-President) asking the British government to press for the withdrawal of the decree.

Suddenly in May – after the collapse of the fumbling campaign in Norway – the blitzkreig exploded: Rotterdam flattened, Belgium overrun, the Maginot Line bypassed. French arteries bombed and machine-gunned by air, killing refugees and retreating soldiers. After a single air raid, Paris ready to surrender. Pétain: '*Il faut cesser la lutte.*' In a desperate week the British forces in France were rescued from Dunkirk – guns and tanks abandoned. And now we waited for the invasion. But under new direction – Chamberlain out and Churchill in.

The NCCL called an immediate Emergency Conference – no time for Executives to meet, delegates to be mandated – but the General Secretaries of eleven national unions (among these the National Union of Journalists, the Electrical Trade Union, the Amalgamated Engineering Union, the Civil Service Alliance and the Federation of Professional Workers) gave their support in a personal capacity to secure and defend, for the safety of the country, all the essential democratic liberties which as they collapsed in France led headlong into defeat. This very effective conference, supported also by H.G. Wells, led to the 'Conference on Civil Liberty and the Defeat of Fascism' a month later at the Central Hall Westminster. It was the largest and most representative since the Council's foundation, with good support from the trade unions, Labour, Liberal and Independent MPs and Fleet Street, in opposition to the plans afoot to introduce something much more drastic than the voluntary press censorship. (British fascists had persisted till the end campaigning against the 'Jews' War'. In May Mosley and his wife were detained under Defence Regulations, and some two hundred of his followers – including Mary Allen the co-founder of the Women's Police Force. His movement was disbanded in July.)

Geoffrey Bing tackled me sternly: 'Have you got a *bike*?' After the invasion the Council would have to operate from some distant secret hideout – the main roads would of course be impassable. My heart sank. I saw myself sleeping in a ditch, up at first light to rough-ride through mud and wet.

The young barrister (son of the Chairman of our Northern Ireland Commission of Inquiry) who had generously been giving us full-time legal help and was now leaving for a post in the tropics was feeling guilty at abandoning the country in its critical danger. (His destination Sarawak was to be overrun by the Japanese and he was to endure for the duration in a Japanese prison camp.) My eldest sister Lydia was going to regular target practice, she had learned how to fire a rifle.

And now with the flat beaches snarled with barbed wire, heavy with tank traps, the railway stations, the signposts at crossroads nameless; the Home Guard drilling with broomsticks; the RAF, with radar, held the air ... over the Channel ports, over the east coast, over the airfields. They held it until they deflected the *Luftwaffe*. The German bombers were forced to turn to an easier target. It was not to be the invasion. Instead it was the blitz.

Ronald's book *British Liberty in Danger* came out in August and was well reviewed. Michael Foot in the *Evening Standard*:

'It is a vital document which should be read by all …' An early consignment of copies was destroyed in the blitz.

London was bombed every night from 7 September to 3 November, and after that intermittently. But the worst quaking cowardly time for me was in anticipation before a single bomb dropped. In the clear autumn nights the German bombers on their trial runs droned overhead, shuffling through the dark at their leisure, quite unopposed. Ronald was breathing deeply stretched vulnerable just under the flimsy roof. Tons of death suspended, the screaming descent, the agony of the Spanish Civil War. I couldn't lie still. I hovered on the landing, leaving our own front door ajar. A draught or an awkward board and Ronald was struggling to wake. 'What is it?' 'Nothing, nothing.' Hurriedly I shivered back into bed.

It was almost a relief when the bombing started. Now I had a good excuse. It was official policy, at any rate at first, to encourage the public to get into shelters, to be accountable, to simplify rescue work. Ronald's readiness to drop off peacefully in bed goaded me into a fierce urge for preservation, to get as far down as possible in the mock haven of the local shelter, the basement just below pavement level of a house a street or two away. Ronald of course came with me, rugs and cushions down in a space on the stone floor. As the sickening thumps came nearer I flattened myself. At dawn, after the all-clear, we emerged bleary-eyed to eat a silent breakfast before starting the day's work.

Our flat was too near the BBC, a nightly target. It was after the flat was twice made inaccessible, cordoned off in an area with unexploded time-bombs, that I found an anchorage outside London. The solidly built ferro-concrete block with its rising tiers of balconies on black and white mock-marble pillars, dominated the roundabout. As the bus slowly circled round I read the notice: 'Centrally-heated Flats Vacant; thirty shillings'. I hopped off and an affable Irish porter showed me round. Compact well-planned flats, sound-insulated, with space and air, good ceilings and access and outlook balconies. A built-in fridge! Convenience fittings, wall cupboards. Most of them standing empty because the complex was on the outskirts of a vast, newly-erected LCC estate. At this end – a cinema, a pub, a shopping centre, a large hospital. In our childhood it had all been green fields and hedges, where on our bicycles we had come to pick blackberries. A token green belt, a patch boggy in places had been left marooned at the outside edge of the development.

Ronald's Bohemian days were only a memory. Now, with his diminished strength he was grateful, in that winter of 1940, for the instant comfort and convenience of a modern flat, and the luxury allowed him at last to stretch out at night on a bed. We had now to make our journey home after work. Caught one evening in a London street with the shrapnel flying, I broke into a trot. When Ronald came up to me as I sheltered in a doorway, he said coldly – a tone so unusual from him that I remember it clearly – '*Never* run.' 'Why *not*?' I cried. 'Because there is no *point* in it.' (After both he and my mother were dead and I was indifferent and invulnerable to danger, I understood the sense of this.) We made the journey back to the flat by underground. But we had to break it half-way after Balham station got a direct hit (with heavy casualties as it was used as a shelter) and wait in a long queue for a bus. One after another they passed full up, meanwhile all the guns on Clapham Common were letting off – a cheering sound after the once impotent silence. In January Ronald had a recurrence of an irregular heart condition that had taken him into hospital in the autumn of 1938. He was away for seven weeks.

But for the NCCL the year started buoyantly with a spate of conferences in big provincial towns, following on the findings of the successful conference on 'Civil Liberty and the Defeat of Fascism'. And on 15 and 16 February a comprehensive conference in London on 'Civil Liberty in the Colonies' with Mr Creech Jones MP in the chair. Detailed memoranda for the delegates had been prepared in advance covering the key issues in the colonies and mandates in the West Indies, in Africa and Asia and in Cyprus. In March there was a lively public meeting on 'Freedom of Expression', which had a very successful outcome. The target this time was the BBC. E.M. Forster in an article in *Civil Liberty* in January exposed the cause and set the scene:

> Until the world learns not to listen, the power of broadcasting remains little less than sinister, and needs watching carefully ...

most of the Board of Governors got the sack when the war started' [including H.A.L. Fisher and Margery Fry] ... at present there are only two [Sir Allen Powell and Capt. C.H.G. Millis] ... doubtless sound business men, but they have, as far as I know, no special interest in culture or the freedom of expression which is one of the causes for which we are supposed to be fighting.

The Board and the Ministry of Information control the policy of the BBC between them. The staff get the kicks. There has been much criticism of the staff, and particularly of the Director General, but as far as one can see they are at present quite without authority ... It is impossible, for instance that they are responsible for the preposterous decree, which bans from the microphone anyone who disapproves of the war, even if he is broadcasting on a subject which has no connection with the war ... The most glaring case so far, is that of Sir Hugh Roberton, the conductor of the Glasgow Orpheus Choir, whose concerts were cancelled because of his pacifist opinions. I hope that even though there is a war on, the Corporation will hear a great deal more about this ...

And beside the Roberton case there are disquieting rumours ... There is certainly a black list of speakers – the name of Mr Middleton Murry has been mentioned ... pacifism again. There is the odd business of Mr J.B. Priestley, of which no convincing explanation has been given, even by Mr Priestley. There is a report that no speaker and no writer in the *Listener* may criticise any Government speaker or member of the government or MP or director of a public utility concern. If this is not fascism, what is?'

A BBC official was told that he would be dismissed as soon as the Corporation learned from the Ministry of Labour that he was registered as a conscientious objector. As well as pacifists, personalities who subscribed to the People's Convention – a left-wing body with Communist affiliations that brought out its manifesto in January – were also to be proscribed.

When Michael Redgrave was banned it made the headlines. He told the audience at our meeting about the prelude in an interview at the BBC: 'Some actors could have built that up into quite a big part but I made nothing of it;' it was 'underplayed', 'tedious' and 'brief'. He refused to discuss his personal opinions which he believed were no concern of the BBC. He ended his speech:

> Here we are in what is called the last outpost of freedom in Europe, and in the last few years have come to us actors and actresses, musicians and writers who ... have chosen to leave their own home ... to learn a new language rather than submit to the regimentation the intolerance of fascism ... And what does that teach us? That if we love our country and hate fascism, let us fight it in whatever form wherever it appears, within, without, fearlessly, always, *Now!*'

Phil Cardew, the bandleader, told about *his* interview at the BBC: 'a glass of wine – the offer was increased to a bottle for the next candidate!' At first he had some satisfaction at being 'an unrepentant sinner', but when he learned that Dr Alan Bush of the Royal College of Music had had a similar interview and that his *compositions* were to be banned he began to realise the implications of the BBC attack.

E.M. Forster speaking at the meeting: 'We are not asking for much. We are not asking for freedom of speech at the microphone, but freedom of speech away from the microphone.'

He announced publicly later that he would refuse all further engagements at the BBC as long as the ban persisted. Rose Macaulay and Dr Vaughan Williams made similar declarations.

Three days after the meeting, Mr Churchill, questioned in the House, virtually condemned the action of the BBC: 'Anything in the nature of persecution, victimisation, or manhunting is odious to the British people.' Special provisions had been made for conscientious objectors as 'a definite part of British policy'. Questioned directly about Sir Hugh Roberton he said, 'I see no reason to suppose that the holding of pacifist views would make him play flat.'

After correspondence with the Director General of the BBC, Mr Forster learned that the bans had been withdrawn and that new Governors had been appointed to the Board. The BBC had been obliged to climb down.

In 1940 Defence Regulations 2D and 94B, giving the Home Secretary powers to close down any newspaper without right of

appeal and to confiscate its printing presses, had been passed
by a small minority and only after assurances that they would
be used only in an emergency such as the threat of invasion.
But in January 1941 Herbert Morrison, the Home Secretary,
chose to invoke the Regulation 2D – in place of Regulation 2C
which required a warning and a judgment in the courts – to
clamp down and ban, without any reference to the all-party
committee, the *Daily Worker* and Claud Cockburn's *The Week*.
Mr Morrison admitted in the House that this was 'preventive'
action, i.e. that neither paper was hindering the effective
prosecution of the war, though the *Daily Worker* was indeed
criticising his policy and administration as Minister of Home
Security.

Civil Liberty in its February 1941 issue carried strong protests
from its President, Henry Nevinson, from Ronald as General
Secretary and from the Treasurer Lord Faringdon, and also
from the editor of the *New Statesman*, Kingsley Martin. The fact
that the protesters disagreed with the policy of the *Daily Worker*
did not weaken their objections to the arbitrary use of powers
in breach of assurances given in the House. On 7 June the
NCCL, jointly with the National Union of Journalists, held a
big conference on the 'Freedom of the Press', at the Central
Hall Westminster, with over 1,000 delegates – among these
representatives from eighteen national trade unions and
associations. Messages of support came from Fleet Street: J.L.
Garvin, editor of the *Observer*, Sidney Elliott of *Reynolds News*
and R.J. Cruikshank of the *Star*; from publishers: F.J. Warburg,
and G. Wren Howard of Jonathan Cape; from writers: H.G.
Wells, Leonard Woolf and Walter Greenwood; from scientists:
Prof. P.M.S. Blackett, Julian Huxley, Professor B. Farrington;
from actors Rex Harrison and Walter Hudd; from Basil
Wright, Director of the Film Centre, and from Labour and
Liberal MPs and peers, and many more.

Frank Owen, editor of the *Evening Standard* speaking at the
conference: the Defence Regulation 2D was 'legislative
dynamite'. The *Daily Worker* was the first victim but both the
Daily Mirror and the *Sunday Pictorial* had been threatened. The
delayed British war communiqués were 'the despair and
laughter of the world'; the government resented criticism and
attempted to check it. When he had challenged the government

figures of the sinking of British ships in the Battle of the Atlantic, 'Mr Alexander threatened to lock me up ... if I had been on the *Daily Worker* he certainly would. I wanted to tell the truth about the Maginot Line and was accused of spreading alarm and despondency.' Paul Rotha, speaking about newsreels, recalled the move of the Foreign Office to get Mr Joseph Kennedy (the American Ambassador) to cut interviews with Wickham Steed and A.J. Cummings out of an American unit newsreel. Mr Sunder Kabadi, representing the *Bombay Chronicle*, traced the history of repression and censorship in India and the colonies. The resolution passed at the conference included a demand for the repeal of Defence Regulations 2D and 94B and that this should be made retrospective so that any action against the *Daily Worker* and *The Week* could come before the courts and be subject to appeal.

On top of the success of this conference the Council was unexpectedly faced with a challenge to its non-party status. Surprisingly this came from a once-good friend who had co-operated with NCCL in more than one of its civil liberty campaigns. A.M. Wall of the London Trades Council made a statement at the Labour Party Conference alleging that the NCCL was under Communist control. A month earlier Ronald had replied, in an article in *Civil Liberty*, to criticism from 'a limited section of the labour movement' that the Council had been going beyond its brief and concerning itself with matters which were a trade union prerogative. Accusations of left-wing involvement were commonly levelled by right-wing detractors against organisations that were active on current issues. These denunciations the NCCL ignored and indeed accepted as a tribute to its effectiveness. But the public criticism voiced at the Labour Party conference was a much more serious matter. The NCCL responded promptly in a letter to the *Times* on 13 June signed by Henry Nevinson, E.M. Forster, Lord Faringdon, W.H. Thompson and Ronald 'categorically denying the statement ... This organisation is not and never has been under Communist control and as long as we are associated with it will not be under that or any other political domination.'

Soon after history took a hand to neutralise the imputation. On 22 June the Nazis invaded the USSR. As the full force of

Nazi armour and airpower concentrated in the East the bombing over England halted. The British public were deeply grateful, and commiserative, and as the newsreels showed how the Russians could take it and the courage and sacrifice of their civilians, admiration and esteem grew. The British Communist Party was now of course whole-heartedly committed in the 'People's War'. So the Communist bogy no longer cut any ice. It went into cold storage. But official vetoes were still rigid, as I was soon to find out, and operating as usual in camera.

Ronald's Health Fails

Ronald and I took our last holiday together in Cornwall, and for comfort this time at a little hotel. On a warm day he ventured into the sea, and was terribly shaken, shuddering uncontrollably, teeth chattering. He made nothing of it, but later a haemorrhage developed behind one of his eyes. He returned bronzed, and still superficially giving an impression of good health. But his doctor told him that he was at risk. He ought to rest for three months, preferably in hospital.

And now, at the end of August, the NCCL was threatened by a financial crisis. The summer was always a lean time for us, as no subscriptions fell due, but this year the shortage was so acute that emergency measures had to be taken: a cut in staff, a halt to the publication of *Civil Liberty*. Financial support had not been falling off. It had doubled in 1939, and increased in 1940. But now we had a much bigger staff: a legal adviser (now that our young lawyers were in the forces), and an accounts clerk (our original honorary treasurer who balanced the books and reported monthly to our Executive no longer available), Elizabeth Allen was our new Appeals Officer, Nancy Bell our area and branch organiser, and there were correspondingly more typists and clerical workers. The big increase in work and output was subject to the heavy wartime increases, roughly doubling the cost of stationery and postage.

I can no longer recall, in this terrible fateful year, exactly when it became clear to me that Ronald's health was permanently impaired, and that he would be obliged to give up his dogged struggle to carry on the arduous work of

General Secretary, and that I must be prepared to take the responsibility of being the prime, if not the sole, wage-earner. My salary (as I discovered recently) was the same as that of a typist. From the first I had been sensitive, because of my personal relation with Ronald, about receiving the kind of salary that would have fallen due to an independently-elected well-qualified assistant secretary. I took on the job because I was there and the work had to be done, and I learnt it as I went along. By temperament I was quite unsuited to a deputising, servicing role and this aspect of the post I never fulfilled. I pegged away on my own doing a bit of anything or everything that came to hand. I never considered myself more than a makeshift – but hard-working and conscientious! Some of the routines involved in the Council's work were to me tedious and uncongenial: the niceties and pedantry of the law, the formalities of Parliamentary processes – debating the placing of an 'and', 'but' or 'whereas' in amendments to Bills – the machinery of conferences and committees. But I plodded on faithfully because all this boring business was inextricably tied up with the vital compelling issues to be defended in that treacherous uncertain political climate. And now my concern that the Council should not lose the sterling services of Nancy Bell was matched by my own need to earn the kind of salary I could expect in my own field. There was another strong reason why I should now make way for another on NCCL. My mother who five years earlier had had what was supposed to be a successful operation for cancer, was now suffering a recurrence of the disease, and had no more than a month to live.

When the Executive met, while Ronald was absent sick, to decide the cut in staff and the other economies it looked as though Nancy Bell was to be sacrificed. I spoke against this. She had given up a good post in safe Oxford to come into the London blitz to work for us. Well-qualified, a dedicated worker, she combined up-to-date efficiency with the old-fashioned virtues: constancy and selflessness. A rather beautiful young woman with a bosomy Victorian hourglass figure, a fair complexion and a ready blush. Like the fated Victorian heroine she was to fade away, sink into a steep decline and die tragically young of an undiagnosed complaint. On the spur of the moment, as I spoke in her favour, I virtually made it clear that I was prepared to be axed. Forster wrote a kind little note to Ronald saying that he and the Committee were impressed by my 'highmindedness'. And later, after I had formally tendered my resignation, his letter inviting me to serve on the Executive (he was writing in place of our eighty-five year-old President who was seriously ill) included in his appreciation the fine word 'homage' – more I feel a tribute to his generous spirit than to my deserving.

That early autumn I was left with the leisure to go to my mother every day, back to the flat at night. She had a very good trained nurse to look after her. In the last phase of her illness, when I left her room late in the evening, and distanced myself, I was no more than an automaton, still in spirit with her, in her room. At the very end, it was impossible to make the break. I stopped in the dark road and turned back.

In the hideous acres of cemetery I stood in the family group beside her grave. For me, the present was torn. Even in my independent life she had been a strong warm centre, at the heart of it. On the other side of the open grave Ronald stood white-faced, the spurious tanned health drained away. His dreadful pallor shocked me back into my own world of action, to face it again.

At a fateful meeting of the Executive, two weeks later in mid-November, Ronald, at the end of his three months' sick leave, had to face the cruel issue of his fitness to continue as General Secretary. It is clear now, retrospectively, that when Elizabeth Allen joined the staff it was in the expectation of eventually taking over as General Secretary, as she knew that Ronald was already a very sick man. She confirmed this when she was interviewed in the late sixties long after she had retired. It was also soon very evident, although this was not a point that she herself made, that in this objective she had the support of key members of the Executive. I had no idea of this at the time, nor I am sure had Ronald. I assumed that, if Ronald's health continued to deteriorate, Nancy Bell, who deputised for him in his three months' absence, might eventually become General Secretary.

I had quite forgotten, but old papers have confirmed, that after this November Executive, the Chairman W.H. Thompson, made the suggestion that Ronald should now take on the role of President – Henry Nevinson had died on 9 November – with an honorarium equal to his current salary. Ronald felt quite unable to accept this. He was not, he thought, of the stature for the honour of the presidency, instead he suggested that he should become Director – he quoted Roger Baldwin, the founder and General Secretary of the American Civil Liberties Union, who had now assumed this post. His function, he maintained, and this he underlined, would be *to direct*, and he went on to outline his duties as he now envisaged them. His general proposition was agreed. And so on 11 December at the memorial meeting for the late President, the grand old champion of liberty and veteran war correspondent, held jointly with the PEN Club, Ronald appeared on the platform at the Caxton Hall as Director of the NCCL and Elizabeth Allen as General Secretary. But the question of the extent of the Director's control and the scope of Ronald's active work was still the subject of discussion by a special sub-committee. If Ronald was determined so was Elizabeth Allen, and the odds of course were against him.

She was a strong-minded woman with an innate Anglo-Saxon sense of superiority, and an undoubted presence. In her own fashion she was as single-minded and dedicated to civil liberty – her very long stint as General Secretary endorsed this – as was Ronald himself. I have no doubt that she appreciated that Ronald was the exceptional right man as founder of the Council to inspire confidence and attract a wide range of influential support – invaluable in the Council's early untried days and in that difficult climate. But now that the Council was well established and that wartime attitudes were radically changing, she had her own ideas how to proceed and she wanted a free hand to inaugurate her regime.

Out of the office, I was not aware how things were working out for Ronald in his new role; he, as usual, was reticent. I still half accepted his own valuation of his physical capacity. He had always cheerfully ignored physical limitations. It was I, thirteen years younger, who flagged first. Observing in the evening after a day's work, it was he who insisted on staying to the very end, the final dispersal, in fact the critical time. Nothing was allowed to deflect him, not his broken leg in plaster, nor the dislocation of the nightly blitz. But there was now a clear danger signal for the future. I was urgently looking for work. In wartime the opportunities were limited. The University Appointments Board (UAB) suggested the Civil Service – certainly not my choice – but as a tentative I took the preliminary hurdle and appeared before the Civil Service Commissioners impressively seated round a circular table. I had the embarrasment of being selected by the chairman as a likely candidate to act as personal assistant to the head of the ATS – today the Women's Royal Army Corps. Coached and pushed into the officer class, I would accompany my boss round the country as she made speeches and took parades, and if necessary deputise for her with the small fry. The picture of myself in cap and uniform, servicing, soft-soaping brass hats of both sexes, competently linking up dates and times of functions with appropriate speeches and transport, filled me with horror. The endless opportunities for precipitating all this into chaos! I excused myself. I must have a London-based post to be near my widowed father.

I circularised publishers. I approached the BBC, and I climbed up the interview rungs of the Corporation ending up with a cup of tea and a cigarette. I was accepted in their intake of graduates, to be tried out in various departments and fitted in to the most likely niche. My contract would arrive in due course. The BBC notified the UAB of my engagement. At the very last the letter reached me. It 'regretted' and slammed the doors of the portal – 'no vacancy in the Corporation'. Now both the UAB and I were made uncomfortably aware that there must be a black – or as I guessed – a red mark against me. Ironically at this time Violet Bonham Carter was both a Governor of the BBC and also a Vice-President of the NCCL. Two more applications for posts, this time in the Ministry of Information (MOI), met the same fate. Now I was in real trouble. Now I knew what it must feel like to be penalised as a Jew – and not only in a fascist country. (A friend of mine, with an unmistakably Jewish name, had had a negative response, not even an interview, to her applications with her honours degree for over thirty vacancies in a variety of posts. After she changed her name, there was no difficulty.) And now the NCCL stepped in to help me. Glenvil Hall, Parliamentary Secretary to the MOI, wrote me a letter expressing goodwill and confidence about my obtaining a post in the Civil Service. Reassured by this, the Appointments Board offered me another vacancy, but now in the more pedestrian Ministry of Works. By a lucky chance, the man who interviewed me was a member of the same golf club as my father. 'When', he inquired jovially, 'would you be free to start? That is ...' 'Tomorrow,' I cut in promptly.

And so I was at my desk and in the 'administrative club' before my alleged past caught up with me – as it did the next week. My immediate boss in the Planning Division, another temporary Civil Servant, was warned against me, I was suspect. I had been associated with the National Council for Civil Liberty. 'So what? I'm a member,' he replied. (I learned all this years later after he had left the service and was back in academic life.) Today with instant computerised records I wouldn't have stood a chance.

Ronald was losing his struggle to master the work he had set himself. There were days when he couldn't make it to the office. He was finishing at home his pamphlet, *Freedom of the Press.* Only occasional days in London. By the end of March he was seriously ill, unable to attend the annual general meeting and give his report on the year's work. He wrote a message for the meeting in a shaky hand from his bed, referring optimistically to 'next year'. The doctor advised that Ronald should go into hospital. Forster visited him there, he had already called to see him when he was at home. Ronald, he said, spoke calmly about his health and was 'still concentrated on the Council and its work'. Ronald meticulously corrected the page proofs of his pamphlet. The April *Civil Liberty* carried an article by him on press freedom (asking why the subsidy for the circulation of *Picture Post* to the Middle East had been withdrawn and objecting again to the repressive Regulation 2D – fourteen months since the *Daily Worker* had been suppressed, with no rational cause now that Soviet Russia was our ally). Ronald wasn't happy in hospital. The routine irked him. As a doctor's son he was too aware of the thermometer that went the rounds from mouth to mouth with a casual dip in between into disinfectant. It was a great relief to him when it was decided he could come home. Now he lay in bed undemanding and uncomplaining, trying to harvest his strength. He dozed with the oxygen spectacles on his nose, the big cylinder standing by his bed. I was out all day in London. Now he could no longer be left alone. My sister Bee found a reliable state registered nurse who arrived each morning before I left and stayed in the evening till I came home. Ronald was sinking. I took sick leave. One day Ronald pulled himself out of the depth: 'We ought to get married …' (It had been on his conscience. It was not in my mind.) I asked him if he wanted to see his wife or his mother: 'She would only fuss.' (He was thinking of his mother.) He told me he was dying happy. He was not sorry to have spent his strength. It was only when he spoke of his last, his best true love, the NCCL, that he wept. He wanted still to be there to look after it.

*

The *Times* obituary remembered Ronald's 'temperately written, well-documented, and in some ways disquieting' book. The Catholic *Universe* recalled 'the glaring occasion for their [NCCL's] support in the renewed outbreak of fierce anti-Catholic attacks' in Northern Ireland, and the 'profound effect' of the investigations and the Report. The *New Statesman* reprinted E.M. Forster's tribute to the man and his work in his address at the cremation, preserved for posterity in his *Two Cheers for Democracy*. Kingsley Martin gave the Empire broadcast and the BBC also carried an obituary on the European service. Reginald Bridgeman wrote the tribute for the *World's News and Review*, *Newspaper World* regretted 'the press has lost a true friend' and *Peace News* 'a loss to the pacifist movement'. Notices in the national press (even the *Daily Mail*!) and the provincial press, telegrams and messages from personalities, from trade unionists and co-operatives in Britain and overseas – from the West Indies and Africa.

But the best memorial Ronald could have was to be the perpetuation of the NCCL, its effectiveness today, and its readiness to play its part in the uncertain world of the future.

9

Starting Again

It was a friend's prodding that sent me down High Holborn to sit hopefully – with no appointment – outside Kingsley Martin's room at the *New Statesman*. 'No good waiting till you're *out*. Do something *now*, while you're still at your desk. *Use* people.'

Victoria was no more the orthodox Civil Servant than I was – even after my ten years. She had come into the Ministry of Information from Fleet Street, formerly fashion editor of the *Daily Mail*. She had made it in journalism in the tough early days for women. She was a fighter, more of a man than most of them. Earlier we had crossed swords in the awkward transition stage when post-war MOI dwindled and settled down into the more humdrum Central Office of Information. But now her militant instincts were awake. By rights I should never have been made redundant (this was in the 1952 Tory cuts of temporary Civil Servants) – 'Appeal! Get it reversed.'

The Civil Service in Wartime

When I started in the Civil Service in the stodgy old Ministry of Works in February 1942, I had been transferred, after a few weeks, into the Planning Division, co-opted for a rush overtime job to prepare a digest of evidence accompanying a White Paper on rural land-utilisation in wartime. And so it happened that when this Planning Division a few months later separated from its parent body of Works to form the new Ministry of Town and Country Planning, I was in at the birth, and in the key planning centre, with the specialists recruited temporarily into the Service. The senior architect and planner was Professor (later Lord) Holford, heading the team of 'liberal herbivore planners', making blueprints for post-war England with its New Towns – Stevenage the first – the innocent precursors of the 'carnivore developers', as one of these architects, Sir Hugh Casson, put it years later. I was lucky to enjoy the informality, the freer liberal climate they created, relaxing the tight convention of the Civil Service. The planners were of course contained in the framework of the established Service, but the Assistant Secretary who headed the Division, a veteran of the First World War, and who earlier in his career had exercised tact and diplomacy as private secretary to both Stanley Baldwin and Ramsay MacDonald as Prime Ministers, was to preside as a benevolent figurehead with an easy rein. We were fortunate too, when the nucleus grew into the fully-fledged, greatly-enlarged Ministry, to be separately housed in a block of spacious old-fashioned flats on one side of St James's Square. On the opposite side was the main Ministry, in the requisitioned Caledonian Club, housing the Minister, and the routine complement of Civil Service divisions: establishment, finance, typing pools, etc., together with a chunk assimilated from the Home Office, including housing. This building stood next door to Eisenhower's 'secret' headquarters, well advertised by a massive Snowdrop, always on duty outside, crowned in his white helmet. One lunch-time, not very long before D-Day, a breeze fluttered a paper off a desk, to send it sailing down into the Square to drop in the gutter. A hundred-percent reliable typist happened to pick up the missive marked 'TOP SECRET'.

I would arrive in the morning wrapped in Ronald's grubby old half-length gabardine raincoat. I sat alone in a big room with a marble mantlepiece, improbably allocated next door to the most senior man, the Assistant Secretary. Was I put there out of harm's way as a dubious character? Certainly his friendly manner never gave a hint. In his style he carried something of the aura of the palmier days of Empire, when the Civil Service was the preserve of those who made it at Oxbridge – no cads. Once in the administrative club, it was assumed that you would of course be Establishment-minded. Yesterday's glamour also touched his faithful secretary. She was the sister of the twenties stage and film star, Clive Brook, the hero of *Journey's End* – who had finally joined the expatriate colony of 'professional Englishmen' in Hollywood.

An outsider in a specialist section and without any professional qualifications in the planning field, I found myself most of the time with absolutely nothing to do. My in-tray piled up with duplicated material, technical papers, establishment memoranda, for my information – nothing for action. At first, I attempted to work my way through all this, digest it each morning. But a daily diet of assimilating paper induced nausea, an aversion to the duplicated page that has persisted to this day. I failed to absorb anything. The planning jargon with its sterilising collective nouns; conurbations, precincts, zones, satellites, densities, amenities, turned everything into cardboard, a rarefied limbo of categories, averages, types – nothing I could connect with my own heterogeneous muddled world.

I spun out my lunch hour as long as I possibly could. A canteen service in the National Gallery for the armed forces and for Civil Servants was catered for by elderly WVS ladies up from the country. With their old-style decorum and perched hats they turned this corner of wartime London into a stall at a garden party as they presided over the queues clustering round the trestle tables while they dealt out portions of beautifully cooked fresh country produce: marrows kept in their striped skins, potatoes in their jackets, green vegetables leafy and juicy – compensating for synthetic mince-type meat substitutes. Old-fashioned puddings, jam roly-poly, apple dumpling. We overflowed from the trestle tables to squat outside in friendly propinquity on the patch of grass in front of the fig trellis, eating in the sunshine. In the air of London Ronald was always with me, and in the life and movement going round Trafalgar Square – ghosts of old demonstrations. Before or after lunch I tiptoed into the entrance next door to listen for a while to a Myra Hess concert.

Back in my high-ceilinged room at the Ministry I whiled away the afternoon propped against the mantlepiece staring hard at my unhappy face in the tall looking-glass, carefully sketching it on minute paper to show at the evening class at the Central School of Arts at the top of Kingsway, to Ralph Coxon who was kind and good-natured. Meninsky appeared sometimes, and stood behind the most promising student breaking his silence at last with a brief comment.

At night, back in my dead flat, out of the current and the stimulus of London, I felt the weight of the next day and the next. But now that I had been caught and held into a regular pattern, all that was required of me was to endure, I only had to trudge on – 'time and the hour ...' The bottle of sleeping pills by my bedside gave me confidence, put me in control. The young doctor, just qualified and filling in at the Ministry before he joined the army, had trustingly written me the prescription. I had explained to him that over-the-counter sleeping pills were useless for me. I needed something extra strong to send me off. The chemist had queried and been reluctant, but after I had signed the poison book he gave them to me. Now the unopened bottle stood there as a talisman.

The flat was on the regular path of the flying bomb – Hitler's secret weapon. Soon after D-Day they started coming over, early in the morning, one after another, like underground trains on a route in the sky. I could hear the tenants on the floor above scuttling down the veranda making for the shelter. Now I had no compulsion to join them, to get low down, to flatten myself. Unmoved I sipped my tea. I felt invulnerable. At the Ministry in its earlier premises in Petty France (outside the high wall enclosing Wellington barracks) when the imminent danger bell sounded, my male colleague, expecting me to make the first move, was obliged at last to cover his own exit with a need to consult the basement library. I would find myself alone on the top floor, flush with, and giving onto the roof and the fire-escape. I was joined by an ex-Naval messenger. He shinned up higher still to get to the topmost point and scan the sky. The flying bomb came hurtling over almost at roof-top level, clearly on its final run before the engine cut out to send it swerving into reverse to flop down silently and explode on contact, discharging its obscene iron excrement. It almost took the messenger's back hair off. He came skedaddling down the ladder, backwards, knees kicking out like pistons, belly thrust forward. Is this how they swarm down in the Navy? To me now it was all comedy. I couldn't take seriously this man-less missile with no hostile brain directing it – a clock-work toy gone mad. Besides, victory was in the air. The Red Army had turned the tide of the war in Europe even before the opening of the Second Front, and in the Battle of the Atlantic we had mastered the U-boat menace – after appalling losses. (Rations cut to a weekly knob of butter, a slice of meat, a real round egg in its shell a luxury!) Now it was only a matter of time.

For a while in the Ministry I was kept busy in the amenities section. In anticipation of holidays with pay, I was given the white-elephant task of compiling a memorandum of the temporary holiday accommodation available in England and Wales. I accumulated a mass of literature – brochures, year-books, pamphlets – collected from every available source, about holiday camps, campsites and so on, and faithfully recorded the details: what and where and which facilities. All of it of course based on pre-war material and in 1944 quite out of date. Now on the vulnerable cliffs the wooden chalets would be tilting drunken, doors burst open letting in the rain, the desolate beach below stiff with tank traps. I was complimented on my effort. It was marred only by the fact that all the way through I spelt accommodation with only one m.

And now regrettably I was to blot my copybook. One fine day all the members of the staff in the administrative and executive grade received a Personal and Confidential minute from the head of Establishment in the form of a letter – 'Yours sincerely' – inquiring into our 'extra-official activities' and asking us to submit particulars of any association, institute or other body to which we belonged; the part we played, as a member of the executive or whatever; and the aims and objects of the association. Professor Holford, as head of the planners, deplored the Establishment minute. He himself intended to decline to submit any information, and he queried the propriety of the inquiry. While he was proceeding in this liberal herbivore fashion, the minute was rudely knocked on the head by a headline in the *Daily Herald*: 'Nosey-Parker is Busy at the Ministry'. It went on to give details about the scope of the snoop. Establishment division promptly back-pedalled. An URGENT follow-up minute was put out: the first minute had been 'misunderstood'. It had been concerned only to learn about associations and institutes connected with *planning* interests.

Although the minute had been duplicated (names of recipients filled in in ink) and no doubt seen by unguarded eyes, everybody seemed to assume that I was responsible. At Whitley Council meetings, where I sat bland and helpful on the staff side (elected to represent another grade), the head of Establishment, a rather keen wolf, who presided in the chair as a big jovial shepherd, would turn a sharp eye in my direction when any matter involving confidentiality arose.

As soon as the Allies overran the launching sites of the flying-bombs, air-raid alarms became the exception rather than the rule. (Hitler's 'secret' weapon No. 2 the rocket-launched explosive was still to come) But now the Ministry had set in train a comprehensive fire-watching system roping in everybody on a rota system. After we had done our tour of inspection we could retire to bed, ready of course to come into action if the alarm sounded. The biggest hazard now as we toured the main building was a confrontation with a nocturnal sewer-rat expecting pickings from the former club premises. The Minister's handsome quarters were in the reception rooms on the ground floor, and in the rabbit-warren upstairs – formerly the premises of the club staff – the clerical and typing pools were squeezed in. I discovered that our fire-watching dormitory was in a stone basement room, its only ventilation through vents onto an enclosed yard where a urinal automatically flushed a noisy torrent every few minutes all through the night, the floor round the beds thick in dust, and squashed cigarette cartons. After an hour or so of breathing dust, listening to water music and groans, I took up my pillow, wandered upstairs to stretch out on a bare office desk. The next morning I minuted the Minister – through the proper channels – I was sure he would be shocked, etc., etc. Establishment tried to pull me up. I was advised, in my own interests, etc., etc. As far as I can now recollect I was obstinate. In the end the basement dormitory was withdrawn from the female contingent and made available to the male personnel! On my next rota I was happy to discover a tiny locked room – the key in the door – with just enough room for the upholstered couch and the wash basin. I spent comfortable nights there – was this the Minister's preserve? Until one night – there was no key in the door. Had I dropped the incriminating hairpin?

For a while Professor Holford harboured me in his room, maybe he felt I might shape into some sort of an assistant. Built on a neat, small rather elegant scale, he reminded me of little Bilee in *Trilby* in the du Maurier illustrations. He had a clarity, a classical approach that effortlessly resolved awkwardness and muddles, perfect self-discipline and Olympian powers of concentration. All this immaculate perfection unnerved me. I still had absolutely nothing to do. When he was out at engagements as was often the case, I answered the phone, and when he was in I tried to think of something to do which would look as though I was doing something.

He sent me to cover a meeting of French planners putting forward their projections for post-war France with material from their colleagues in the occupied country. The platform was filling up in the little theatre – the Savoy, I believe, or was it at the Institut Français in Knightsbridge? A towering figure strode onto the stage – General de Gaulle! Back in Churchill's plane from North Africa, where he had been recruiting for the Resistance. This was the first time I had seen him, though I had of course heard his defying rallying voice after his escape from the fall of France. The French audience stood up to acclaim him. Did we burst into the 'Marseillaise', or was that only in my imagination? Then the business of the meeting. I was expecting some stimulating, perhaps thrilling tidings from occupied France. But nothing of the kind. This was strictly professional, planning experts adumbrating the prosy generalised French equivalents of the English planning jargon – zones, conurbations and so on, but on a big scale, railway systems, docks, motorways, canals. It went on and on getting duller and duller and more and more complicated, as my scribbling pencil tried to sort something coherent to take back.

A letter from the Civil Service Commission invited me, as one of a small group, to take part as a guinea-pig in an experiment to try out a new intelligence test for civil servants. The pundit who devised it was, as I recollect, Sir Cyril Burt, a member of the Advisory Committee to the War Office on Personnel Selection, later debunked for falsifying his 'scientific' evidence. We had first of all to identify and pick out shapes and patterns and solve arithmetical puzzles – the kind of thing a bright, practical ten-year-old would enjoy and do smartly. I was crawling along painfully still hesitating at the top of each page when the metronome signal was given to turn over to the next. After the juvenalia we had to resolve high policy and strategy. It was foxy because it involved theorising about an ambivalent situation: how to proceed in governing a country, under military stress from outside and facing militant opposition within. The implicit assumption that the government in power must be worthy and the militant opposition bad – patently false in the context of occupied Europe – tangled the answer, designed, it seemed to me, more to identify politics rather than policy. The results of the experiment were announced promptly. I was placed in the moron class, in the lowest category, E, with 25 per cent. It was immediately after this that I was accepted by the MOI as a commissioning editor with an increase in pay of £100 – very little today, but quite a useful addition in 1944. I also had the satisfaction of removing myself to another ministry at the right moment. The civil servant who had originally tried to queer my pitch by warning my boss against me (as a dangerous woman) had now himself applied for my services in his own section, in another mind now evidently as to my reliability and competence.

I was migrating from the Ministry of Town and Country Planning under my own steam, not directed by the service, leaving a neutral role among the leisurely blueprints of specialist post-war planning, to get into the active hive of wartime propaganda journalism. I was interviewed for the post by the head of Publications Division, Robert Fraser, (later Director General of the Central Office of Information, and after that knighted and the first Director General of IBA) and happy to find that now, in this culminating year of the 'People's War', my experience with the NCCL was all to my credit! Of course by this time I also had the hallmark of respectability as an Administrative Grade civil servant of two years' standing. We discovered mutual acquaintances, among them the friendly editor of *Vogue* who had lent a hand each month with the lay-out and paste-up of *Civil Liberty*. It was to be my job as a commissioning editor to help promote awareness of British efforts on the home front by commissioning articles for placement in the North American market. Writers with names were ready in wartime to do their bit – 1,000 words for seven guineas, 2,000 for ten, as well as an eager army of freelance and specialist journalists.

I was introduced into Victoria's room as the new editor. She was firing off her typewriter like a machine-gun, banging out an article for export. Down the corridor were C. Day Lewis and Laurie Lee, and editors and journalists from Fleet Street, including my immediate boss. I was aware at once, that first day of the brisk tempo, everything geared to a lively pace, a quota of newsworthy articles, vetted (by service chiefs), sub-edited, matched up with pictures, issued each week. The constant activity was just what I needed, after the dead calm of the Ministry of Town and Country Planning.

The MOI while it lasted was stimulating. But after the end of the war the whole edifice crumbled. All its stars returned to their peacetime occupations, the editors and the journalists with the mettle back into Fleet Street. The Ministry dwindled into the Central Office of Information. Victoria and I and the others were left with the rump and were translated into the conforming Civil Service category of Information Officers, in the Executive Grade, with tags, Higher and Senior.

After the War

The lifting of tension at the end of the war, the end of repression and the black-out and a celebration of life and victory, I associate with a small exhibition of pictures lent by Picasso and Matisse that opened in a gallery somewhere in Kensington. I remember how a small boy ran in ahead of his mother and caught by surprise in the express-train blast of colour and assertion by Picasso – burst into tears! After a heady draught of the major artist, I found another delight to pass on to the elegant rhythms and harmonies of Matisse. I had not realised how much I had been starved in the war years and before that by the self-imposed disciplines as we concentrated on the fight for civil liberty.

The post-war electorate was ready for and demanding radical change. The people had been toughened and united by austerity, and in shared hardship and danger social barriers had come down. Labour came in with a big majority to introduce the welfare state, the health service, to nationalise key industries, to repeal the Trade Disputes and Trade Unions Act of 1927 and to assist instead of opposing the inevitable transition from Empire to Commonwealth. But for those naïve enough to expect the reality of a socialist Britain, the dream soon faded. The Labour Party lacked the vision or the will to agree on a socialist foreign policy, and Ernie Bevin, the strong trade unionist, was a disaster as Foreign Secretary. To the warm approval of the Tories, he carried on Conservative policy of propping up reaction in Greece – with wartime partisans now treated as the enemy. The Cold War was fatally accepted and cemented, clamped into our way of life. In Palestine his harsh policy towards the Jews provoked their militants into terrorism, with a backlash of anti-Semitism stirring again. After Jewish terrorists were hanged by the British army in control in Palestine, reprisals were threatened if more captured Irgun fighters met the same fate. When the executions went ahead, two British intelligence unit sergeants were kidnapped and found hanged. The *Daily Express* published a front-page photograph. Over the Bank Holiday weekend, crowds of some hundreds in Liverpool smashed and looted Jewish shops, in Bethnal Green a hostile crowd threatened a meeting of Jewish Ex-Servicemen, incidents occurred in other parts of the country, some synagogues were vandalised.

Mosley, like an evil bluebottle smelling another opportunity, made a comeback, heading what he called his Union Movement. Some of his old associates, active again in Kensington and the East End were cashing in, putting themselves in the right, on the same side as the British army.

A few weeks after the backlash at the murder of the British sergeants, the *New Statesman* of 30 August 1947 published an article (reprinted by the NCCL) 'Well It's a Free Country Isn't It?', a first-hand account by a Labour MP of a street meeting the previous Sunday in Bethnal Green:

> Five policemen stood in a row behind the speaker. Ten formed a cordon in the road twenty yards ahead of him. Others were on the pavements, and more were among the crowd beyond the cordon. Round the inside of the ring formed by the policemen walked the Chief Superintendent in a smart grey suit ... Sometimes he directed a policeman towards an interrupter in the crowd.

'We are fascists and we're proud of it ... I love Mosley ... He was less likely to be a traitor than Herbert Morrison, the conscientious objector. And what about "Ikey" Strachey? ... Now Britain was a fifth-rate nation, dictated to by four thousand Jews ... There was only one way to stop terrorism ... Take out whole Jewish families in Palestine and shoot them against a wall and do the same to Jewish families here ...'

[Someone] had the temerity to shout 'Down with fascism!' Three constables advanced towards him and removed him from the crowd. It was an offence to say 'Down with fascism' in England on 24 August 1947.

' ... no corpses at Belsen ... a lie told with the co-operation of newspaper photographers. The war was a mistake. We had fought the great German race.'

The [Union Movement] closed with the police driving the audience away and not allowing them to stop near anyone selling an anti-fascist newspaper: the fascist ones had been sold during the meeting ... Perhaps it is of no importance that the fascist meetings have been growing ... that they now are being held regularly in Brighton, in Liverpool, in the East End and other London districts ... Perhaps Mosley really means it when he says that he is not engaged in politics but in publishing his books through Mosley Publications ... But there is a law about incitement to violence which the police of Bethnal Green and Dalston have apparently not been told about. Possibly Mr Chuter Ede [the Home Secretary] might care to spend a Sunday evening in the Ridley Road area and then look it up ... and even consider legislation to forbid the formenting of racial strife.

The author of the article was Woodrow Wyatt.

Mr Chuter Ede twice in 1948 invoked the Public Order Act to ban both fascist meetings and anti-fascist opposition to them. In each case he followed the precedent laid down in 1937 and banned *all* processions – under Section 3(3) of the Act, although he had the option under Section 3(1) to ban *any* procession likely to cause serious public disorder. And so in the aftermath of the victorious war to defeat fascism – as many believed was the objective – we were back again in the ambivalent pre-war situation, only this time it was under a Labour government.

The COI had left its MOI premises in Russell Square and

was now accommodated in Mortimer Street off Baker Street, in blocks of modest-sized flats, with their pantries and bathrooms adapted as best they could to serve as offices. Above my room, upstairs, Dora Russell and Lena Chivers (later Lady Jeger) were engaged on a project which had its origin in wartime: a periodical in Russian on the British scene and the British way of life, for circulation uncensored in the USSR with official Soviet state blessing and co-operation. It had been launched at a time when comradeship and fraternity were the order of the day, when the USSR was taking the weight of the war in Europe, lifting the bombing from this island, and at last turning the tide. The public saw newsreels of the heroism of Russian civilian resistance, women digging trenches in the snow. For a time it was commercially viable, acceptable to the public to show, in a light-hearted film, the *Demi-Paradise*, communism and capitalism in friendly amity; British captains of industry as wise old birds and the hero, a young Soviet engineer on a trade mission to Britain played by Laurence Olivier – the blunt ingenuous young patriot with no-nonsense cropped hair – a year before he appeared in his film, *Henry V*.

Dora Russell who radiated warmth and enthusiasm, introduced me to the Fleet Street Forum. This was an information and discussion group of journalists concerned at the danger to peace in the accelerating Cold War. It met in the upstairs rooms of pubs in the Strand and off Fleet Street. Its leading lights from the Central London Branch of the NUJ (I was a member then) were Ritchie Calder, Ted Castle, and Geoffrey Goodman as the honorary secretary. Its projected programme for the autumn of 1952 included a discussion opened by Aneurin Bevan on peace and the press, Vicky, the cartoonist, back from Moscow, cross-questioned by David Low (both of these supporters of the NCCL) and a live issue in the news in the cruel Korean War: the allegation by China of germ warfare dropped by American planes, with a report by the scientist Dr Joseph Needham returned from China with his investigating team that included Geoffrey Bing – ex-Major in the 1939 war, and now Labour MP for Hornchurch.

The work I was doing at COI did not directly touch on politics, but the blight of the Cold War conditioned and angled the general tone and the policy, killing what had once been a lively interest. Wartime impetus and incentive flagged and died.

It was at this time that I came disconcertingly face to face, in the room down the corridor, with 'your actual fascist', or rather yesterday's fascist, today's alert Information Officer, recently recruited into our section – thirtyish, confident, easy-going, personable. I had come to check on some press-cutting or other in an agricultural context. The *Observer* had recently highlighted a new development in British farming, with a full-spread picture of chickens dangling from the moving belt on their mechanical way, as live feathered birds to go on to be processed into cleanly burned bare carcasses. The end of their tightly-caged span as hormone-jerked egg-extruding machines, after their final journey packed live in superimposed crates, to be finished on the last factory line. We were then still sensitive to the basic conditions of factory farming – animals permanently exiled from their natural habitat of free air, sun and grass; calves penned in the dark, hooves slipping on utilitarian slats, craving roughage and still fed on liquids to keep the flesh white. Today the flicked-over picture on television of a beak pecking through a gap in the wire, the sweating rumps of concentrated pigs, scarcely merits a yawn, followed by the perky comedy cartoon hen giving her victory salute to advertise her own succulence, the tasteless flesh occasionally taking its revenge in salmonella poisoning. I must have made some reference when I approached my colleague to this 'technologial advance' – how Mosley came up I have no recollection. While he was checking through press-cuttings in answer to my query, he volunteered, as a casual matter of interest, that he himself had been a Mosley follower in his youth, and now, he went on, he was experimenting with battery hens in his suburban garden. An open drawer revealed a pretty little pair of binoculars. He had liberated them for sixpence! The slot fee trustingly imposed for their release and hire for the duration of the performance and for the benefit of the once solidly respectable occupants of front stalls and dress circle! 'The March of Time!'

* * *

Kingsley Martin's door opened. A man came out and I went in. From time to time since I left NCCL I had been in touch with

Kingsley Martin. While I was still an eager new broom at the Ministry of Works, on a grey morning absurdly early I boarded the Embankment tram. A crowd of cleaners piled on still game after their dawn stint in Whitehall and in spite of the night's air-raid warnings. And now in an 'All Clear' mood as the tram rollicked along, they shrieked with joy. Rising to his audience the conductor pranced down the galloping gangway hand on hip. 'Mr Wrongsky!' they cheered him (Russia was all in the news), 'All different!' 'Passing Scotland Yard,' he warned them. One of the 'girls': 'I don't want no more passes!' and so on. Unquenchable cockneys – just right for an MOI booster in a People's War film strip). I typed out a couple of paragraphs and sent them to Kingsley Martin.

'I think I can use it,' he scribbled back. He put the little piece in his own column in the *New Statesman*. But he took it for free! He had been accustomed when I was with the NCCL to receiving pieces about civil liberty, and at that time it was a favour for him to place them (without a fee) in the *New Statesman*, so this was the slot I still fitted into. That year I was paying double income tax. Civil servants were taxed a different way from the public at large, the one currently, the other retrospectively, I got caught both ways. To save the pennies, I made do with just the morning paper, and stopped buying the *Star* or *Standard*. I cycled two-and-a-half miles to the underground and padlocked the bike in a dank shed adjoining the station. The ancient custodian had his own bucket under the counter. When I came to get the cycle out last thing, the shed stank of urine. The lonely old man wanted to chat to almost his last customer. I backed out nodding and smiling, holding my breath. At that time even the slenderest little remittance would have been very welcome.

Now, as I came in, after the lapse of years, to make direct contact again, I told Kingsley Martin that my term in the Civil Service had come to an end. So – I was looking for something … vaguely congenial … I added, 'I remembered what you said to me at Ronald Kidd's funeral.'

The *New Statesman* had carried E.M. Forster's tribute delivered at the cremation, and in the same issue Kingsley Martin had contributed his own appreciation of Ronald and his work. In this he referred in passing to the Thurloe Square '*riot*'! This was typical Kingsley Martin recalling a left-wing issue and transposing it all in his memory. I wrote briefly recapping the facts – not of a riot but more of a rout: the peaceful meeting in a quiet Kensington Square, well away from the flash point of the fascist meeting, and just about to close when the mounted police moved in, forced the frightened crowd taken unawares to retreat into the narrow confines of the square and pinned them against the railings and punished them with their batons. He thanked me for 'refreshing his memory' and printed the letter. He also contributed an article on Ronald for *Civil Liberty*. Probably he was very busy at the time. But again there was this inverted Midas touch, so that what he handled, with the best intentions, emerged a little tarnished and diminished. At a time when letters and telegrams of shock and regret were flowing in to the Council's office it was not the moment to recall – and in the Council's own journal – with a light touch the urinal outside the Council's first office, and the Bohemian side of Ronald's temperament. The chairman of the Executive had let me see a copy first, and Kingsley Martin accepted all my amendments with the greatest good nature. Later, and at short notice, he was asked to broadcast an obituary on the Overseas Service – I had no chance to see his script beforehand. In the BBC ambience, the Bohemian Ronald vanished. He became a sort of old-fashioned Whig, and even, at the close, 'in the best sense of the word' and with a small c, 'a conservative'! 'I hope you like it,' Kingsley Martin wrote when he sent it to me.

But now he was curious to know what it was that, ten years ago, he might have said at Ronald's funeral.

'You said, "Let me know if at any time I can be of any help to you." '

'Did I say that!' He was quite touched. Moved by his kindness … all those years ago … lingering for a moment in sentiment in the past.

'And so … as I'm sort of looking around …'

He came briskly and cheerfully into the present: 'Well there's *absolutely nothing* for you here.'

'No, of course not …' I waited a moment or two longer, but there was in fact absolutely nothing more to come.

As I went down the moving stairs at Holborn, I remembered

again the cocktail party – in 1938, I believe – in the palmier days of the NCCL when it was in Upper Regent Street. The idea was to canvass and boost funds for the NCCL. Kingsley Martin held it at his house in Great James Street, his first wife Olga was the hostess, a slim, taut, little wooden doll. I remember sipping the slenderest little thimbleful of sherry, while Dorothy Woodman, expansive, rather untidy, worked her way round vigorously, sorting out the crowd, sizing them up, nobbling them for her own Union of Democratic Control. Young lawyers (some of them working for the NCCL) whom she could use, patrons for the cash, useful contacts. She pinned them down energetically with a cheery no-nonsense benevolent forcefulness. Impossible to compete. Ronald was talking to Victor Gollancz, who agreed to let the NCCL circularise his Left Book Club membership – now a formidable total. But it turned out to be only a cocktail agreement. It never materialised. In the end we did get just a quarter-page rectangle for an advertisement in one issue of *Left News*.

I remembered too one morning in 1940 in the middle of the blitz, Ronald and I on our way to work ran into Kingsley Martin in Great James Street. He was looking haggard after a nasty night's bombing.

'The trouble is,' he confided to Ronald, 'I couldn't stand torture. I couldn't stand up to it.' He was already in the hands of the Gestapo!

Ronald, fresh-faced in the early morning and with his calm good looks was solidly reassuring and protective. He turned the subject, spoke about this and that, raised a point of special interest for Kingsley Martin on the next Executive's agenda. The editor recovered himself, was soon joking and resilient. As we separated, on our own, I couldn't resist laughing at him, making a fool of him. Ronald's silence discouraged me, cut me short.

And there is no doubt that Kingsley Martin was fundamentally kind. People were human beings to him, not just officers, cogs. He was fortunate and wise in finding the right match for his temperament in Dorothy Woodman with her certainties, her robust good sense, her boundless vitality and courage. At the end of 1941, when Ronald and I were no longer in the Council's office, Ronald 'promoted' as Director and away ill, and I had resigned from the staff, he wrote Ronald a friendly letter:

> I hear that you are ill for which I am indeed sorry and that Miss Crowther-Smith is leaving the NCCL. I realise what this must mean to you both. Miss Crowther-Smith and you are far more than anyone else responsible for founding and running the NCCL and you have really given your lives to it for many years ...

* * *

I came up into daylight out of the underground. Kingsley Martin had been a tonic. I had only been going through the motions, doing what was expected of me, the sensible thing, but without any real intention of climbing into a good or better job – because, of course, I didn't want one. In the conventional sense it didn't exist for me any more. I would never ever again sit at my appointed desk, day after day, to follow some imposed directive. I was going to be my own boss. I would discover as I went along how to earn my living. First I was going to try freelancing – I had my redundancy money.

Working with Ronald for civil liberty had been the turning point to give me an interest and an incentive for life. And for a while, at any rate, I had played a part. I had lent a hand doing something really worthwhile. Ronald with his strong, generous, uncompromising nature had given me the ballast – of necessity I had acquired the fortitude – and now I was ready to tackle the future.

I had been lucky indeed to have been kicked out, made redundant. Now I could shake off the dust – and start again.